BABE RUTH SLEPT HERE

BABE RUTH SLEPT HERE
THE BASEBALL LANDMARKS OF NEW YORK CITY

By Jim Reisler

Diamond Communications, Inc.
South Bend, Indiana

BABE RUTH SLEPT HERE

10 9 8 7 6 5 4 3 2 1

Manufactured in the United States of America

Diamond Communications, Inc.
Post Office Box 88
South Bend, Indiana 46624-0088
Editorial: (219) 299-9278
Orders Only: 1-800-480-3717
Fax: (219) 299-9296

Library of Congress Cataloging-in-Publication Data

Reisler, Jim, 1958 -
    Babe Ruth slept here : the baseball landmarks of New York City /
by Jim Reisler.
        p.   cm.
    ISBN 1-888698-15-2
    1. Baseball--New York (State)--New York--History. 2. Baseball
players--New York (State)--New York--History. 3. Buildings--New
York (State)--New York--History. 4. New York (N.Y.)--Buildings,
structures, etc.--History.   I. Title.
GV863.N72N487   1999
796.357'09747'1--dc21   98-30819
                                                              CIP

TABLE OF CONTENTS

"It's a fickle town, a tough town. They getcha boy. They don't let you escape with minor scratches and bruises. They put scars on you."

— Reggie Jackson, Yankees outfielder, 1981

"I won't be active in the day-to-day operations of the club at all. I can't spread myself so thin. I've got enough headaches with my shipping company."

— George Steinbrenner, buying the Yankees, 1973

"I'm from the generation that forgives baseball everything."

— Pete Hamill, Daily News, *1981*

For Tobie and Julia, my all-stars

AN INTRODUCTION

When it's 9:30 in New York, it's 1937 in Los Angeles.

Groucho Marx said that. And whatever he meant, the inference is clear: In the pantheon of United States cities, New York is hands-down, flat-out, number one. Gotham. The enchilada. The straw that stirs the drink, as Reggie Jackson might have said.

You know the litany of complaints about New York. It's big, too big. There's pollution, crime, subways that smell, and cab drivers who speak funny languages, got their licenses two weeks ago, rarely stop, and average 163 miles per hour — in traffic. It's expensive, too expensive. Want to grab dinner in Midtown? Cashed in your trust fund?

Ah yes, that's New York, but despite everything, there's nothing else quite like it. Nothing even close. To live there can be maddening, but intoxicating. Want to catch a play? Meet me in Times Square. BROADWAY! And that tall building? The Empire State Building. Not just any other building — the one King Kong scaled in the movies. That river over there? The Hudson, the mighty Hudson, which is more than just a river: It's a school of painting. In New York, even street corners have a history.

Baseball is a colorful part of that story. It's at Yankee Stadium that the Babe smote (a great word deserving of a comeback) his majestic home runs. It's where the early baseball god John McGraw cussed and stormed his way to success, and where a man actually leaped to his death from a building on 5th Avenue, wondering how the Dodgers did that day. New York is where the Black Sox scandal was hatched. It's where Christy Mathewson rose to fame and where Lou Gehrig was born. Baseball history is likely to be around the corner in New York, across the street and up the alley.

That's what this book is about — the baseball landmarks of a great American city, some of which you've heard about, like Yankee and Shea stadiums, some that aren't there anymore, and plenty you probably never even knew about, like the tenement where Hank Greenberg was born and where Joe Pepitone was found on the night he was arrested with a lot of drugs. Collectively, and with a healthy irreverence but utmost respect for the National Pastime, it's quite a story.

It's interesting how people considered quintessential New Yorkers are typically from somewhere else. They can move there from Where-eversville, USA, live in Manhattan, practice their art, and if they're good and go to the right parties — presto — they're a New Yawkah. F. Scott Fitzgerald was from

Minnesota. Cole Porter, from Indiana; Bobby Short, musical idol of the smart set today, is from Kentucky.

That goes for baseball. Mathewson was from Factoryville, Pennsylvania, John McGraw from upstate New York, and Babe Ruth from Baltimore. Then they all became, well, New Yorkers. Had they played in Cincinnati or Cleveland, sure, they'd still have been Hall of Famers. But in New York — largely because they were in New York, mind you — they were on the national stage and became icons. Sure, Willie Mays spent most of his career in San Francisco, but his start is a New York story — how he came up with the New York Giants, lived in Washington Heights near the Polo Grounds, and really did play stickball with the neighborhood kids.

This book is about them too — where they lived, dined, got into occasional trouble, and yes, played stickball. It's about the present, but mostly about a vanished time in America when baseball was king, there were no teams west of St. Louis nor teams that dressed in teal, and your dad actually dressed up to go the game.

And it's about a time in New York, when there were three baseball teams, of which at least two were usually pretty good, and games were played mostly during the day and always on grass. That just may be New York at its most romantic — the city of the black & white Weegie photograph, a place in which men always wore hats, egg creams were the rage, and a good cup of coffee was as close as the local automat.

So, with that, here are some rules of literary engagement:

- Don't take it too seriously;
- Don't get huffy about things we may have missed, like the apartment building, where, in 1943, the Dolph Camilli family lived, which you know about because it was down the street from where your neighbor's cousin went to Hebrew School — the landmarks are not chosen scientifically;
- Don't go looking for some of these landmarks because they might not be there anymore — John McGraw's pool hall is now a parking lot and Lou Gehrig's birthplace is a nursery;
- Don't walk too fast, as Satchel Paige once said, because it angries up the juices; and,
- Above all, sit back and enjoy.

By the way, it's still 9:30 in New York.

ACKNOWLEDGMENTS

This book was compiled primarily from the microfilm of old newspapers, mainly *The New York Times*. Many of the quotations used here appeared in *The Times* and are periodically referenced throughout the text.

A number of other books and publications were enormously helpful and are cited where appropriate. Several books were invaluable, such as Ray Robinson's biographies on Christy Mathewson and Lou Gehrig; and Lawrence Ritter's *Babe Ruth: A Life in Pictures*, and his landmark, *Glory of Their Times*. Both Robinson and Ritter were also kind enough to meet with me and were gracious in their encouragement to pursue this quirky topic. Thank you to both.

Other books like Richard Scheinin's *Field of Screams* and Dan Gutman's *Baseball Babylon* were also solid sources. And so were a number of volumes put together by the Society for American Baseball Research (SABR). Publications such as *Early 19th Century Baseball Stars* and *The Federal League of 1914-15* were very useful. Mark Rucker was at the helm of most of the publications.

Among the most influential people in helping to put this book together were the publishers at Diamond Communications, Jim and Jill Langford, and their able assistant, Shari Hill. All were exceedingly encouraging and supportive. A Ballantine break for all.

Jim Langford's idea to have Jack Kavanagh edit this volume was a stroke of genius. Jack is a giant in the field of baseball writing, and his deft touch, common sense, and enormous font of knowledge of both baseball and the English language shaped this book. A sincere thank you, Jack, for all your work and especially for your friendship.

And finally, a special thank you goes to my wife, Tobie; and, our daughter, Julia. Throughout this project, both were patient, understanding, and more fun than a Sunday doubleheader at Yankee Stadium. I hope they enjoy reading this book as much as I did in putting it together.

CHAPTER ONE

110 RIVERSIDE DRIVE

THE BABE SLEPT HERE

"I had a better year than he did."
— Babe Ruth, 1930, on being told his salary
was more than President Herbert Hoover's

THE MAN WHO SOLD THE BABE
Harry Frazee kicks off the curse
270 Park Avenue

"Harry Frazee's experience in baseball was stormy and immensely profitable," *The New York Times* wrote in 1929.

Well, that's putting it mildly. The occasion for such editorializing was Frazee's death that year at 48, a victim of Bright's Disease. By then, "The Curse," as it's known in baseball circles, was reaching a decade. Now, with the millennium upon us, it's approaching 80 years.

The Curse is the inexplicable inability of Frazee's team, the Boston Red Sox, to win a World Series. Setting that streak in motion — the last Red Sox World Championship is still 1918 — is Frazee's unloading of one Babe Ruth from his team to the Yankees in 1920.

Frazee made $125,000 for the deal, the greatest ever paid for a player up to that time. But the ultimate price was far greater: In 1919, Ruth hit 29 home runs for the Red Sox; in 1920, he hit 54 for the Yankees, followed by 59 in 1921, which was also the first of his seven American League pennants and four World Championships with New York.

But picture Frazee on January 6, 1920, the day the blockbuster deal was announced: At the time, Frazee was the era's big-time theater mogul and owner of baseball's best team — Ruth and the Red Sox were World Champions in 1915 and 1916 as well as 1918 — he was nonetheless a man in dire need of cash.

The reason was Frazee's philosophy, as Lawrence Ritter puts it in his book, *Babe Ruth: A Life in Pictures*, that the ballclub, in his mind, "was just another musical comedy." In the seven years Frazee owned the Red Sox, he sold off all his stars to raise money to finance his stage ventures. Frazee's most notable show was the 1925 musical, *No, No, Nanette!* His last venture, *Yes, Yes, Yvette!*, in 1927, was a failure and cost him millions.

It was all indicative of the boom-and-bust life and times of Harry H. Frazee. Born poor in Peoria, Illinois, the fast-talking Frazee entered the entertainment world at the age of 16 as an usher and a box office attendant in his hometown theater. Within a year, he was touring the Western US as an advance agent for a small theatrical company.

Still in his early 20s, Frazee became a producer and laid the foundation of his fortune, producing several successful musical comedies. In New York, he built the Longacre Theatre and acquired both the Lyric and Harris theaters, changing the name of the latter to the Frazee. He was also a big man around town, entertaining at his Park Avenue home and hosting Charles Lindbergh in 1927, on the aviator's return to New York after the historic solo plane trip to Paris.

The Ruth deal was made while the Babe was playing golf in California. Yankee Manager Miller Huggins was dispatched to the West Coast to let the newest New York star know of the sale.

On meeting Ruth, Huggins used the occasion to hold forth of the evils of the fast life in the big city. Ruth's response, according to Ritter's book: "If [Yankee owner Jacob] Ruppert wants me on the Yankees, you will tell him he'll have to tear up that $10,000-a-year contract and give me a new one for $20,000."

Ruth got his salary doubled. That year at spring training in Jacksonville, he also experienced the inconvenience of Prohibition, which didn't slow him down a bit. And it was during that spring training that Ruth's roommate, Ping Bodie, uttered his famous line.

Asked what it was like to room with his wild teammate, Bodie said he had no idea.

"What do you mean?" the reporter said. "I thought you room with Babe Ruth."

"No," said Bodie, "I room with Babe Ruth's suitcase."

Mercifully, Frazee's baseball tenure ended in 1923, with the Sox by then a last-place team. That year, the Yankees won their third straight American League pennant and Ruth hit 41 home runs. The Curse was underway.

THE BABE GOES BIG-TIME
The emergence of Christy Walsh, sports' first agent
570 7th Avenue

That Babe Ruth remains larger than life more than 100 years after his birth has a lot to do with merchandising and publicity — perhaps more than the home runs and World Series victories. Credit, in part, goes to the quick thinking of a forceful young man named Christy Walsh.

Ruth was the toast of New York when he first met Walsh. As an impulsive big spender, he made a lot, spent extravagantly and saved nothing — never slowing down long enough to realize that his earning potential was greater, far greater, than the salary he made hitting a baseball.

In 1920, Ruth earned $20,000, an enormous sum for the day. In 1921, he made $30,000, which, in 1922, went up to to $52,000 for the next five years. The Yankees had offered $50,000, but Ruth insisted on the additional $2,000, thinking, "It would be nice a make a grand a week."

How fortunate that around then, Ruth met Christy Walsh, who managed to slip into Ruth's suite at the Ansonia on the pretense of delivering a case of bootleg beer from the neighborhood deli. A California native and a lawyer with an interest in the sports and entertainment business, Walsh was a young man with a money-making idea.

"Mr. Ruth, how much do you get for those newspaper articles you write?" Walsh asked. He was referring to the brief stories that Ruth or a local sportswriter ghostwrote after each of his home runs.

"Oh, $5, I think," Ruth said. "And why is it any of your business, anyway?"

"Mr. Ruth, I can get you hundreds of dollars for each article," Walsh countered. "And in addition, I can guarantee you $1,000 within 60 days from similar deals."

That got the Babe's attention, and later, after serious negotiations, they came to an agreement. From then on, all of Ruth's commercial ventures were cleared by Walsh, who, in the process inadvertently became sports' first agent.

And so, for the rest of Ruth's career, Walsh served as the slugger's business and financial advisor. It was a lucrative partnership: Under Walsh's guidance, Ruth earned perhaps twice the amount from endorsements and barnstorming tours than he did from the Yankees. Walsh also insisted he regularly invest a portion of his earnings, making Ruth a wealthy man in retirement.

By the way, Ruth got that first check for $1,000, but in 30 days — not the 60 days that Walsh had promised during their first meeting. The enterprising Walsh had borrowed the money to get off on the right track with the Babe.

Walsh grew to be a friend, as well. On November 15, 1922, Ruth, after a poor, suspension-filled season attended a baseball writers' dinner at the New York Elks Club, with Walsh's urging. Speaker after speaker stood to criticize the Babe for his errant behavior, including New York State Senator and future mayor, Jimmy Walker. It was there that Beau James told the Babe that, "the cheers of yesterday have a short echo." Ruth pledged to change his wayward ways, telling the gathering through his tears that he'd mend his ways and get in shape.

"So help me, Jim," Ruth told Walker, but speaking to the entire room. "I'll go the country and get in shape."

Ruth kept his word and returned to form. He even tamed his lifestyle somewhat, with Walsh and Claire Ruth working to keep him baseball-focused. Walsh even worked on the Babe's infamously uncertain table manners, as in the time they attended a formal dinner party and the matronly hostess asked the Babe whether she might pass him the creamed asparagus.

"No thank you," said Ruth, ever the gracious guest. "It looks delicious but I never eat asparagus. It makes my urine smell."

Later, after Walsh suggested that the Babe should watch his language, Ruth was dumbfounded. "Whaddaya want, Christy?" he said. "I was pretty proud of myself. I said 'urine' didn't I?"

With success, Walsh's syndicate at 570 7th Avenue expanded its stable of athletes from Ruth to other top jocks, including Lou Gehrig, John McGraw, and, of Notre Dame football fame, Knute Rockne. After the 1927 baseball season, Ruth and Gehrig went on an extensive, Walsh-arranged barnstorming tour, playing for the "Bustin' Babes" and "Larrupin' Lou's."

Despite Ruth's substantial post-baseball income, the ever-attentive Walsh, along with Claire, the Babe's second wife, created a household budget system for the Babe. Whenever Ruth needed money, Claire signed a $50 check for him. "It was a tiring thing for both of us," she said later, "but it served the purpose of cutting down on such Ruthian habits as tipping $100 for a 35¢ ham sandwich."

Walsh was there until the end, serving as a pallbearer at Ruth's funeral in 1948.

THE HOUSE THAT BUILT THE HOUSE THAT RUTH BUILT
White Construction Co.
95 Madison Avenue

Back in 1922, when $2.5 million was a lot of money instead of a year's salary for a mediocre utility infielder, a cathedral rose in the South Bronx. It was Yankee Stadium, known for good reason as "The House That Ruth Built." Its winning teams in pinstripes helped turn the ballpark into the world's most famous sports stadium.

How extraordinary then that the original construction of this most distinguished of ballparks went quickly — in less than a year — and all for the advertised price of $2.5 million. The money came from the wealth of the Yankee owners, colonels Jacob Ruppert and Tillinghast Huston.

Performing the massive construction job was one of New York's own, the White Construction Company. Work began without ceremony in the drizzle of May 6, 1922 on the 11.6-acre plot of land purchased the year before from the William Waldorf Astor estate. It was directly across the river from the Polo Grounds, which the Yankees then shared with the Giants.

Workers had been on an ambitious work schedule, trying to complete the massive ballpark for the 1922 World Series. "A little teamwork will be necessary to accomplish this happy result," said Bernard Green, the engineer representing the Osborn Engineering Company of Cleveland, which drew up the initial plans for the ballpark.

The teamwork was overmatched and the new ballpark didn't make it for that fall's Yankees vs. Giants World Series. It was played entirely at the Polo Grounds. But they made it for the following season, turning in the process, some 45,000 cubic yards of earth, 2,000 tons of steel, and 18,000 cubic yards of reinforced concrete into a three-tiered colossus of a ballpark. Yankee Stadium's grandstand and bleachers alone required 600,000 lineal feet of lumber, four miles of piping for rails, and 500 tons of iron.

It's April 23, 1923, opening day for the Big House in the Bronx. (National Baseball Hall of Fame Library, Cooperstown, New York)

Opening ceremonies took place April 23, 1923 under crystal blue skies, before the Yankees took on Boston. Governor Al Smith threw out the first ball, which, "contrary to the usual order of things," said one account, was not "a wild throw." And the Babe, with characteristic timing, belted the ballpark's first home run — a three-run shot to right that iced a 4-1 Yankees' victory.

A capacity crowd of 74,200 crammed the new ballpark to the rafters for the opener. Another 25,000 milled around outside hoping to get in, but couldn't. The big crowd, which dwarfed baseball's previous record crowd of 42,000, was orderly and got to and from the stadium easily, thanks in part to the smooth working of the subway, "which handled the heavy traffic without a break," according to reports.

But hey, this was New York and even the most mannerly of big crowds needed a small obligatory token of unrest. That was provided by two men who were arrested before the game for ticket scalping, one of whom, Sebastian Calabrese, 35, of 255 East 23rd Street, was nervy enough to try to sell his $1.10 grandstand seat for $1.50. He and Abraham Cohen, 23, of 547 Howard Avenue, Brooklyn, who had tried to sell his $1.10 ticket for $1.25, were jailed to await court appearances on misdemeanor charges. No word on whether they were Yankee fans.

THE HOUSE THAT RUTH BUILT
Yankee Stadium
East 161st Street, off the Major Deegan Expressway, The Bronx

Yankee Stadium today.

What New York baseball landmark needs less of an introduction than Yankee Stadium? It is "The House That Ruth Built," where the Babe, Lou Gehrig, Joe DiMaggio, and Mickey Mantle had quarters. Renovated in the mid-1970s, it remains America's most famous sports palace for America's most successful and best-known franchise.

Ghosts of the great ones pervade Yankee Stadium. Casey Stengel is said to have watched a long drive go past his centerfielder and bounce around behind the monuments, where his outfielder had troubled picking it up. "Ruth, Gehrig, Huggins — someone throw the ball," he yelled.

His reference was to the fascinating historical artifacts that adorn Yankee Stadium. Beyond the left center field wall, between the bullpens, is monument row — a series of plaques to former Yankee greats, of which there are many. Ruth, Gehrig, DiMaggio, Mantle, Stengel, and Miller Huggins have plaques, as do Jacob Ruppert, Ed Barrow, Thurman Munson, and a couple of non-Yankees. Pop quiz: Who are they? Pope Paul VI and Pope John Paul II, both of whom celebrated Mass at the stadium.

The park has changed somewhat through its 75 years; right field in Ruth's day, for instance, was 280 feet, whereas today it's 312 feet. Capacity has dropped over the years from the original 80,000 or so to today's 57,000, largely because outfield seats were gradually replaced with chairs in the 1930s and 1940s. Also, in 1937, changes in the bleachers shortened straight-away center from 490 feet to 461 feet.

Other odds and ends:

- In 1937, DiMaggio caught a Hank Greenberg drive that was actually behind the center field flagpole.
- Mantle, for whom the tape measure home run was developed, hit a ball on May 22, 1963 that struck the upper deck facade in right field, missing by six feet, the first fair ball hit out of Yankee Stadium. No major league home run has yet to leave the stadium.
- But one ball is "said to have left the park." In 1934, Josh Gibson is reputed to have hit the only fair ball out of the park, his feat coming near the left field foul pole in a Negro National League game. Actually, an inner fence kept the ball inside the park.
- Bleachers in right center were often called "Ruthville" and "Gehrigville" for the men who hit a fair share of home runs to the area.
- The origins of the expression, "out in left field?" In Ruth's time, youngsters crowded the right field bleachers to be near their homer-clouting hero, according to a Hall of Fame librarian. The story goes that people not sitting in right field weren't only uncool; they were slightly daft. You know, "out in left field."

Throughout the majestic ballpark's history there has been one constant — America's greatest and most dominant sports franchise. There have 31 World Series played at Yankee Stadium, with the Bombers winning 23 of them. In his first 14 years as a big-leaguer, Mickey Mantle played an astounding 12 World Series; Gil McDougald played eight in his 10 big-league seasons. For a child of the 1950s and '60s, autumn meant going back to school, the leaves changing colors, football, and the Yankees playing the Series — it was a rite.

Success brought both admiration and an intense dislike (jealousy?) of baseball's all-time best team. "It may be noted that the Yankees are the least popular of all baseball clubs, because they win, which leaves nothing to 'if' about," A. J. Liebling once said. Added comedian Joe E. Brown in a much-repeated quote: "Rooting for the Yankees is like rooting for US Steel." Said Wait Hoyt, a former Yankee as he faced a group of razzing opposition players as a member of the Pirates: "Shut up, you guys, or I'll put on a Yankee uniform and scare the s— out of you." DiMaggio put it more succinctly: "I'd like to thank the good Lord for making me a Yankee."

BELLYACHE HEARD 'ROUND THE WORLD
St. Vincent's Hospital and Medical Center of New York
7th Avenue (& West 11th Street)

"He was the most uninhibited human being I have ever known; he just did things," John Drebinger of *The Times* wrote of Babe Ruth. More to the point, what didn't the Babe do, when it came to eating, drinking, womanizing, and just plain hell-raising?

By 1925, Ruth's prodigious talents in hitting a baseball were finally eclipsed by his legendary excesses off the field. In early April, with the Yankees working their way north from spring training, Ruth was hitting, but not feeling well. Who stopped to notice? The year before, Ruth had again dazzled the baseball world, leading the league in batting average (.378), home runs (46), and runs scored (143). And for the third time in the previous four years, he had 200 or more base hits.

But 1925 was different. On February 6, his 30th birthday, Ruth tipped the scales at 255, a good 40 pounds over his optimal playing weight. Later that month, he got the flu and did little to curb either his appetite or alcohol intake during his illness. As the team barnstormed its way north, playing the Dodgers along the way, Ruth fell ill in Atlanta, but insisted on accompanying the team on to Chattanooga, where he hit two home runs. He belted another the next day in Knoxville and got sick again that night with stomach cramps.

On April 7, only a week until the regular season, the teams took off for Asheville, North Carolina on a winding and uncomfortable train trip through the Great Smoky Mountains. The ride made several players nauseous; meanwhile, Ruth came down with a fever, and collapsed on arriving at the Asheville train station. When the train missed a connection, rumors flew that the Babe was dead.

The Babe got better, as the train continued north. But with the teams approaching Washington, Ruth again passed out, smashing his head against a sink as he fell. Back in New York at Penn Station, his unconscious body was passed on a stretcher through the window to an ambulance that sped him to St. Vincent's Hospital. Getting him out of the train and to the hospital took seven men and the use of heavy sedatives.

Ruth was operated on April 17 for what was described as an "intestinal abscess." His recovery took a long time — Ruth remained at St. Vincent's nearly seven weeks and didn't return to the lineup until June 1.

So what exactly caused this intestinal problem? *The Times* hypothesized it may have stemmed from a big breakfast of fried potatoes. And years later, Claire Ruth actually wrote that the Babe had hurt himself sliding into first base. Taking the prize for the most inventive description of the illness was one W. O. McGeehan of *The New York Tribune* who wrote that Ruth's illness was a stomachache from eating too many hot dogs, peanuts, and soda, in what became celebrated as "The Bellyache Heard 'Round the World."

The Babe's teammates knew better: "Ruth hadn't been drinking that much pop, and it wasn't even a bellyache," one old Yankee told Roger Kahn in *How the Weather Was.* "It was something a little bit lower than that." The modern belief: Ruth had suffered an attack of gonorrhea and syphilis.

BASEBALL'S MOST FAMOUS TELEGRAM
The story of Johnny Sylvester
National City Bank of New York
55 Wall Street

This much is clear: On October 6, 1926 in game four of the World Series, Babe Ruth hit three home runs to trigger the New Yorkers' win over the St. Louis Cardinals.

Legend has it has Ruth belted each home run as a promise to a dying boy in Essex Falls, New Jersey. Thanks to Babe's promise and a later visit, for real, to the boy's sickbed, by the Yankee slugger, Johnny Sylvester not only became the most famous 11-year-old in 1926, but, as the story goes, he recovered. At least that's the Hollywood version.

"Boy Regains Health as Ruth Hits Homers," the headlines trumpeted. Nice copy, and yes, Ruth did like kids, but come on. Was it true? More than 60 years later, nobody really knows. The myth of a sentimental press or an overzealous press agent? Hard to say, but probably closer to the truth ... maybe. Even Hollywood contributed to the hype, having the Hollywood Babe, played by William Bendix, promising a home run to a dying Johnny in a scene from the 1948 stinker, *The Babe Ruth Story.*

Suffice it to say that the story of Johnny Sylvester, though clouded in myth, is more-or-less accurate. Sylvester himself went to his grave swearing that indeed, he was the inspiration for those long-ago Ruthian heroics of 1926.

One reason for doubt about the story is the range of illnesses ascribed to the young boy. He was said to be suffering everything from blood poisoning to a spinal infection, a back problem, and a sinus condition. Singularly, they're not ailments that would kill anyone — collectively, they were enough to slay a horse.

A more accurate picture emerged years later from Sylvester's son, John, Jr., who said his father received an infection from a wound to his forehead, suffered when he fell from a horse, while riding in his home town of Essex Falls, near Montclair. The boy's father, Horace C. Sylvester, a vice president of the National City Bank, maintained a weekend estate there.

The hype kicked off when the elder Sylvester sent out what proved to be among America's most famous telegrams — an urgent plea to the Yankees, in St. Louis at the time for the Series — for an autographed baseball as a present to the sick boy. Back came an airmail package containing two balls — one signed by the Yankees and another signed by the Cardinals. And on the Yankee ball was a special message from Ruth: "I'll knock a homer for you on Wednesday."

A follow-up note from the Babe "to my sick little pal," on October 9 — the day of game six — said, "I will try to knock you another homer, maybe two today." But not even Ruth could deliver that time, as he went homerless and the Yankees lost. They lost again the next day, giving the Series to St. Louis.

That, at least, is believable, since Ruth was a genuine friend of children and a frequent visitor to hospitals and orphanages. But in the case of Johnny Sylvester, there were no hospitals, rendering the scene in *The Babe Ruth Story*, inaccurate since it takes place in a hospital.

Newspapers of the day told of Johnny's doctors, who marveled at the boy's quick recovery following Babe's note. "His fever began to abate at once and the favorable course was hastened ... after he had listened to the radio returns, clutching the autographed baseballs," gushed *The Times*.

But less than a week after the Series had ended, Sylvester really had improved and Ruth really did visit the boy at his home in New Jersey. Again the hype, with newspapers breathlessly reciting the conversation between the ballplayer and the boy:

"Glad to meet you Johnny," the Babe said. "How you feeling?"

"F-fine," [Johnny] said. "I'm sorry the Yanks lost."

Ruth met Johnny en route to a barnstorming game in Bradley Beach at the

Jersey Shore, where he hit two doubles for the team, "The Kings of Swat," in a 3-1 loss to the Brooklyn Royal Colored Giants.

As for Johnny, he recovered to become a healthy young boy. A decade later, Johnny graduated from Princeton University and later served as a lieutenant in the US Navy during World War II. A scene in the most recent *Babe Ruth Story*, the 1992 version starring John Goodman, shows a nattily-dressed, earnest Johnny visiting Ruth on the field before the ballplayer's last game in 1935.

Sylvester tells the slugger that largely in part to his kindness, all those years ago, that he has completely recovered. "Glad to hear it ... good to see you again," says Ruth.

So Sylvester walks away, out of earshot. "Who the hell is Johnny Sylvester?" Ruth asks a teammate.

There is still another version of the legend — again with a similar theme, in which Sylvester visited Ruth another dozen years later, as the ex-ballplayer was gravely ill with throat cancer. In this version, Sylvester returned his most cherished possession — the ball Ruth had autographed for Johnny two decades before.

For his part, Sylvester became a businessman, serving as President of Amscomatic, Inc., a packing equipment manufacturer in Long Island City, Queens. He died in 1990 at the age of 74, swearing to the end that yes, every word of his unique relationship with the Babe was true.

THE BAMBINO GETS HITCHED AND SETTLES DOWN ... SORT OF
Roman Catholic Church of St. Gregory the Great
140 West 90th Street ... 110 Riverside Drive (& West 83rd Street)

He was the Bambino, the Sultan of Swat or simply the Babe — "the only sports legend I ever saw who completely lived up to advanced billing," Jimmy Breslin once said.

As the greatest player and personality to don a baseball uniform, Babe Ruth lived life fast, furiously, and loved the limelight so much that on a trip to Paris, he wanted to go home because he wasn't recognized. Said Ruth: "I swing big, with everything I got. I hit big or I miss big. I like to live as big as I can."

He knew himself well. It's difficult to think of Babe Ruth actually putting down roots anywhere. Yet, for most of his more than 25 years in New York, he was an Upper West Sider, living in a half-dozen or so apartments between 70th and 90th streets, bounded by Riverside Drive to the east and Broadway to the west. The Babe was even married in the area, tying the knot in 1929 with the former Claire Hodgson at Roman Catholic Church of St. Gregory the Great.

Out the door of St. Gregory The Great stepped a newly-hitched Babe Ruth.

Actually, life for Ruth on the Upper West Side had started a few years earlier in the Ansonia Hotel on Broadway at 73rd Street, where he lived from 1920 until he was married Hodgson. During most of that time, Ruth was married to his first wife, Helen, but the couple were by then estranged.

They separated in 1925, by which time Ruth had already met and taken up with Hodgson, a striking young Georgia-born illustrator's model and Broadway dancer. Despite his lusty behavior, Ruth was a staunch Catholic, not remarrying until after his first wife, Helen, died in a fire.

At the time, Hodgson was widowed with a young daughter, Julia. Claire soon became Ruth's trainer, finance manager and all-around taskmaster, in addition to being his wife. Although club rules prohibited wives from accompanying the team on road trips, Claire traveled with the Babe. It was a shrewd move, since Claire managed to control his legendary excesses, which had included overeating, drinking, and entertaining women in every American League port-of-call.

After they married, the Ruths moved to Hodgson's 11-room, seventh-floor apartment, down the hall from her mother at 345 West 88th Street. Their wedding was typical of the attention Ruth attracted, as America's most famous athlete-turned-folk-hero: The April 18, 1929 ceremony was held just before 6 AM to avoid the crowds, but word got around and within a half-hour, the number of onlookers had swelled to 200.

Babe Ruth, family man, with his young daughter, Dorothy. He had two daughters, both adopted. (National Baseball Hall of Fame Library, Cooperstown, New York)

The day was supposed to be the opening game of the season, at the Stadium against the Red Sox. But rain throughout the day postponed the game and the newly-married couple, after breakfast back home, went to a theater matinee instead. As for a honeymoon, Ruth said he guessed that he would spend it, "on the baseball field."

Marriage meant instant responsibility for the once-randy Ruth. In addition to Hodgson's daughter, Julia, the couple in 1930 officially adopted Ruth's daughter, Dorothy, from his first marriage. And with time and the responsibility of a couple of daughters to support, "he began calling Claire, 'mom,'" writes Lawrence Ritter in *Babe Ruth: A Life in Pictures.* "Not that it was so surprising," Ritter says. "After all, he'd never really had a 'mom' before."

The Babe lived here.

In 1942, the Ruths moved to another 11-room apartment — this one at 110 Riverside Drive at 83rd Street. Here Ruth lived out his baseball retirement — he died of throat cancer in 1948 at 53. Claire lived on another 28 years, covering the apartment with photographs, portraits, plaques, awards, and memorabilia from her husband's fabled career. She died of cancer in 1976 and is buried next to the Babe at Gate of Heaven Cemetery in Hawthorne, Westchester County, some 25 miles north of Yankee Stadium (see page 239).

BOMBERS HIT THE BIG SCREEN
THE BABE RUTH STORY and *PRIDE of the YANKEES*
Astor Theater
45th Street & Broadway

Too bad Babe Ruth left his Memorial Hospital sickbed, where he was dying of cancer, to see the July 26, 1948 opening of the film of his life. What a stinker; he should have stayed in his room.

You have to wonder about a film that bills itself as "No Greater Entertainment In Our Time." We're not exactly talking *Ben Hur* here. In fact, *The Babe Ruth Story*, starred a wooden William Bendix as the Babe and a grating Claire Trevor, who had the same name as Claire Hodgson Ruth — but little else. In short, it was a Grade-B bomb, barely appropriate for late-night cable.

"The pattern of the drama, with its Horatio Alger stamp — rags to riches and romance — is obviously contrived, and the personal characterizations are all of them second-grade stock," sniffed *The Times* in a review. No wonder the Astor went out of its way to proudly advertise that it was air-conditioned; there wasn't much else to boast about. Even Bendix said years later that the film embarrassed him.

The Babe implored by a tear-soaked kid not to let his dog, Pee Wee, die? Or the paraplegic kid who — miracle of miracles — gets to his feet after the Babe says, "Hello." Yup, both scenes are in there. Too bad that much of the Ruth mythology is based on such trite stuff.

The most positive part of the film was Ruth's appearance at the opening. Insulated by a police cordon from a pushing, cheering crowd of more than one thousand gathered outside — the Bambino was still a hero — Ruth walked slowly into the theater, supported under both arms, perspiring heavily and seemingly too exhausted to manage much more than a weak smile to spectators.

At least the film raised money for a good cause, the Babe Ruth Foundation, which gave underprivileged kids a chance to play baseball. On hand to greet the Babe at the film were Mayor William O'Dwyer, Mrs. Eleanor Gehrig, and former teammate Joe Dugan.

Ruth, his body ravaged with the cancer that would kill him in less than a month, was too sick to endure the entire film and left before it was over. He returned to Memorial Hospital that night and never left. Said Ruth to Connie Mack on the day before he died: "The termites got me." On August 16, 1948, the Babe died at 53.

What was it about the Astor? Some six years and a month before Ruth's film debuted, another film of note, *The Pride of the Yankees*, about the life and death of Lou Gehrig, opened there as well.

The 1942 film, starring Gary Cooper as Lou and Theresa Wright as Eleanor, wasn't well-reviewed at the time, but has survived to become a tear-jerker of the standard spring cable line-up. That's when the stations celebrate the start of another new baseball season by showing *Pride of the Yankees*.

Cooper even received an Academy Award nomination for his portrayal of Gehrig, but lost out to James Cagney, who took the Oscar for *Yankee Doodle Dandy*.

Not bad for Cooper, who grew up in Montana and admitted he knew next-to-nothing about Gehrig. And not bad for filmmaker Sam Goldwyn, even more of a baseball illiterate, who thought there were 10 bases on a diamond and had to ask what position Gehrig played. It didn't matter, because once Goldwyn saw a clip of Gehrig's poignant Yankee Stadium farewell, he knew he would make the film.

Goldwyn felt Gehrig's story represented more — much more than a baseball game. So what we have, as *The Times* reported, "is the story of a simple, shy young man who works hard to provide for his parents, meets and marries, after a while, a pleasant girl and then, when things are looking brightest, is ironically struck out by a fatal illness."

In other words, *Pride of the Yankees* was, well, really kind of average. That its story line is well known may have hurt its quality. On the other hand, the film was rushed and completed only a year after Gehrig's death in 1941. The result: box office appeal and one of the top 10 hits of 1942.

Goldwyn did his best to compensate for Cooper's lack of the most basic baseball skills. The actor was a righthander, creating a dilemma since Gehrig was a lefty. To help on fundamentals, old ballplayers such as Lefty O'Doul and former Dodger Babe Herman were hired to work with Cooper. That proved fruitless and movie makers eventually reversed the tape of Cooper batting right-handed. Said O'Doul: "He threw the ball like an old woman tossing a hot biscuit."

Very little is written about the July 15, 1942 opening of the film. But its enduring quality was evident from the start. During World War II, writes Ray Robinson in his 1990 biography of Gehrig, American soldiers repeatedly asked Cooper to recite his famous farewell speech during the actor's tour of military bases. Fumbling his lines at first, Cooper thereafter made sure he was ready and performed it flawlessly.

THE BABE'S LEGACY
The Babe Ruth Foundation gets started
Sherry Netherland Hotel, 781 5th Avenue

Historians focus on the excesses of Babe Ruth — how far he could hit a baseball, the famous 18-egg omelet breakfasts, and his fondness for women and booze.

But there was another side to Ruth — the quiet, unpublished trips to orphanages, similar to the one where he grew up; his genuine love for kids; and, in particular, his little-known creation on October 7, 1947 of the Babe Ruth Foundation. Its purpose: raising money for underprivileged children.

Not much is written about the Babe Ruth Foundation. The evidence comes mainly in the form of a museum piece — the front page of the minutes to the Foundation's formative meeting at the Sherry Netherland Hotel, in the residence of baseball Commissioner Albert B. "Happy" Chandler.

The Sherry Netherland was a little different from the kind of place in which Ruth was most familiar. Built in 1927 at 59th Street and 5th Avenue, the hotel's 525 rooms and 40 stories quickly became one of the city's most elegant residential addresses. No wonder it was billed as "more than a place to live — a new way of living."

The Babe was there, signing the ledger, "George Herman Ruth," one of the few times he used his full name. So were the seven other board members, who included Chandler, Eleanor Gehrig, American League president Will Harridge, and National League president Ford Frick.

Ruth was already sick, his throat ravaged with the cancer that killed him less than a year later. Earlier that summer, Ruth's pain had become so bad that his doctors decided to treat the cancer with an experimental new drug, a synthetic relative of folic acid, part of the Vitamin B complex.

By October, when the Foundation met, Ruth's pain had lessened enough for the Babe to occasionally play golf and entertain visitors.

It's hard to know how much the Ruth Foundation actually raised. But, it did make a difference: What is thought to be the last photo of Ruth, taken July 29, 1948 from the Babe's bed at Memorial Hospital, where he died three weeks later, shows him accepting a check for the Foundation.

CASE CLOSED
The Babe's pants are back
35 West 36th Street

Sounding like a character out of "N.Y.P.D. Blue," New York City Detective Brian Costello described the moment he and fellow Detective Mary Anne Greene finally cracked the baffling case. "They got greedy," he said of the criminals in question, "and they got stupid."

"We didn't ever expect to get it back," he added, turning his attention to the recovered crime items that had consumed so much of the city's attention and newsprint for close to a week in May 1995. Costello spoke before the usual bank of tape recorders and microphones that mark the most important press conferences at the Midtown South station house on West 35th Street.

A case of diamonds recovered? No. A cache of drugs with a zillion dollar street value? No again. In this case, the subject of this piece of New York City police sleuthing was a pair of pants — Babe Ruth's pants.

So here were Costello and Greene talking about pants and the other recovered items, including a 1967 Tom Seaver rookie card. And here was the suspect, one William Wilson III of 305 West 145th Street, sheepishly admitting to his crime, saying he gave up these invaluable items of baseball's past because he was scared. The 39-year-old Wilson even took the opportunity to boast to police about the strikeout record he set more than two decades ago at Trenton High.

Wilson said he stole the Babe's pants when he hopped into the unattended car of Mark Lassman, a baseball card memorabilia dealer from Davie, Florida. Lassman, in town for a card show at the Westchester County Center in White Plains, had the uniform, worth some $50,000, as well as $250,000 in baseball cards inside the trunk of his rented Mercury Sable, which he had left outside Lazare Sportswear, 35 West 36th Street.

The story should end there; instead, it gets weirder. Actually, the mysterious case of Babe Ruth's pants started years earlier when Ruth, according to Lassman, first wore the heavy, off-white size-50 shirt and size-44 pants for the 1924 season. Ruth is said to have also worn the uniform, playing himself opposite Gary Cooper as Lou Gehrig in the 1942 film, *Pride of the Yankees.*

On to the weird part: According to Lassman's partner, Edward Lenahan, the uniform was then purchased from the Yankees by Western Costume

Company in North Hollywood, California and remained with the company through the filming. But in the 1950s, the uniform vanished, its whereabouts unknown until the early 1980s, when it was found among the property of Dennis Walker, a collector and victim of an apparent mob hit in a Las Vegas hotel room.

Some years later, the Walker murder and the missing uniform were the subject of an episode in the television program, "Unsolved Murders." Shortly after the show, Lenahan said, another collector named Malcolm "Sonny" Jackson visited the Suffolk County police and turned in the uniform.

There's more. The uniform remained with the police until 1992 when Jackson sued to get it back. He, in turn, sold the uniform to Thomas Catal, the owner of Mickey's Place, a Cooperstown, New York sports memorabilia store. Catal, who believed the uniform to be a costume only, said he paid $1,500 and sold it to Lenahan for $2,500.

Back at the Midtown South station house, detectives gave some insight into the case. They found the Babe's uniform in Wilson's apartment; other memorabilia turned up in an abandoned building down the block and in Morrisville, Pennsylvania.

Wilson apparently stole the merchandise by shattering a window and opening the trunk from inside the car. Detective Greene said she knew what she had and used a middleman who tried to sell the memorabilia back to Lassman.

But then, as Costello related, they got greedy and things went awry. Thank goodness that the Babe's pants are safe — for now.

CHAPTER TWO

THE BRONX

"The secret of success as a pitcher is to get a job with the Yankees."
— Waite Hoyt, 1927

END OF THE ROAD FOR THE IRON HORSE
Christ Protestant Episcopal Church, Riverdale

A steady rain matched the mood on the day they remembered Lou Gehrig. This gloomy June 4, 1941 day was three years since Gehrig had pounded the ball in his last full season as a Yankee superstar and only two years from the day he had gone to the Mayo Clinic and heard the news about the crippling disease, ALS (Amyotrophic Lateral Sclerosis), that would waste his body.

Gehrig's death on June 2 wasn't a surprise. It was met nonetheless by a tremendous outpouring of grief for the humble, 37-year-old baseball superstar. More than 1,500 telegrams arrived at the Gehrig's nearby home at 5204 Delafield Avenue in Riverdale. President Roosevelt sent flowers and Mayor La Guardia ordered flags in New York City to fly at half-staff.

At Gehrig's old work address, Yankee Stadium, his former teammates lined up in front of the stands in a minute of silence. At Christ Church, 5,000

Lou Gehrig at the end of his career: Note the 1939 New York World's Fair patch on his arm. (National Baseball Hall of Fame Library, Cooperstown, New York)

people filed past his bier. The following day's private funeral service produced yet another outpouring of grief from Lou's friends and teammates, as hundreds stood outside in the rain along the outer ridge of the Henry Hudson Parkway.

It was a short, dignified ceremony, lasting no more than eight minutes. Near the end, the Rev. Gerald V. Barry read the Episcopal service for the dead, pausing to say there would be no eulogy at the request of the Gehrig family. "We need none," Rev. Barry said, "because you all knew him."

The immediate family accompanied the body to Fresh Pond Crematory in Middle Village, Queens. Gehrig's ashes then were taken to the family vault of Yankee general manager Ed Barrow, at Kensico Cemetery in Valhalla, Westchester County. In September 1941, they were transferred to a permanent resting place in the family plot at the same cemetery.

HAMMERIN' HANK GETS HIS START
663 Crotona Park North

Not much eluded New York's resident baseball genius John McGraw in his 30-some years as Giants manager. But when he passed on a young slugger from the Bronx named Hank Greenberg, he missed the opportunity of a lifetime.

McGraw had long sought a premium Jewish ballplayer as a way, he figured, to attract Jewish fans to the Polo Grounds, and to counteract the enormous draw of a Yankee slugger named Ruth. "An outstanding Jewish player in New York would be worth his weight in gold," McGraw told writer Fred Lieb in a 1935 interview in *The Sporting News.* But he passed over Greenberg without batting an eyelash in what ranks as perhaps the city's greatest blown opportunity to sign a legitimate home-grown star.

"I knew that New York kids sometimes went to the Polo Grounds to shag flies when the Giant irregulars hit in the morning, and I asked for permission to join them," Greenberg recalled in his 1989 autobiography *Hank Greenberg: The Story of My Life,* written with Ira Berkow. "Back came the word from John McGraw: 'Henry Greenberg had already been scouted by the Giants; he would never be a ballplayer.'"

So Greenberg signed with the Tigers in 1929, went on to hit 311 major league home runs and was elected to the Baseball Hall of Fame, all of which proved McGraw wrong — very wrong. As for Greenberg's relationship with another New York team of note, the Yankees, he turned them down as a scholastic player at James Monroe High School: "I was a slugging first baseman," the ballplayer explained in his autobiography, "and the Yankees had the greatest in Lou Gehrig."

Greenberg wasn't the major league's first Jewish player. But as the Tigers' star slugger during the 1930s and '40s, he was a stirring symbol of success to Jews everywhere, particularly as a world war rumbled across Europe and the Far East. That was particularly so for youngsters, whose Eastern European Jewish parents generally considered participation in sports a waste of time. Indeed, in 1934, when Greenberg decided to play on the first day of Rosh Hashanah, the Jewish New Year, hitting two home runs in the process against the Red Sox, telegrams flooded in from rabbis across the country telling him that he had made a grave mistake.

Things were a little different that same year, on Yom Kippur, the Jewish day of atonement. Greenberg decided to skip that day's game against the Yankees, choosing instead to attended services at a Detroit synagogue. When Greenberg entered the synagogue, it erupted in applause. "I was embarrassed; I didn't know what to do," Greenberg said in his autobiography. "I was a hero around town, particularly among the Jewish people, and I was very proud of it."

Born a few minutes after midnight on January 1, 1911, Greenberg lived at first in Greenwich Village with his family in a second-floor tenement apartment at 16 Barrow Street. About six years later, they moved to 663 Crotona Park North, then on the outskirts of the city, which Greenberg compared to living in the country. Although Greenberg was not particularly observant in adulthood, his was an Orthodox home, where both Yiddish and English were spoken.

Greenberg's father, David, owned the Acme Textile Shrinking Works on the Lower East Side. Neither of Greenberg's parents appreciated their son's growing attachment to baseball. As a strapping kid — at 13, Greenberg stood 6'3" — he built a sliding pit in the family backyard and only had to cross the street to Crotona Park to find a game.

That as much as anything encouraged his interest in baseball. "Sports were my escape," Greenberg wrote. "Many of the very things that were social liabilities were assets in sports. I felt comfortable with athletics and I think that had a lot to do with why I spent most of my time in Crotona Park, or sliding into the pit in my backyard."

At first, the youngster stood around the edges of the park as sides were picked. Eventually, both sides wanted him for their games, in which an old ball was taped together with adhesive tape. Later, at Public School 44, Greenberg played both baseball and basketball.

After graduating from James Monroe High School, he enrolled at New York University on an athletic scholarship but dropped out to sign a professional contract for $9,000 a year. A year later, he was in the majors and by 1933, he was a full-fledged star, spending 12 of his 13 major league seasons with Detroit. He led the American League in home runs five time and runs batted in four times.

Greenberg was the American League Most Valuable Player in 1935 and again in 1940. He was elected to the Hall of Fame in 1956, the first Jewish player and one of two to be chosen — Brooklyn's Sandy Koufax is the other. He died in 1985 at the age of 75.

BATTLE IN THE BRONX
Show me the money!
Crotona Park

Don't think for a moment that the game they played years ago was any kinder and gentler.

The date: July 6, 1914. The place: the lower ballfield at Crotona Park, where later, Hank Greenberg would play. On this lazy Sunday afternoon, it was home to the amateur Bronx Orioles, locked in a tight duel with their cross-Bronx rivals, the Kingston Athletics.

Not quite the Jints and the Bums at the Polo Grounds, but a passionate rivalry all the same, with a crowd in the thousands.

As was the custom in those days, the teams played for a side bet of $10, with the money held by a man who was supposedly neutral. No big deal. Then the A's won, 10-4. Still, not a big deal. But when they turned to where the stakeholder had been sitting and found him gone, quite suddenly, it was a very big deal.

A fight started. Nobody could say where and how it got going exactly. But within minutes, players were fighting players and fans fighting fans. "Bats, masks, and shin guards were used by members of both teams," reported *The New York Times*, "and spectators flung themselves into the battle armed with brickbats and pop bottles."

A contingent of policemen from the Tremont Station did their best to quell the disturbance, dispersing the crowd and making some arrests and discovering a real tragedy — a man killed in the melee. Pronounced dead at Fordham Hospital was Henry Schaeffen, a clerk, of 1462 Brook Avenue, whose skull was fractured by a brick.

In all, there were several arrests and more than a dozen injured. Nobody was ever arrested in the death of Schaeffen. And the stakeholder? Never found.

LIFE IN THE FAST LANE ... AND PERFECTION
Grand Concourse Hotel
2000 Grand Concourse

World Series perfection? Christy Mathewson came close in 1905 with three shutouts. In more recent years, Sandy Koufax and Orel Hershiser were practically unbeatable. But in a game of improbables, Don Larsen's World Series perfection stands out.

For one glorious autumn afternoon in 1956 at Yankee Stadium, Yankee Don Larsen achieved the pinnacle of pitching success, setting down his opponent — who else but the snake-bitten Brooklyn Dodgers? — with 97 pitches, 27 outs, and no hits, no walks, or errors. It was the only Series perfect game in history, courtesy of a journeyman player whose late-night, carousing lifestyle earned him the apt nickname, "Sourmash Don."

"He was tired in the morning, afternoon and night — especially if there was a game scheduled," manager Jimmie Dykes once said of Larsen. To writer Jimmy Cannon, he was a "midnight kid who doesn't miss many laughs."

Larsen came to the Yankees after the 1954 season in a whopping 18-player deal with the Orioles. It was an odd deal on several fronts, since not only were the conservative, lordly Yanks inheriting a player of questionable habits; they were adding a man with a previous year's record of 3-21.

But manager Casey Stengel saw some promise in the 6'4" righthander. Despite a stint at Denver in the minors and a spring training driving encounter with a telephone pole at 2 AM — he "must have been out mailing a letter," Stengel said afterwards — Larsen finished with an impressive 11-5 mark in 1956.

Larsen's home as a Yankee was the ballplayer's home away from home in those days, the Grand Concourse Hotel. A number of Yankees, including Mickey Mantle, in his first few years in the majors, and several of the New York football Giants made the then-elegant hotel their home during the season. In Larsen's case, it served as a refuge of sorts from a broken marriage and a place to unwind from his many hard nights.

Like the night before the fifth game of the '56 Series: Having pitched four days before in game two, he had gone to bed before midnight and been shelled by the Dodgers the next day, not lasting beyond the second inning. Growled Larsen after absorbing the loss: "That's the last time I'll ever go to bed early."

True to form, Larsen went out for drinks with some teammates the night before starting game six. A teammate, Bob Cerv, was quoted as saying he left Larsen at 4 AM. Said Larsen later: "I got no comment at all on that night."

You know what happened next. Pitching for the Dodgers was Sal Maglie, who was good, limiting the Yankees to five hits. But Larsen, with his no-windup delivery was better, throwing an assortment of fast balls, sliders and slow curves, all delivered with pinpoint control. With two out in the ninth, Dale Mitchell, pinch-hitting for Maglie, took a 1-2 fastball for strike three and the improbable had happened.

Wrote Shirley Povich in the next morning's *Washington Post*: "The million-to-one shot came in. Hell froze over, a month of Sundays hit the calendar. Don Larsen pitched a no-hit, no-run, no-man-reach-first game in a World Series."

The euphoria didn't last. With his marriage troubles continuing, Larsen that night dispatched $420 to the lawyer for his estranged wife, Vivian. They eventually divorced.

FORDHAM FLASH AT REST
Woodlawn Cemetery
233rd Street & Webster Avenue, next to Van Cortland Park

There is a tale about Frank Frisch, related as the Giants were traveling by train and a stranger entered the club car. He placed a strange-looking valise at his feet and introduced himself to some ballplayers as a man who had made his way around the country giving lectures on snakes.

Then he reached into his bag and produced a squirming snake.

"This one," he announced with pride, "is the fastest thing on the continent. As fast as you young men are, none of you could ever catch this snake."

"Frisch could," said Giant Ross Youngs.

"I doubt it," the snake man replied. "You've never seen this snake on the loose."

"Maybe not," said Youngs, "but I've seen Frisch."

Frisch was Frank Frisch, the "Fordham Flash." Born in New York and educated at Fordham, where he captained the baseball, football, and basketball teams, Frisch was signed by the hometown Giants and wound up in the Baseball Hall of Fame. He is even buried in the city — his resting spot set amid a rolling landscape of 3,500 trees and extraordinary diversity of sculpture in Woodlawn Cemetery.

Frisch earned his nickname. "Then there was Mr. Frisch, which went to a university and could run fast, besides," Casey Stengel recalled. "He was the first second baseman, too, that didn't pedal backwards when the ball was hit down the line. He'd put his head down and commence running like in a race, and he'd beat the ball there."

Frisch started running in 1919 after joining the Giants of John McGraw and didn't stop for 19 years, compiling a .316 batting average as a switch hitter. He was also part of the Giant World Series victories of 1921 and 1922 over the Yankees, as well as National League pennants the next two years; the Giants lost the '23 Series to the Yanks and in '24 to the Senators.

Along the way, Frisch developed a reputation as one of the most competitive, tempestuous figures in the game. When he collided with McGraw in the mid-1920s and was then traded to the Cardinals, fans at the Polo Grounds were outraged. But his fiery personality proved just as popular in St. Louis, where he played all over the infield and won three more pennants as a player and another two as playing manager of the famous Cardinal rowdies, "The Gashouse Gang." In later years, he also managed the Pirates and Cubs, before retiring in 1951 to the announcing booth.

The stories are legion. As a player, Frisch was once thrown out of the game in the Polo Grounds and took off for the centerfield clubhouse by a roundabout way to annoy the umpires. A wrong turn or two later, he was out on 8th Avenue, still in uniform and locked out of the ballpark. As a manager, Frisch once was ejected for arguing, and drew a five-game suspension the next afternoon for arguing again.

Considering such stormy behavior, how ironic that Frisch should end up amid the gentle rolling hills of Woodlawn. But, like a lot of hotheads, he was different away from the ballpark, a gentle raconteur who enjoyed listening to a large collection of records and planting flowers in his New Rochelle backyard. Of particular interest to Frisch in later years were a couple of Cardinals he named Musial and Slaughter.

Frisch spent his final years in Rhode Island. A widower, he married a wealthy woman who urged he sever his ties to baseball. In 1973, she refused to accompany him to Florida for spring training, whereupon Frisch angrily began to drive and had a fatal auto accident in Delaware. As Stengel would say, "which is why his place of death is Delaware, where you wouldn't expect."

HAZARDOUS TO YOUR HEALTH?
Jimmy's Bronx Cafe
281 West Fordham Road

It would be major news anywhere else but New York. But in the wacky world of Steinbrenner-era Yankee baseball, news that major league baseball had ordered its players to stay away from Jimmy's Bronx Cafe amounted to a one-day tabloid frenzy — barely a blip on the journalistic radar screen in the general scheme of things.

Here was the newest and most prominent Yankee at the time, Ruben Sierra, a part-owner at Jimmy's, warned to keep out of his OWN club. "Anything can happen anywhere, not just in Jimmy's," a perplexed Sierra told *The Daily News* after the August 1995 warning.

Long the hot spot for the city's Hispanic population and a favorite spot for ballplayers, musicians, and politicians alike, Jimmy's had become the scene of at least two shootings in 1995 alone, which worried baseball officials.

Police believe the shootings may have been caused by incidents that originated outside the club. In fact, a major league baseball official cited the "unsavory characters" who frequented the restaurant.

"Unsavory characters?" asked Jamie Rodriguez, Jr., Sierra's business partner and the "Jimmy" for whom the club is named. "They go to Yankee Stadium all the time. You get 40 desk appearance tickets a night at games. If baseball knows of undesirables in my place, tell law enforcement and have them locked up."

Fair point. For starters, Jimmy's doesn't even look like a nightclub; it's a rectangular, sparkling white, Miami-looking kind of place, just off the Major Deegan Expressway with the architectural flourish of a car dealership, which it was in a previous life. Inside, beyond the framed silver satin tuxedo of band leader Tito Puente and assorted ballplayers' jerseys, is a Caribbean-style seafood restaurant, bar, and nightclub.

A taste of Miami in the Bronx: Jimmy's Bronx Cafe.

Then, there's Jimmy himself, a 6'3" combo of charisma and schmooze, and known in the papers as "the Latin Toots Shor." On most nights, you'll see the 35-year-old Rodriguez making the rounds carrying his patented rum and Coke and making sure that people are enjoying themselves. And chances are you'll see Bronx Borough president Fernando Ferrer, or, depending on what team is in town, a major leaguer or two.

Jimmy's bio reads like a Horatio Alger novel. A high school dropout, Rodriguez sold lobsters under the Bronx River Parkway and soon expanded into his first restaurant, Mariscos del Caribe.

In 1993, Rodriguez opened Jimmy's. He sponsors dozens of Little League teams and even opens the restaurant every Sunday for a church meeting, and the word is that Jimmy is now moving into the more rarefied Upper East Side social circles; among his recent visits are to the Armani show and a *New York Magazine* party.

Another venture of late — attending the February 1998 Duke of Windsor auction at Sotheby's, where he paid $22,000 for three suits, including lederhosen the Duke wore in 1937. According to newspaper reports, Rodriguez plans to frame the lederhosen and place them next to Tito Puente's tux.

That wouldn't happen in Cleveland. Only in New York. And only at Jimmy's.

CHAPTER THREE

BROOKLYN

"They brought me up to the Brooklyn Dodgers, which at that time, was in Brooklyn."

— *Casey Stengel, Mets manager, 1962*

HOUSE OF CARDS — TOPPS CHEWING GUM CO.
Bush Terminal
269 37th Street

So, it was Mom who threw out your baseball cards.

Remarkable how she found them, digging deep within your closet to retrieve the battered shoebox, and, with the agility of Brooks Robinson going deep in the hole, tossing them straight into the trash. Of course, nothing else amid the clutter was touched — not the piles of old sweat socks, not the sixth-grade geography notes, nor even the summer camp woodworking trophy. And never mind that you haven't bought a baseball card since you were 12 — they're gone, long gone, and it still hurts.

"That bit about their mothers, they always say that," says Shirley Festberg, who helps her son, David, run the Baseball & Hobby Shop on Flatbush

Avenue. "Then they look around the store and say their collection was bigger than ours — two or three times bigger."

Festberg is sitting a few years ago amid stacks of old cards, yearbooks, and autographed baseballs and sorting through a bundle of vintage Joe DiMaggios and chain-smoking as she talks about the kinds of customers who buy baseball cards. "Adults, kids and almost all male," she says. "A lot of the older collectors relate to things and people they remember, like Mickey [Mantle] and the Babe."

The Festbergs make a nice living in the baseball-card business, which in itself is a tribute to the staying power of the national pastime and the enduring hobby that the Topps Chewing Gum Co. helped to launch. Sure, there are all kinds of companies making baseball cards these days — Fleer and Donruss among them — but get a sampling from most collectors today and you'll find that Topps still rules.

The first baseball cards were introduced with cigarettes in the 1890s and dominated the trading card field through the early part of the century. Those early cards were crude by today's sleek standards — most of the photographs were taken in an artist's studio with the action simulated to resemble game conditions. Indeed, it wasn't unusual to see players catching or hitting a ball suspended from a string or sliding into a base on a wooden floor.

Particularly memorable at the turn of the century were the T-205 and T-210 sets, including the famous T-210 Honus Wagner card, which sold for nearly $500,000 a few years ago. Included in packs of cigarettes, the cards were notable for their superior colors and were the product of German inks. World War I put a stop to the ink supply and the sets were discontinued.

In 1933, Goudey (Big League Gum Co.) cards with bubble gum were introduced and featured more realistic poses and heavier cardboard.

But card manufacturing took another hit when it was suspended during World War II to divert raw materials to war use. Production resumed in 1948, when the Bowman Company issued a series of small, black-and-white cards.

In 1951, enter Topps — redefining the modern standards of baseball cards and touching off a furious marketing war in the process. Ironically, it was later that year, with its first series, that Topps issued a Dodger Ralph Branca card, but not one for Giant Bobby Thomson, whose miracle ninth-inning home run off Branca won the National League pennant that year.

During that era, both Topps and Bowman fought to obtain exclusive contracts with most of the established big leaguers. For competitive reasons, you won't find Indians' righthander Bob Feller on many Topps cards, while Duke Snider of the Dodgers is rarely on a Bowman. In the valuable 1952

Topps set, complete with player statistics on the backs of the cards and considered the prototype of today's cards, there were five players who declined use of their photographs. Even without them, the set in mint condition now sells for $20,000.

By 1955, Bowman had left the baseball card business, giving Topps a virtual monopoly in the field. In those days, players received $50 a season for the use of their pictures. Their fee has since jumped to $250, with benefits that can earn a player more than $2,000 a year. As the prices grew, so did the company's selection, which now includes cards for league leaders, record breakers, and all-time greats.

In 1982, Fleer and Donruss successfully challenged Topps' monopoly and signed contracts with the Major League Baseball Players Association that allowed them to produce baseball cards without the bubble gum.

Baseball cards without gum? That's like Amos without Andy and Crosby without Hope. Beavis without Butthead? Well, maybe not, but you get the idea: It's almost un-American. Thanks goodness for Topps, which has kept the gum, satisfying the purists and proving that you don't tinker with tradition. And despite a move in recent years to a new swank headquarters in the Wall Street area, Topps continues to churn out the cards and help to create a new generation of youngsters to supplement their baseball fix with collecting.

Back at Shirley Festberg's shop on Flatbush Avenue, a man with a lingering passion for the Dodgers, is sifting through one of the notebooks of cards from the 1950s. "Look ... a Pee Wee Reese," he shouts triumphantly. "I've been looking all over for this and here it is." The man is happy, the Festbergs have another sale and all is well in baseball card country.

DA FLAG IS BACK
Brooklyn Historical Society
128 Pierrepont Street, Brooklyn Heights

Okay, it's not plundered art treasures returning to Russia from Germany after World War II, nor a priceless marble frieze that Lord Elgin looted from the Parthenon, on its way back to Greece. But for Brooklynites, there is enduring satisfaction that the lone Series flag the Dodgers won while in Flatbush is back in the borough.

For two years only, that banner — white lettering on a blue background that reads "World Champions, 1955 Dodgers" — fluttered high above the right-center field wall at Ebbets Field. Then, as fast as you can say, "Carl Furillo," it was gone, mysteriously disappearing in 1959 from a Dodgers hospitality suite while the Dodgers of the Los Angeles variety were beating the Chicago White Sox in that year's World Series.

What happened? And how did the flag find its way back to Brooklyn some 38 years later, to its current resting place at the Historical Society? Whatever the answer, "it belongs back in Brooklyn," said Johnny Podres, who shut out the Yankees in the seventh game in the '55 World Series, earning the enduring affection of Dodger fans everywhere. "Some of my blood is on that thing."

According to a Historical Society official, a group of Brooklyn sportswriters, shedding a collective tear for the dearly-departed Dodgers, were responsible for lifting the nearly 17-foot flag. For a time, it was kept in a Roslyn, Long Island basement on the theory that it should be shared with the public, and was eventually presented to the Baseball Hall of Fame in Cooperstown, New York, until a worthy home could be found back in Brooklyn.

It stayed in Cooperstown until April, 1995, when the Historical Society threw a fund-raising dinner to honor the 40th anniversary of the World Series triumph. And so, at the suggestion of Dodger owner Peter O'Malley, it was brought back via United Parcel Service, the flag now a little frayed at the edges.

A reception of 150 of the aging faithful dining on hot dogs and egg creams on white linen tablecloths decorated with pitchers' mounds made of moss and offset by napkins of Dodger blue, welcomed the flag back.

That Peter O'Malley is the son of the borough's most hated man, Walter O'Malley, who moved the Dodgers to Los Angeles, is an irony not lost in the borough, where the wounds are still deep for many who miss the team. "This act in no way mitigates the pain O'Malley caused to the borough," said one such fan.

Today, the flag is showcased in the Historical Society's Dodgers display along with seats from Ebbets Field, old bats and uniforms once worn by Podres and Jackie Robinson. Back where it belongs.

KING SANDY STARS ... IN HOOPS
Jewish Community House
7802 Bay Parkway (& 78th Street)

There isn't the kind of affection reserved for Bensonhurst's Sandy Koufax that there is for other former Dodgers like Pee Wee Reese or Duke Snider.

Koufax's best years weren't with Brooklyn, for whom he won a grand total of 10 games in three years. Stardom came later, in Los Angeles, where Koufax, after a handful of mediocre seasons there as well, became arguably the most dominant pitcher of the 1960s. Today, that doesn't inspire affection, as much as awe.

Who wudda thunk it? Back in Bensonhurst, before Koufax even signed with the Dodgers, he was best known as a basketball player. And it was at the Jewish Community House, where he developed his talent for the game that sent him to the University of Cincinnati with, yes, a basketball scholarship.

Set up like any YMCA or community house, the "J" as it was known, became Koufax's "second home," as he explains in his 1966 autobiography, *Koufax*. It included a weight room, handball court, pool, steam bath, and "the heart of the place," he says, which was the basketball court.

Koufax discovered basketball in the fall of 1949 when he entered Lafayette High School. "I had suddenly developed outsize hands and feet," he writes in the book. "The hands were a great help for basketball and the feet didn't particularly hinder me. While I never really had a good shot, I could — believe it or not — run very well and, most of all, I could jump. I could jump through the roof. I could jump as naturally as I could throw. I just could."

At the J, Koufax played basketball on weeknights, weekends, and every opportunity he could find to hone his skills. "I suppose it gets down to a matter of space," Koufax explains. "In Brooklyn, every square foot of recreational area has to be used — and that's about all the space you need to set up a basket."

In fact, baseball really didn't enter the picture until Koufax's freshman year at the University of Cincinnati, where he was talked into pitching for the baseball team. When he struck out 58 batters in 38 innings, the scouts came running.

Back home for the summer, he joined a sandlot team, "Nathan's Famous," sponsored by the Coney Island hot dog landmark and drew the interest of the Dodgers' Scout Al Campanis. Signed by the team as a "bonus baby," he stayed with the big club for two years, as stipulated by major league rules. So, less than two years after leaving Lafayette High School, Koufax was a Dodger.

A 6'2" and 210-pound lefthander, Koufax had speed but no control. "He couldn't hit the side of a barn door at 60 feet," said Tom Lasorda, who was demoted to the farm in Montreal to make roster room for Koufax. "But he had that burning desire to whip control problems."

In the early days, teammates hated batting against Koufax, not knowing where he was likely to put the ball. Despite those few victories in his first few seasons with the Dodgers, the hints of greatness were there: On August 27, 1955, in his second major league start, Koufax pitched a 14-strikeout, two-hitter against the Reds.

In 1961, Koufax won 18 games and led the major leagues in strikeouts. Before he was done only five years later, he had led the league in ERA five times, pitched four no-hitters and won 20 games three times. Koufax's record over those last four years: 97-27, making Brooklyn fans happy that a native son had conquered the mountain, but frustrated that it had to happen a continent away in Los Angeles.

Koufax, wracked by painful arm problems, retired in 1966 at the age of 31. Five years later, he was elected the Baseball Hall of Fame, making him the answer to a good trivia question: Cooperstown's youngest elected member.

SAD END FOR A LANDMARK
The Hotel St. George
51 Clark Street, Brooklyn Heights

There was a time when The Hotel St. George was one of THE places to go in Brooklyn. An elegant, grand dame of a 2,800-room hotel, it hosted Johnny Weismuller, who once swam in the mirrored basement swimming pool, the city's largest indoor pool. Revelers danced away the evenings in the grand ballroom here, and dined in the rooftop restaurant.

The Hotel St. George was also home to several Dodgers of note, many of them single, and others living on their own with families back home. In the first part of the century, many Brooklyn ballplayers lived near the ballpark, using the subway to get back and forth. It didn't hurt that the Brooklyn Heights hotel, along with others like the Hotel Bossert and the Towers Hotel, were a short walk to the main Dodger office at 215 Montague Street.

Dodger Manager Wilbert Robinson and his wife took a suite at the St. George when it opened in 1929; they stayed until he retired in 1931. Over at the Bossert, Leo Durocher had a suite, as did Carl Furillo, Johnny Podres, and Gino Cimoli. Down the street at the more elegant St. George, Andy Pafko and Joe Black kept apartments, a 20-minute subway ride to the Lincoln Road station, and from there a short two-block walk to Ebbets Field.

Hotel living for ballplayers was typical back then, with single players from each of the three New York teams tending to cluster at the same places as their teammates. For the Yankees, Concourse Plaza, near 161st Street and a stone's throw from Yankee Stadium, was the preferred place. Many Giant players lived at the Somerset Hotel, at 72nd Street and Columbus Avenue; the Braddock, at 126th Street and 8th Avenue; and, the Colonial, at 124th Street and 8th Avenue. Typical for single players was to marry, start families, and then move into the suburbs of New Jersey and Westchester County.

The presence of ballplayer celebrities only helped the reputation of places like the Hotel St. George, which for years was considered Brooklyn's finest, a stately 31-story building that towered over the neighborhood's brownstones. How sad it was, then, when the hotel nearly burned to the ground in 1995 — one more reminder that Brooklyn had changed for the worse.

A huge 16-alarm fire that deployed 500 firefighters, 50 engines, and 27 ladder trucks gutted the once elegant landmark. Charged with setting the fire was a 61-year-old retired city laborer, Louis Foressie, who told police he accidentally set the fire while ransacking a vacant section of the hotel in search of copper wire he could sell, possibly to support his drug habit.

Here is how much the building had changed: The fire caused the evacuation of several hundred transients and HIV-infected homeless people housed by the city in the building.

But if you think that's unfortunate, consider the case of one family residing at the hotel, Sidney and Norma Buckholtz. Tough year for the Buckholtzes: Earlier that week, they had fled their vacation home in Speonk, Long Island, a step ahead of an enormous wildfire that consumed thousands of acres in Suffolk County.

Then they were rushed out of their apartment at the Hotel St. George. Said Norma Buckholtz to *The New York Times*: "We are double evacuees, but we are very grateful and very lucky that no one was hurt."

BUMS HERE
555 Flatbush Avenue (& Church Avenue)

In the 1940s, this building was home to several Dodgers and their growing families. Arky Vaughan lived here for a time, as did Cookie Lavagetto, Pete Reiser, Bruce Edwards, and Joe Hatten.

THE OISK DELIVERS FROM THE HEART
Lafayette Place & 98th Street, off 4th Avenue, Bay Ridge

"If you've ever been in love, you can relate to it — a love affair with extreme emotional ups and downs," says onetime Brooklyn hero, Carl Erskine.

No, Erskine isn't trying out the lead to his new gothic romance. The World Series hero and lifetime 122-game winning pitcher is discussing the unusually close relationship that he and his Dodger teammates of the late 1940s and early 1950s shared with Brooklynites, the onetime Flatbush faithful.

Even criticism was okay in Erskine's book. "They'd lambaste you when things were bad, but it was almost like an endearment," says the 72-year-old Anderson, Indiana bank president. "There was such an emotional involvement on the part of the community with the team in large part, because it was so personal."

When Erskine was on the road, neighbors looked in on his wife, Betty, and children, to make sure they were comfortable. After pitching — win or lose — the local grocer would leave a bag of groceries on his family's stoop, which in his case, was this quiet street in Bay Ridge, also home for a time to the families of Dodger mainstays Pee Wee Reese, Duke Snider, and Clem Labine.

Nearly a half-century later, Erskine grows almost misty-eyed remembering. "Once you get past the cold facade of a New Yorker, there was a kind of intimacy," he says. "Here were Betty and I — two kids from Indiana with small children — and what happened to us in Brooklyn was a beautiful thing. The ties we developed in Brooklyn … still carry on. It was special."

Even after Erskine moved to Los Angeles with the Dodgers in 1958, his wife continued to call their Brooklyn pediatrician for advice. Says the old righthander: "All the players had their own intimacies with Brooklyn people."

In Erskine's mind, the Yankees were "the uptown sophisticates," the Giants were "the rough riders, the New Yorkers," whereas the Dodgers were "the orphans, a team coming off a long history of not winning very often."

"We were the poor kids on the block, something that actually enhanced our popularity in the borough," he says. "We went through a lot together. After all, we died a few times together."

And so it goes in a love affair reaching back more than 40 years.

BIRTH OF BASEBALL'S ANTHEM
Hammerstein's Victoria Theatre
Bedford Avenue & Fulton Street

Quick now — name the most popular baseball song of all time. If you answered, "Take Me Out to the Ballgame," give yourself a well-deserved Ballantine break.

Every red-blooded baseball fan knows at least the first verse of this smaltzy, waltzy little ballad, sung for generations at most seventh-inning stretches at the old ballyard. But how this song, written some 90 years ago from language taken from a subway ad, became an American folk classic is an intriguing tale.

There are more than 100 recorded versions of the song. In the 1949 MGM musical, *Take Me Out to the Ballgame*, the title song got the attention of some real all-stars, as Frank Sinatra sang it, Gene Kelly tap-danced to it, and Esther Williams swam to it. In the updated 1950 version, the Dodgers' Roy Campanella and Ralph Branca, along with Phil Rizzuto and Tommy Henrich of the Yankees, teamed with Mitch Miller and the Sandpipers.

There are lots of other, better songs about baseball. What's particularly ironic about about this one is that the song's composers, Jack Norworth and Albert Von Tilzer, had never even seen a major league game, nor had any interest in the sport when they composed their ode to baseball. That they composed THE song that became the national pastime's national anthem is about as unlikely as Shoeless Joe Jackson performing the soliloquy from Hamlet.

Norworth wrote the lyrics to "Ballgame" on a 1908 subway ride, getting the idea from an ad promoting baseball at the Polo Grounds. Ride the subway these days and you can compose some catchy lyrics to a song based on the English translation of a cockroach ad.

Norworth gave the lyrics to Broadway show tune producer Albert Von Tilzer — he of the famous five Tin Pan Alley composing brothers — who promptly composed the memorable music. But when Norworth introduced his song to his act at the Amphion Theater in Brooklyn, it bombed.

Figuring he had a dud on his hands, Norworth forgot all about it, until three months later when he re-introduced the song during the ninth act at Hammerstein's Victoria Theatre vaudeville show and the crowd went wild. So what happened? The positioning of the galaxy perhaps — and good timing.

Actually, the song's sudden popularity may have had something to do with the exciting National League pennant race of that year, won by the Cubs over the Giants and Pirates by a single game. Another craze of the era — the spread of popular music through nickelodeons — also may have contributed to its popularity. Indeed, when Norworth discovered he had a hit that night at the Victoria, he found the song had proven so popular in the meantime that several acts before him had blended the song into their acts as well.

So Norworth had a hit — one of many, including "Shine on Harvest Moon" in a prolific career of some 3,000 songs. Actually, "Ballgame" was more than a simple chorus we all sing at the ballpark. It includes more verses than the standard ditty and tells the tale of one Katie Crosby, a baseball-mad young woman who turns down her beau's invitation to a show, insisting instead he "take me out to the ballgame."

The song inspired what has been called a "golden age" of baseball songs, which is hard to fathom since most appeared to be forgettable imitations of the Norworth/Von Tilzer classic. Even George M. Cohen tried by co-writing a suspiciously like-sounding song called, "Take Your Girl to the Ballgame." Said Norworth of that effort: "Who ever heard of a baseball song with, 'in the stands it's so grand if you're holding her hand at the old ball game?' Nobody holds hands at a baseball game.'"

Then again, how would Norworth know? Both he and Von Tilzer lived long and artistically productive lives, but never showed the slightest interest in baseball. It took Von Tilzer more than 20 years to see his first game. Norworth wasn't in much of a hurry either, finally making it to Ebbets Field on June 27, 1942, when the Dodgers had a day for him.

So how could these two men who could care less about the game write the baseball song that is embedded on the conscience of America? Explained Norworth years later: "A friend of mine, Harry Williams, wrote 'In the Shade of the Old Apple Tree,' and he never saw an apple tree." Enough said.

CAVE OF WINDS
Dodger headquarters
215 Montague Street, Brooklyn Heights

"This ball," a reflective Branch Rickey once mused, holding up a baseball. "Is it worth a man's whole life?"

It was for Rickey, arguably the single most influential front-office figure in the game's long history. Rickey, given to such bursts of philosophy, could have been anything he wanted. Debates raged about his true character — whether he was the world's most pious man or simply its biggest huckster. To journalist John Gunther, Rickey was "a combination of God, your father, and Tammany Hall." Said ex-Dodger Gene Hermanski: "He had a heart of gold — and he kept it."

Local tabloids called him, "The Mahatma." And in the years this nattily-dressed, stubbornly Victorian man was building all those great Dodger teams, the press conference room at 215 Montague Street — Dodger headquarters — was known as "The Cave of Winds." At one of those press conferences, in response to a question from John Drebinger of *The New York Times*, Rickey spoke for 20 minutes. When he wanted to know if that was a sufficient answer, Drebinger replied, "I've forgotten the question."

In a nearly 60-year career as a major league player, manager, and front office maven, Rickey paused long enough to spearhead one of baseball's seminal events — signing the game's first black player, Jackie Robinson, to a Dodger contract. The deed, done with a simple stroke of the pen in November 1946 at the Dodger office, transcended the game, assuring Rickey's spot in the history books.

By then, Rickey had already left a considerable legacy — building the great Cardinal teams of the 1930s, in part, by developing the modern farm organization. By 1949, based on his remarkable success in both Brooklyn and St. Louis, an estimated three of eight major leaguers had been developing in one of the two systems. It was Rickey's 1912 St. Louis Browns that were among the first teams to take spring training in Florida.

Challenging baseball's long-standing policy of segregation was more than a simple recognition of a good ballplayer who happened to be black. While Robinson's signing was, in effect, a business decision to tap a rich reservoir of under-utilized talent, its roots sprang from Rickey's deep-seated need to right a wrong.

"I had to get the right man, off the field," Rickey said. "I couldn't come up with a man to break down a tradition that had centered and concentrated all the prejudices of a great many people, north and south, unless he was good. He must justify himself on the principle of merit. In Jackie Robinson, we found the man [who] was eminently right off and on the field."

Rickey came from a devoutly Methodist family who adhered to the Wesleyan tradition of social liberalism, education, self-discipline, and hard work. In 1904, when Rickey was coaching at Ohio Wesleyan University, his only black player was denied a room at the Oliver Hotel in South Bend, Indiana before a game against Notre Dame.

In The Cave of Winds: Jackie Robinson & Branch Rickey. (National Baseball Hall of Fame Library, Cooperstown, New York)

Rickey stood his ground, refused to check out, and the player, Charles Thomas, kept his hotel room. But it was the sight of Thomas, tears welling in his eyes, that forever stayed with Rickey.

"The tears spilled down his face," Rickey said of Thomas. "Then, his shoulders heaved convulsively and he rubbed one great hand over the other with all the power of his body, muttering, 'Black skin, black skin … if I could only make it white.' He kept rubbing and rubbing as though he could remove the blackness by sheer friction."

Not everyone was a Rickey admirer. To Leo Durocher, who managed for him, Rickey was, "the cheapest, the shrewdest, and the most hardhearted of men." Jimmy Powers of *The Daily News* had another description of Rickey: "El Cheapo," a reference to his low-priced stogies and notoriously tough tactics during player contract negotiations.

Rickey joined the Dodgers as team president in 1942 and stayed eight years before leaving in a power struggle with owner Walter O'Malley. In later years, he worked for Pirates, before returning to the Cardinals. In 1962, he attended Jackie Robinson's Hall of Fame induction, and was himself inducted in 1967, one year after his death.

THIS IS NEXT YEAR! — BUMS DOOD IT!
Dodgers Cafe
24 DeKalb Avenue

The greatest moment in Brooklyn Dodgers history ended this way, courtesy of Vin Scully at the microphone: "Howard hits a ground ball to Reese. He throws to Hodges ... the Brooklyn Dodgers are World Champions!"

It was 3:43 PM, October 4, 1955. In their 49th World Series game and eighth championship appearance, the Dodgers had won their first and only World Championship. Perhaps best of all, they had beaten the Yankees — yeah, those Yankees — and at Yankee Stadium, formerly the Temple of Doom.

A significant date, this October 4. On that day in 1861, Union forces converged to form the Army of the Potomac. Three years later, the Erie Canal opened, and on October 4, 1940, Hitler and Mussolini met at the Brenner Pass. But in Brooklyn, no earthly event could match the events of 1955, when years of frustration were wiped out with this tense, pitchers' seventh-game duel. Final score: Bums 2, Bombers 0, thanks in large part to Johnny Podres, the winning pitcher, and to Sandy Amoros, with a game-saving catch.

"So enduring had been the impression that Brooklyn could never win a World Series that the folks from Canarsie to Greenpoint undoubtedly will be checking their newspapers today just to be sure," wrote Arthur Daley in *The New York Times* on the sweet day after. "No game today."

The jinx was over. The Bums had done it — "dood," in Brooklynese. In the moments after the game, from 3:44 PM to 4:01 PM, New York Telephone officials reported a flood of phone calls, the greatest in the borough since

V-J Day. Pandemonium ruled the borough; cars blew horns out on Flatbush Avenue, Kings Highway, and Ocean Parkway; cowbells clanged and firecrackers cracked on street corners outside houses, stores, and bars from Bay Ridge to Bensonhurst.

A magical night in Flatbush: It's Oct. 4, 1955 and Dodger fans celebrate their team's only World Series triumph. (National Baseball Hall of Fame Library, Cooperstown, New York)

And outside the Dodgers Cafe, a noisy crowd cheered the victory over the Yankees with handmade signs that read, "Yes Dodgers" and "Bums? Champs!" It was nothing unusual that memorable day in Brooklyn, but worth bringing up as another example of the spontaneous celebration that can still bring a tear to middle-aged Flatbush faithful.

Motorcades raced through the streets. Effigies of Yankees hung from lampposts and strangers hugged. In Ciudad Trujillo, Dominican Republic, a baby was born and named Podres Garcia. And at Joe's Delicatessen at 324 Utica Avenue, owner Joe Saden was so utterly overwhelmed at the magnitude of the Dodger victory that he set up a sidewalk stand and gave away free hot dogs. Imagine!

Some Dodger fans even took their case straight to the heart of darkness — The Bronx — which, until 4 PM October 5, 1955, would have been to court certain bodily harm. But once Brooklyn won, many fans worked their way from bar-to-bar within sight of the Stadium, even performing an impromptu celebration on the lawn of the Bronx Courthouse. What symbolism! And downtown in Manhattan, businessmen dumped confetti fashioned from desk pads and vouchers from rooftops and windows in another display of spontaneity.

Back in Brooklyn, borough president John Cashmore was so excited that he was moved to utter his undying commitment to keep the team in Flatbush at all costs. That August, with the Dodgers, alone in first place, 14 games ahead of their nearest competitor, the National League had granted permission for them to schedule eight home games for 1956 in Roosevelt Stadium, Jersey City. It was Dodger owner Walter O'Malley's way of lobbying for a new ballpark.

But in this delicious moment of triumph, Cashmore didn't seem dismayed, even as he ordered a survey for a new Dodger ballpark at Atlantic & Flatbush avenues. "They must never leave Brooklyn," he said.

That night, at the Dodger victory party at the Hotel Bossert, Duke Snider was given the honor of blowing out the candles in the victory cake. So numerous were outsiders at the party that O'Malley hired an extra room to take care of all the celebrants. Podres was carried out of the party. Others were too.

This was more than a win in a baseball game. It was sweet revenge for the years of inferiority, for all the jokes about Brooklyn in the war movies and for all the times the Dodgers had come ever so close. The fact that it came against the seemingly invincible, big-city, fat-cat Yankees was poetic justice in the extreme.

Sadly, it was the Dodgers' high-water mark. In 1956, they played those "home" games in Jersey City. A year later, the team left Brooklyn.

FREDDIE FITZSIMMONS – PITCHER, BUSINESSMAN
Freddie Fitzsimmons' bowling alley, bar, and restaurant
120 Empire Boulevard

First things first: Giant and Dodger mainstay "Fat" Freddie Fitzsimmons, as he was known, was not really fat. A bit chunky perhaps and built more like a defensive end than a pitcher, but not fat. However, the unfortunate nickname, "Fat Freddie," sounded good to sportswriters, so it stuck.

The Sporting News dealt with the subject gingerly after Fitzsimmons died in 1979: The 5'11" righthander who weighed 215 "was inclined toward fatness despite a relatively Spartan life," it wrote. Said Fitzsimmons back in his playing days: "Maybe I just eat too much."

So what? The winner of 217 games in an eventful 19-year major league career, Fitzsimmons had a unique delivery, pivoting on his right foot until he was virtually facing center field before turning to deliver the pitch — usually a knuckleball. But he was also quick and catlike off the mound and was widely considered the best fielding pitcher of his generation.

Fitzsimmons may have been more suited to bowling than baseball, a theory that became closer to the truth when "Fat Freddie," traded to the Dodgers in 1937, after 12 years with the Giants, opened his Brooklyn bowling alley. With 40 Brunswick lanes, it included a bar and restaurant — and was conveniently near Ebbets Field.

Fitzsimmons was 36, elderly by baseball standards, when he got to the Dodgers. His best years were behind him; pitching for the Giants, in 1928, Fitzsimmons posted his only 20-win season (20-9) and followed with seasons of 15-11, 19-7 and 18-11. Yet, the Dodgers had the upper hand as Fitzsimmons won 47 more games, including a stellar 16-2 record in 1940.

The bowling alley — "street level ... air conditioned," trumpeted the ad in the telephone book — became a Brooklyn mainstay, and so did Fitzsimmons. In 1941, his 6-1 record in 12 starts helped Brooklyn take its first pennant in 21 years. But pitching in a scoreless duel against the Yankees in game three of the World Series, Fitzsimmons was hit by a vicious line drive above the left kneecap by the opposing pitcher Marius Russo.

He pitched two more years with the Dodgers, but never regained his old form. "Guess I should have learned to duck," Fitzsimmons told *The New York Times*.

In 1943, Fitzsimmons replaced Bucky Harris as the Philadelphia Phillies manager. He quit two years later with the Phillies in last place. Fitzsimmons later coached the Giants, the Boston Braves, and the Cubs, in addition to a stint as general manager of the Brooklyn Dodgers of the NFL. He retired to California in 1966 after more than 40 years in the game — and long after the bowling alley had closed. Fitzsimmons died in 1979: he was 78.

WAIT A MINUTE — WE CAN MAKE A BUCK
Union Grounds
Marcy (NE), Lee (SW) & Rutledge (SE) Avenues, Williamsburg

It was inevitable — with the popularity of baseball sweeping the country in the 1860s, it became a business. And the real moment of truth can probably be credited in part to the decision of one William Cammeyer, whose Union Grounds was the first enclosed baseball field, to charge admission. The price on that fateful April 19, 1869 afternoon: 10¢.

Just how baseball reached that point can be traced to the extraordinary spread of the New York game that Alexander Cartwright and the Knickerbockers had invented some 25 years before — and tried to keep to their own social class.

But social restrictions didn't work. Baseball's popularity grew wildly — from the shipwrights and mechanics who, in the late 1850s, formed the famed Eckford Club after Brooklyn shipbuilder Henry Eckford, to teams like the Mutuals, composed of firemen, and the Manhattans' team of policemen. By the summer of 1856, the metropolitan area hosted a whopping 53 baseball teams.

That same year, *Porter's Spirit of the Times* reported that every available green plot within 10 miles of the city was being used as a playing field. Brooklyn, then known as the "City of Churches," was fast becoming a city where baseball was king, prompting one New Yorker to comment: "God speed the churches and ball clubs of our sister city."

Baseball's feverish grip reached an early peak in 1858 with a three-game series at Fashion Race Course on Long Island in which a team of New York all-stars edged a group of Brooklyn all-stars. To reach the games, fans clogged up both roads and the Flushing Railroad. Oh yes, admission was charged — 50¢.

Maybe that's how Cammeyer got his grand idea. His Union Grounds, which opened May 15, 1862 at the intersection of Marcy, Lee & Rutledge avenues in Williamsburg, occupied the Union Skating Club's ice skating rink. The wooden bleachers with outfield fences more than 500 feet distant, became the home to several of the area's best teams — the Mutuals, Eckfords, and Atlantics.

"These grounds, if managed properly — and there is little doubt but that they will be — could be made not only to prove very profitable," wrote *The Standard*, "but a credit to the section in which they are located."

The bottom line? Baseball could be profitable. Union Grounds had its heyday through the 1870s, when it served as home to several teams and was used during the winter as a skating rink. It lasted until 1889, as home to the Dodgers of the American Association.

RED STOCKINGS CALLING
Capitoline Grounds
Putnam Avenue (N), Nostrand Avenue (W), Halsey Street (S) & Marcy Avenue (E), Brownsville

Further evidence that baseball was a business came with the famous visit to Capitoline Grounds of the sport's first all-professional team, the legendary Red Stockings of Cincinnati.

Financed by a band of Ohio investors, the Red Stockings brought glory to Cincinnati, not to mention an unblemished 65-0 record in 1869 — a year when they managed to turn a profit of $1.39. Success came largely through the efforts of the team's manager, Harry Wright, the British-born son of a cricketer, who could play some ball and more importantly, saw the commercial potential of his vision.

Wright paid himself $1,200 a season, but paid his younger brother, George, the shortstop, $200 more. Good move: George hit .519 in 1869, socking a downright Ruthian 59 home runs and fielding flawlessly.

The Red Stockings were the pride of Cincinnati. "I don't know anything about baseball," said a native. "But it does me good to see those fellows. They've done something to add to the glory of our city."

No wonder Brooklyn's growing baseball-mad populace was excited when, in 1870, the Reds came calling at Capitoline Grounds to play Brooklyn's Atlantics. To historians, it was among the game's first titanic struggles.

The Red Stockings entered the game on their usual roll, taking the season's first 27 straight games for 92 straight wins. They came to Brooklyn as heavy favorites, as some 15,000 New Yorkers crossed the East River by ferry and then took horse-drawn carts to the ballpark.

Capitoline Grounds occupied the intersection of Halsey Street and Putnam, Nostrand & Marcy avenues in the Brownsville section of Bedford-Stuyvesant. Built in 1862 by Robert Decker, the park was part of a farm leased to Decker's father by the Lefferts family.

In New York, the Red Stockings attracted big-time interest. "Hundreds who could not or would not produce the necessary 50¢ for admission looked on through cracks in the fence," reported *Harper's Weekly*. "Others were perched in the topmost limbs of the trees or on roofs of surrounding houses."

Oddsmakers made the Red Stockings 5-1 favorites. And for a time, the game went as predicted: Cincinnati grabbed a quick three-run lead, but the Atlantics rallied, with two runs in the fourth and two more in the sixth to go ahead by one. Excitement mounted, and after nine innings, the score was deadlocked at five.

The Atlantics were more than happy with a draw against the great Red Stockings. But Harry Wright insisted that wasn't good enough and argued unless the captains of both teams mutually agreed that the game should end in a tie, they should continue. Enter Henry Chadwick, the chairman of the Rules Committee of the National Association and the highest authority on hand, who ruled in Wright's favor. On went the game.

At first, Wright's strategy appeard to pay off — the Red Stockings scored two runs in the 11th inning, but the Atlantics stormed back to tie it in the bottom of the 11th. Then, with a man on first and only one out, the next Atlantic batter hit a grounder to Red Stockings' first baseman Charlie Gould who let the ball pass between his legs, stumbled after it and chucked it over the third baseman's head as the winning run crossed the plate. Shades of Bill Buckner against the Mets. Victory — Brooklyn.

After the game, Harry Wright sent the following telegram to *The Cincinnati Commercial*: "JUNE 14. ATLANTICS 8 CINCINNATI 7. THE FINEST GAME EVER PLAYED. OUR BOYS DID NOBLY, BUT FORTUNE WAS AGAINST US. THOUGH BEATEN, NOT DISGRACED."

BASEBALL'S FIRST STAR
The fast times and death of Jim Creighton
Green-Wood Cemetery
500 25th Street (& 5th Avenue)

James Creighton, Jr. was more than baseball's first star. His untimely death gave the game its first bona fide pilgrimage site — a trip to the granite obelisk with the crossed bats over his grave at Green-Wood Cemetery became a mandatory ritual for the BIG fan.

Creighton, the game's first great pitcher and outstanding batsman, was only 18 when he made his debut with the Brooklyn Niagaras. Although the rules at the time banned any snapping of the wrist when delivering the pitch, Creighton somehow managed to deliver the ball toward the plate with alarming speed and a spin "as swift as sent from a cannon," as an eyewitness put it. Mixed in were an assortment of what he called "dew drops" — off-speed pitches to keep batters off-guard.

In an era when pitchers were expected to deliver the ball to help the batter make contact, here was Creighton throwing it by them and defying the norm. And here he was, deceptively winning game after game and making the Niagaras the envy of the baseball world.

In time, Creighton was lured either by an offer of money or a job to Brooklyn's Stars, then to the Excelsiors. In 1860, as the nation braced for Civil War, Creighton had other things on his mind — leading the Excelsiors on the game's first major barnstorming tour, striking out batters, and winning games from teams in upstate New York to Canada, Pennsylvania, Maryland, and Delaware.

He became a hero, lauded as much for his field exploits as his deport-ment. Young players imitated Creighton's delivery and some are said to have even named their teams after him.

On October 14, 1862, batting for the Excelsiors against the Unions of Morrisania, Creighton hit a home run, circled the bases, and collapsed. The force of his swing had ruptured his bladder and he died in agony four days later at the home of the father, James Sr., at 307 Henry St. Creighton was all of 21.

An early-baseball pilgrimage spot: Jim Creighton's grave.

So grief-stricken were his Excel-sior teammates that the team presi-dent, feared that news of the tragedy would dissuade parents from encour-aging their sons to play baseball. Re-sorting to a case of early baseball spin-control, he said Creighton had actually died playing cricket.

To honor their fallen comrade, the Excelsiors set up the monument, topped by a marble baseball at Green-Wood Cemetery. Perhaps 12 feet high, it's as tall as a Baltimore Chop and hard to miss. It is also just down the winding cemetery trail from the resting spot for a couple of other Brooklynites with baseball ties — Henry Chadwick and Charles Ebbets.

PLAY BALL! BASEBALL'S THIRD MAJOR LEAGUE
Washington Park
3rd Avenue between 1st & 3rd Streets, Red Hook

The Federal League was the baseball's last serious attempt to establish a third major league. Started in 1912, the league lasted only four years, but gave the established National and American leagues a colorful run for their money, particularly after establishing itself at two spots in the critical New York market.

The New York strongholds were Harrison Park in Newark and the hastily rebuilt Washington Park in the Red Hook section of the borough, where the forgettable Brooklyn Tip-Tops stumbled to consecutive second division finishes in two undistinguished seasons.

Outlaw baseball leagues are an American tradition. No exception here: John T. Powers of Chicago, who organized the Wisconsin-Illinois League in 1905 had bigger things in mind — a professional league using players unaffiliated with other professional clubs that pooled their resources to make a profit.

Powers formed his next venture, the outlaw "Columbian League" in 1913, which then evolved into the Federal League. Convinced that baseball's bursting popularity could support eight primarily Midwestern teams, Powers kept the peace with organized baseball by restricting league rosters to free agents and, in cases of teams in major league cities, scheduling league games when the major leaguers were on the road.

The Federal League's low profile ended in 1914, when a faction of owners led by "Fighting Jim" Gilmore, a Spanish-American War vet, self-made coal baron, and owner of the league's Chicago franchise, forced Powers out of office with the intention of going big-time. From then on, the renamed Federal League added several ingredients to a beefed-up league — expansion into more lucrative Eastern cities, modern stadiums, and a more aggressive pursuit of established major league stars.

As part of the master plan, the new Brooklyn franchise announced its intention to resurrect old Washington Park, home of the NL Brooklyns before Ebbets Field. Those efforts paralleled successful efforts in Pittsburgh to bring back old Exposition Park, the one-time home of the Pirates, and in Chicago, where Charles Weeghmann constructed an all-concrete and steel park called Weeghmann Park, which became Wrigley Field.

Chances are the man on the bicycle doesn't know that this nondescript wall in Brooklyn, now part of a Consolidated Edison maintenance yard, was part of Washington Park, where the Dodgers and Tip-Tops once played.

At the time, Tip-Top owners, the brothers Robert and George Ward, who named the team after their popular brand of bread, had tried to merely expand on Washington Park's existing wooden grandstand. But Brooklyn building codes forced them to totally raze the old structure and, as in Chicago, erect a new concrete and steel grandstand.

For Washington Park, it was the third leg of an odd life that had started in May 1884 and housed the Dodgers for five years, until it was destroyed by fire exactly one week before another, more deadly tragedy struck — the Johnstown Flood. The park was named for General George Washington, whose headquarters in the Battle of Long Island during the Revolutionary War, was in Gowanus House, which still stands on the same block. And the team's clubhouse during part of the park's life: a stone building actually occupied for a time by Washington.

Rebuilt in less than a month, Washington Park housed the Dodgers again from 1898 to 1912. The new park, rebuilt in wood by the Dodgers, was actually catty-corner to an earlier version of Washington Park. Total seating capacity for the renovated park was 18,000, including a covered grandstand, with the longest dimension a reasonable 400 feet in center field, where the scoreboard rested on supporting legs so a fair ball could roll underneath.

Construction delays and cold spring weather kept the Tip-Tops from opening their 1914 season until May 11 against Pittsburgh. As throughout the entire eight-team league, ticket pricing was identical to the major league clubs — $1 for box seats, 75¢ for reserved grandstand, 50¢ for pavilion seats, and 25¢ for the bleachers. In keeping with the religious sentiment in "The City of Churches" and the laws of New York State, the Tip-Tops scheduled no home game for Sundays.

At the home opener, the Tip-Tops were already mired in fifth place, when Tom Seaton lost a tight 2-0 pitching duel to Pittsburgh's Howie Camnitz before more than 15,000. Both pitchers, former major leaguers, were among a number of former big leaguers who jumped to the new league. Among the others, many of whom were at the end of their playing careers, were future Hall-of-Famers Edd Rousch, "Three Finger" Brown, Eddie Plank, and Chief Bender.

Player raids that continued into the Federal League's 1915 season brought on lawsuits and legal skirmishes with the major leagues. It also created the need of strong franchises in the high-profile New York market. That got a considerable boost in the Tip-Tops' first home game in '15, when Benny Kauff, newly acquired from the defunct Indianapolis franchise, belted a three-run home run to help defeat the Buffalo Feds.

But upbeat beginnings couldn't save the Federal League. Kauff won the batting title at .344, but the Tip-Tops fell to seventh place in the standings, beating out only the lowly Baltimore Terrapins. That did little to stop the declining attendance at Tip-Top games, even though the team, in desperation, slashed the 25¢ bleacher tickets to a dime and were actually planning to play night baseball — a full 20 years before its introduction in Cincinnati.

Things got worse when Federal League officials failed to persuade Judge Kenesaw Mountain Landis to dismiss the league's prolonged suit against organized baseball. The end came December 17, 1915 at the Waldorf Astoria Hotel, where the NL/AL baseball establishment agreed to put up a sizable sum to compensate debt-ridden Federal League backers in exchange for disbanding the league. As part of the peace treaty, Chicago's Weeghmann was given controlling interest of the National League Cubs; and Phil Ball, the ice-making magnate, of the American League St. Louis Browns.

And Washington Park? Along with ballparks in Newark and Pittsburgh, it became one of three Federal League stadiums to have its ownership assumed by the major leagues. Unfortunately, the rebuilt ballpark had no hope for survival as a profitable baseball operation and it was eventually torn down, although it's unclear precisely when.

Today, a two-block wall of the former park runs along an industrial section of 3rd Avenue between 1st and 3rd streets. Painted gray over red brick, the wall includes bricked-in arched windows that once opened into the players' clubhouses. It is part of a building that houses Consolidated Edison trucks and tools.

There is no plaque to commemorate what is possibly the oldest standing wall of any ballpark in the US.

MARIANNE MOORE – POET, RESIDENT INTELLECTUAL, DODGER FAN
260 Cumberland Street, Fort Greene

Sure, the Hildas, the Sym-phony and other Ebbets Field loonies got the ink. Leave it then to Pulitzer Prize-winning poet and longtime Brooklyn resident Marianne Moore to account for the intellectual wing of Dodgerdom.

"These men are natural artists," Moore once said of Dodger ballplayers. "I remember Don Zimmer playing at third base. He was moving toward home plate when a fly came toward him. He had to get back to third and he backhanded it with his left hand."

In one respect, it is difficult to see why Marianne Moore cared so passionately about the Dodgers. She won just about every notable prize for poetry and literature, taught for many years, lectured, went to church, and kept company with the New York literary crowd. Baseball? "How *jejune*," you can hear her scholarly colleagues editorializing.

On the other hand, Moore once wrote a poem about a race horse named Tom Fool, kept company with Casey Stengel, and lived in a snug fifth-floor apartment at 260 Cumberland Street that was crammed with bric-a-brac from porcelain to ivory animals, a walrus tusk, feathers, and old coins. When asked by the Ford Motor Company in 1955 to name a new line of the company's cars, she suggested, "The Intelligent Whale," "Varsity Stroke," "Turtletopper" and "Hurricane Hirundo." Ford didn't like any those names, so they came up with their own: "The Edsel."

Why baseball? Like many good writers, Moore was intensely aware and proud of living in Brooklyn. She avidly rode the subways and often dispensed tokens to visitors as they were leaving her apartment. And judging by her enormous range of interests, Moore possessed an insatiable thirst for intellectual stimulation and knowledge, of which the Dodgers were an integral part.

A quick glance through the 1967 book, *The Complete Poems of Marianne Moore*, reveals a wide range of subjects, including her homage to the '55 Champion Dodgers, entitled "Hometown Piece for Messrs. Alston and Reese," a long poem written to the cadence of "Li'l baby, don't say a word: Mama goin' to buy you a mockingbird." Among the poem's more memorable lines: "Hope springs eternal in the Brooklyn breast."

Moore lived on Cumberland Street for 37 years, moving in 1966 to 35 West 9th Street in Greenwich Village. By then, the Dodgers' move had forced her to switch allegiances to the Yankees, a decision she used to form a great friendship with Michael Burke, Bomber owner of the pre-Steinbrenner-era. She died in 1972 at the age of 84.

"HIT SIGN, WIN SUIT" — ABE STARK
1514 Pitkin Avenue, Brownsville

Abe Stark is an example of one of the quirks that makes America great — a poor kid made famous by a sign. Yeah, a sign.

"Hit Sign, Win Suit" read Abe Stark's message underneath the right-center field scoreboard at Ebbets Field. It became more than an ad for Stark's clothing store at 1514 Pitkin Avenue in Brownsville; immortalized in a *New Yorker* cartoon and as background in countless wire photographs of Dodger games, the sign made Stark famous to a generation of baseball fans.

Nobody knew how many suits he actually gave away. It doesn't matter, because Stark shrewdly engineered his peculiar brand of celebrity to an unlikely second career of sorts, as New York City Council president and Brooklyn borough president. He won three terms as borough president of Brooklyn after having served as City Council president from 1954 to 1961, but he never realized his real ambition to become mayor.

"A good businessman would make an excellent mayor," Stark once said. "New York City is the biggest business in the world. It takes a businessman's viewpoint and man with an open heart toward every human problem."

Stark was a businessman and philanthropist for 30 years before entering politics. Born in 1894 to impoverished Russian immigrants on New York's Lower East Side — his father was a tailor — Stark was 11 when he quit his newsboy job to become a handy boy at $2.50 a week at a clothing store in Brooklyn, where his family moved in 1910.

In 1914, when Stark was 21, he opened a men's clothing store in partnership with two others. In 1915, he started the Pitkin Avenue store, launching his career as one of Brooklyn's best-known businessmen.

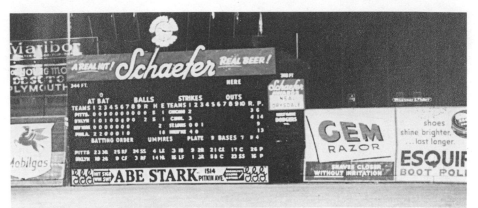

The Ebbets Field scoreboard says the game is over. Wonder if anyone hit the sign and won a suit? (National Baseball Hall of Fame Library, Cooperstown, New York)

Stark's sign ran along the concrete base of Ebbets Field's scoreboard. *The New Yorker* cartoon showed a businessman — presumably Stark —wearing a suit, with glove in hand, standing in front of the sign to cut down on the free suits. Could he have played the carom off the wall as well as Furillo? We'll never know.

HISTORY IN THE STACKS
Brooklyn Public Library (Main Branch)
Grand Army Plaza

Now, it can be told: Buried deep in the stacks of the Brooklyn Collection at the Brooklyn Public Library is a little-known treasure.

It is baseball's earliest known photograph. It shows 12 dapper gents — three of them seated and dressed formally with top hats, and the other nine wearing 19th century baseball uniforms, which, unfortunately give them more the look of hotel bellboys from a Marx Brothers film.

They are probably Manhattan's Gotham Base Ball Club of 1856. Unfortunately, the photo, which was published twice in *The Brooklyn Daily Eagle* in the 1930s, is a copy; the original is lost.

This intriguing footnote to baseball history is courtesy of Tom Shieber, a scholar of early baseball history and the author of a story about the photo, which appeared in the 1997 edition of *The National Pastime*, published by the Society for American Baseball Research (SABR).

For years, baseball historians have thought the well-known, half-plate daguerreotype of six members of Manhattan's Knickerbocker Base Ball Club was the sport's earliest known. That photo is thought to date to the 1840s and to include baseball founder Alexander Cartwright. But as Shieber argues, there is doubt as to whether it is a baseball team at all.

"The best we can say about the daguerreotype is that it may be a portrait of six members of the Knickerbocker Base Ball Club," he writes. "It may also be a portrait of Alexander Cartwright and five unidentified companions, some of whom played baseball. We cannot state for sure that this is definitely the earliest known baseball photograph."

How a photo of the Gothams of Manhattan got to Brooklyn is another mystery. The reverse side of the photo identifies the teams as the 1855 Atlantics of Brooklyn, but the names of the players, Shieber reveals, were all ones who played for the Gotham club. *The Daily Eagle* had unwittingly published a photo of a Manhattan team, thinking it was their own.

Besides, the photo probably doesn't date to 1855, Shieber says. Only two boxscores are known in which the Gothams' lineup is an exact match for the players listed; both are from October 1856.

So, now you know.

BROOKLYN'S BASEBALL BABYLON
Hugh Casey's tavern
1828 Flatbush Avenue

Ah, Brooklyn of the '40s and '50s — a magical place to grow up where neighbors looked out for one another and things like divorce and the shame of out-of-wedlock births happened elsewhere. At least that's the usual rose-tinted revisionist history lesson you get when talking to most natives of the borough from that era.

Sure, it was better there than it is today. Family units were stronger and it was safer. But scandalous stuff still happened; people just didn't talk about it as much and newspapers seldom reported it either. A case in point: Hugh Casey, the Dodgers' hard-living, hard-throwing righthander, who demonstrated that baseball Babylon, Brooklyn-style, was indeed alive and well.

On the mound, Casey rode the crest of good Dodger teams of the 1940s.

He was ahead of his time in some ways as baseball's best relief pitcher at a time when the teams were just discovering the value of the hard-throwing, late-inning game saver. He was the winning pitcher in one of the most famous World Series games of all-time — game four of the '47 Series when Dodger pinch hitter Cookie Lavagetto doubled home two runs to beat the Yankees and deprive Bill Bevins of a no-hitter with two outs in the eighth. Altogether, he pitched in six of the seven games of the Series that year.

And at his bar, in the shadows of Ebbets Field, Casey played host to a happy swarm of teammates and their wives in 1947 to celebrate the team's clinching of the National League pennant. Celebrations erupted all over the Brooklyn that night, but Casey's joint was the focal point, as reported in *The Herald Tribune*: Joining him in a booth at the tavern were Pete Reiser, Hank Behrman, Harry Taylor, Bruce Edwards, Vic Lombardi, and Johnny Jorgensen. Notably absent from the celebration were Pee Wee Reese and Jackie Robinson.

The Dodgers lost that World Series but had a good season, anyway. And Casey pitched well, going 10-4 in 1947 and 2-0 in the Series. But it would be Casey's high-point as a Dodger; in 1948, he hurt his back, won only three games, and was out of the majors a year later.

But Casey's real troubles were just beginning. On November 2, 1949, Hilda Weissman, a 24-year-old saleswoman from 1580 Eastern Parkway, gave birth to a son. Nothing unusual there, except the following year, a three-judge Special Sessions Court determined that Casey was the father of the illegitimate child. It was a verdict the pitcher vehemently denied to his death.

And death came sooner than expected. On July 3, 1951, the 38-year-old Casey, back in Atlanta, took his own life, firing a 16-gauge shotgun into his neck — moments after denying anew that he was the father of the Weissman child. The pitcher's last words, as reported by his estranged wife, Kathleen, who tried to talk him out of suicide over the telephone: "I am completely innocent of those charges."

In court, Casey had insisted he had never had relations with Weissman beyond greeting her as a customer at his bar. Kathleen, who later insisted the breakup of their marriage had nothing to do with the court decision and testified at the hearing that she believed her husband. Said her husband, just before pulling the trigger: "I can't eat or sleep since going through all the embarrassment ... I swear with a dying oath that I am innocent."

Kathleen, meanwhile, had another compelling slant on the reasons behind the suicide. "What he seemed to feel most was this was his first year out of baseball," she said later, adding that he was upset that his restaurant wasn't doing well.

Said Weissman, by then happily married to a furrier: "I'm sorry, very sorry ... It's a shame he had to commit suicide; he must have been a very unhappy man."

WALT WHITMAN ANOINTS "OUR GAME"
106 Myrtle Avenue

"Well — it's our game; that's the chief fact in connection with it; America's game; it has the snap, go, and fling of the American atmosphere; it belongs as much to our institutions, fits into them as significantly as our Constitution's laws; is just as important in the sum total of our historic life."

Walt Whitman said that. So, could America's greatest 19th-century poet have told the difference between a hard slider and a split-fingered fastball? Probably not. Was he even a fan? It really doesn't matter, for Brooklyn's first and most significant writer recognized the symbolic implications of baseball, comparing its mid-19th century explosion of interest to the restless energy of the young, growing country itself.

America's enormous size and its tremendous energy fired Whitman's fervid mind. Indeed, his celebrated 1856 volume, *Leaves of Grass* — so misunderstood and little read when it was first published — celebrated the success and potential of the young country with supreme optimism and vigor. Celebration of the volume came with time.

For a good portion of his working life, Whitman lived in Brooklyn Heights, spending his time as editor of *The Brooklyn Freeman* at a house at 106 Myrtle Avenue. Like many New Yorkers of his era, Whitman was sentimentally attached to the waterfront, particularly enjoying ferry trips to Manhattan to attend opera and other cultural events.

When *Leaves of Grass* was published, Whitman was, in fact, in the midst of several jobs, working for a time as a reporter at several newspapers and a real estate speculator in addition to writing poetry. In 1862, he went south to Fredericksburg, Virginia, to look for his brother George, who had been injured during a Civil War battle, which inspired him to take up work as a nurse in hospitals in Washington, DC. He never moved back to Brooklyn, living in later years in Camden, New Jersey, where he died in 1892.

ST. GIL — HONORARY BROOKLYN GUY
St. Francis Xavier Catholic Church
3472 Bedford Avenue

Here is how Brooklyn felt about Gilbert Ray Hodges: "It's really too hot for a sermon," Father Thomas Redmond of St. Francis Xavier Catholic Church told his surprised congregation one Sunday in May 1953 when Hodges, then the muscular Dodger first baseman, was mired in a batting slump. "Keep the Commandments and say a prayer for Gil Hodges."

They did. Meanwhile, Hodges took care of his hitting problems — belting 31 home runs, driving in 121 runs and batting .302 to lead the Dodgers to that season's World Series, where he hit .364.

And it was some years later, in 1969, when Hodges managed the formerly-laughable Mets to the pennant and a five-game World Series triumph over Baltimore — a year after the team had lost 101 games — that cemented Hodges' status as a beloved New York baseball deity. In a sport littered with rough characters, the only criticism uttered about Hodges when this gentle giant of a man and deserving Hall of Famer died in 1972, was that he smoked too much.

"It's a good thing he's a nice guy," teammate Pee Wee Reese once said of Hodges. "With his strength, he had to be a peacemaker."

Hodges' baseball skills are well-documented. A 6'2" and 210-pounder with a bodybuilder's physique, he was an unusually graceful first baseman who hammered 370 career home runs during 16 big-league seasons with the Dodgers, the last four of them spent in Los Angeles.

No wonder they prayed for Hodges in Brooklyn — and not just Catholics, but Protestants, Jews, and the rest of the borough. Hodges was a true Bum, a naturalized Brooklynite feted for his accomplishments and forgiven for his slumps.

For all his success on the diamond — he played in seven World Series and six All-Star Games — he is perhaps most remembered for his image as the devoted family man who may have been from somewhere else but adopted Flatbush as his own. And nothing personified that spirit as three things — Hodges' 1948 marriage to Joan Lombardi of Brooklyn, running the 48-lane bowling alley that bore his name, and the couple's home at 3472 Bedford Avenue, where Mrs. Hodges still resides.

Hodges personified the kind of work-in-town, live-in-town ballplayer that Dodger fans cherished. Compared to today's utility infielder/millionaire types, this Dodger straight arrow might as well have been from Mars — after their marriage, the Hodges family moved in with Joan's parents on Hawthorne Street; then to Foster and Ocean Avenue; on to 32nd Street and Avenue K; and, finally, to the house on Bedford Avenue in Flatbush.

Most of Hodges' spare time was devoted to the couple's three daughters and a son. And, he could often be found at the bowling lane — a kind of Brooklyn institution in its own, complete with four grandstand seats salvaged from Ebbets Field.

"He's a devoted family man," Joan said when he was named manager of the Mets before the 1968 season, after five years as manager of the Washington Senators. "[He is] devoted to his family, his work, his religion. There's only one thing he can do with the Mets — his best."

As Mets manager, Hodges' best meant instilling in his young charges the feeling they could be winners. As the strong, silent type, he suffered through a losing 1968 season, before leading the Mets to the promised land; a superb pitching staff, led by '69 Cy Young Award winner Tom Seaver, helped too.

Tugging at Hodges were persistent health problems. His first heart attack came in 1968 during a game in Atlanta. But Hodges recovered and exactly one year later, the Mets clinched the National League Eastern Division pennant. The second and fatal attack came in 1972 after playing 27 holes of golf in West Palm Beach, Florida, where Hodges had spent a spent an afternoon during one of spring training's frequent work stoppages. He was a day shy of his 48th birthday.

Gil Hodges' memory lives on through his wife, and through the Gil Hodges Elementary School, a long fly ball from where he once lived as one of the borough's beloved figures and honorary local guys.

A DYNASTY GROWS IN PIG TOWN
The life and times of Charles Hercules Ebbets
1466 Glenwood Road

Long before Roy Campanella, Duke Snider, the Dodger Sym-phony, Hilda Chester, and other Dodger-like icons, there was Charles Hercules Ebbets, namesake of the late, great Ebbets Field and a man synonymous with the team that made the borough forever baseball-mad.

"It always will be Ebbets and the part he played in the promotion of base-ball in Brooklyn that will remain as his greatest monument to the game," *The Times* wrote. "Mr. Ebbets was one of the best known and best beloved men in baseball."

When it opened in April 1913, Ebbets Field was the premier ballpark of its time. Built on a site once known as "Pig Town," it housed about 23,000 — later about 33,000, when a left-field and center-field double deck was added in the early '30s. Along the way, Ebbets Field became the quirkiest, rowdiest, best-known, and best-loved ballpark in baseball.

It looks like Duke Snider is stepping to the plate at Ebbets Field in what is probably the 1947 World Series. (National Baseball Hall of Fame Library, Cooperstown, New York)

Several baseball innovations can be traced directly to Ebbets. *The New York Times* credits him with inventing the rain check. He was a staunch pro-ponent of Sunday baseball at a time when Sunday Blue Laws ruled the land. He argued hard to establish a permanent schedule for World Series dates. And the system of drafting players in which tail-end teams got first pick and pennant winners got last dibs? Yup, Ebbets again.

Baseball flowed in Ebbets' veins. In his 20s, he sold scorecards at Wash-ington Park for Brooklyn's first professional baseball club, which was a mem-ber of the Interstate League, a kind of forerunner to the American Association. That Brooklyn club won the last American Association pennant in 1889, switched to the National League in 1890, and took that flag too.

Ebbets rose quickly, acquiring stock in the club and assuming its presidency in 1898 at the death of Charles Byrne. Working quickly, he managed the club that first year and bought up star members of the disbanded Baltimore franchise the next year. Bingo: pennants in 1899 and 1900.

Alas, Ebbets stopped winning pennants for 16 years. But not even a championship could match the happiness of perhaps Ebbets' most lasting legacy — the opening of his new ballpark, the aptly named Ebbets Field. It opened April 9, 1913 with a Robins 3-2 exhibition win over their cross-town rivals, the Yankees.

"The day was made to order," gushed *The Times*. "It was one of the nicest little spring days the oldest inhabitant of Flatbush could remember. And the sky ... it was the same glorious canopy of pale blue, arched from horizon to horizon and flecked here and there with filmy clouds of white."

Ebbets, who lived at 1466 Glenwood Road, died in 1925 at age 66 on a day when the Giants beat the Robins at Ebbets Field. As a tribute, both teams lined up around the plate as players and spectators alike paid silent tribute. He is buried in Green-Wood Cemetery.

EBBETS FIELD
Shrine no more
Bedford Avenue & Sullivan Place, Crown Heights

Marty Adler was a student at Brooklyn College on the day the Dodgers left Brooklyn forever. "It was September 24, 1957 and we beat Pittsburgh 2-0; everybody knows that," he says. "It's like a birthday. You just don't forget."

As president of the Brooklyn Dodgers Hall of Fame, Adler keeps alive not just the memory of baseball's most colorful team, but the legend of their ballpark, Ebbets Field. Situated within a narrow sliver of land in Crown Heights, the ballpark seated 33,000 and was usually packed for home games.

"The fans were practically in there with you," says Preacher Roe, a Dodgers pitcher from 1948 to 1954 and a 22-game winner in 1951. "They got on you sometimes — you were bums if you lost — but they were always with us and knew their baseball. If you were from Brooklyn, you were a Dodger fan."

Ebbets Field fit snugly within the confines of its crowded urban landscape. Most any Brooklyn native above 50 knows full well of Ebbets Field's many well-known quirks. A sampling:

- At the park's April 9, 1913 opening, an American flag, a press box, and the key to the bleachers had been forgotten;
- Abe Stark's famous sign in right field, "Hit Sign, Win Suit," (see pages 55-56);
- The Schaefer Beer sign on the top of the right-center scoreboard that notified fans of the official scorer's decision — the "H" in Schaefer lit up for a hit, the "E" for an error. The sign was built after World War II;
- The right-field wall and scoreboard offered caroms at many angles and the scoreboard jutted out five feet from the wall at a 45-degree angle. The overhang of center field's second deck extended over the field;
- On September 24, 1924, 500 fans entered the park by battering down the center-field gate with a telephone pole;
- In the early 1940s, Lonnie Frey of Cincinnati hit a ball against the screen on the top of the wall between the scoreboard and the right-field foul pole. But when the ball bounced into a small opening where workmen had just removed a rotted 2-foot-by-4-foot shelf and never came down, Frey had himself a home run. The next day, in an effort to prevent similar occurences, the repair work was finished, this time with an angled shelf placed over the opening;
- Joe Adcock of the Braves hit the only home run over the ballpark's roof;
- Hilda Chester and her cowbell (see pages 217-218).

When the Dodgers left Brooklyn for Los Angeles, it left a wrenching emotional void in the borough. Adler again: "The Dodgers unified everyone in Brooklyn. Without them, we lost part of our identity, our rallying cry. It was very bad."

In fact, it was one of a series of considerable blows — among them, the decline of Coney Island and the closing of two other venerable institutions, the Brooklyn Navy Yard and its main newspaper, *The Brooklyn Eagle* — from which the borough has yet to recover.

News of the end came midway through the 1957 season, leaving an intense hatred among Dodger faithful for team owner Walter O'Malley, who pushed the move. To this day, O'Malley's name is vilified in Brooklyn, "ranking a close third on the most-hated list, close behind Hitler and Stalin," says Adler, only half-kidding.

Like a lot of people at the time, Roe figured the team would stay and

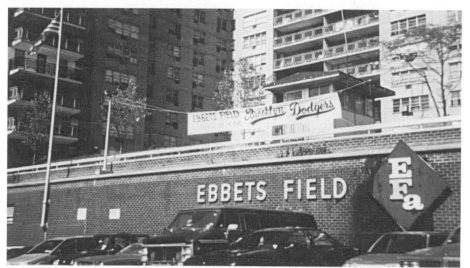

They paved paradise and put up a parking lot. The Ebbets Field Apartments, where a ballpark once stood.

build a bigger stadium. In 1960, he was invited to the ballpark's demolition, but didn't go. "I couldn't have taken it," he said.

Demolition started February 23, 1960. As Gay Talese wrote in *The Times*, "Men swung sledge hammers, the dugout crumbled and an iron ball crashed like Pete Reiser against the wall."

Present at the demolition were some 200 people, including former Dodgers who did show up — Carl Erskine, Roy Campanella, and Ralph Branca. Campanella was awarded his old locker and a pot full of ballpark dirt, swept up from behind home plate.

The festivities included a brass band playing "Auld Lang Syne" and long-time Ebbets Field public address announcer Tex Rickards, saying for the last time, "Ladies and Gentlemen, now coming in to pitch for the Dodgers, Number 13, Ralph Branca."

Just then, Branca — this time a middle-aged businessman dressed in a camel's-hair coat — emerged from the dugout and smiled. Overhead, for the last time, the flag flew, unintentionally left upside down, which is the international sign for distress.

And with that, the big crane headed in from center field, "with the speed of Ernie Lombardi," wrote Talese. With its iron ball painted white with stitches to look like a baseball, it came spinning, like a Hugh Casey fastball, toward the wall and demolition of a shrine was underway. The same wrecking ball was used four years later to demolish the Polo Grounds.

In 1963, the Ebbets Field Apartments opened on the site of the former ballpark. When Jackie Robinson died in 1972, it was renamed for the late Dodger. Across the street stands the Jackie Robinson Intermediate School. And the school's retired assistant principal? Marty Adler.

FIFTEEN MINUTES OF FAME
The man who caught Maris' 61st
1418 Neptune Avenue, Coney Island

The world is full of variations on Andy Warhol's line that everyone is famous for 15 minutes. No word on whether the late pop artist was a ball fan, but if his line applies to anyone, it's to one Sal Durante of 1418 Neptune Avenue, Coney Island.

Every baseball fan knows how Roger Maris, a solid-but-not-great Yankee, for one magical season, 1961, scaled the mountain, setting a new single-season home run record. Maris' record-breaking 61st dinger — not broken until 1998, when Mark McGwire hit 70 homers and Sammy Sosa, 66 — came against Red Sox rookie pitcher Tracy Stallard to win the game 1-0 for the Yankees on the season's last day, October 2, 1961.

Maris' home run that broke Babe Ruth's single-season home run record of 60, was a 2-0 waist-high fastball that sailed into the lower right field deck of Yankee Stadium. And making an impressive one-handed catch of the historic homer was Durante, a 19-year-old truck driver attending the game with his fiancee, Rosemarie Calabrese.

Durante and Calabrese had bought right-field tickets for all three games of the weekend Red Sox series in slim hopes of catching the home run ball hit by the left-handed slugging Maris. Ironically, the right-field stands were about the only place a crowd had gathered that Sunday afternoon at Yankee Stadium — the modest attendance of 23,154 that day left the ballpark less than half-full.

Durante's youthful reflexes earned him a well-publicized $5,000 reward from Sam Gordon, a Sacramento, California restaurateur, as well as a round-trip passage to the 1962 World's Fair in Seattle and two season passes to the 1962 Yankee home games. Gordon paid Durante almost right away — flying to New York after the game to present the check to the young Brooklynite the next morning, live on the CBS-TV program, "Calendar."

As Maris swung through #61, Durante secured his unusual place in history by leaping onto his chair — Box 163D, seat 4 — reaching up and snaring the line drive. For a moment, he and a multitude of others hoping to catch it themselves fell into a heap, but Durante held the ball, despite jabs and punches from those nearby.

Stadium police then whisked Durante quickly away, toward the waiting television cameras and newspaper scribes to meet Maris. Regarding the reward money, Durante struck a modest chord: "All I want to do," he said, "is give the ball to Maris."

Even Maris, who left the dugout to meet Durante as the Yankees batted in the fifth inning, was impressed. "What do you think of that kid?" he asked Red Sox catcher Russ Nixon, as he stepped up to the plate in the eighth. "The boy is planning to get married and he can use the money, but he still wanted to give the ball back to me for nothing. It shows there's some good people left in this world after all."

For Maris, #61 ended what had been an agonizing ordeal of intense media scrutiny. The soft-spoken, 27-year-old North Dakota native had the double burden of competing, not just against the ghost of Ruth — the game's most enduring deity — but in a tight homer-for-homer race for the record against his teammate and the game's most popular player of the day, Mickey Mantle, who finished with 54 homers that year. Maris didn't enjoy New York either, choosing to live quietly on his own in Queens.

Adding to Maris' burden was Baseball Commissioner Ford Frick's humiliating proposal that an asterisk be placed next to #61 in the record books. It would explain that Maris benefited from a schedule that expanded from the 154 games of Ruth's day to the 162 games of Maris' era and today.

But no asterisk ever appeared in any record book. Contemporary pride prevailed over historic sentiment. So, why the fuss in the first place? Years before, Ford had been a sportswriter who had ghostwritten for Ruth.

Meanwhile, Durante goes down in the record books as the man with the game's most profitable seat. For the record, he and Rosemarie married October 29. He later became a bus driver in Brooklyn.

SAY IT AIN'T SO, JOE PEP
An ex-Yank is busted
Rockaway Avenue & Newport Street, Brownsville

"I discovered the city, the Copa and all that," Joe Pepitone once said of his bittersweet eight-year career as a New York Yankee. "And I found I could hit .996 on the street. It probably took 60 points off my average."

For honesty alone, Pepitone makes the all-star team. From the start, the Brooklyn born-and-bred Pepitone ignored the Yankee hierarchy at a time when it still mattered. Signed by the Yankees for a $25,000 bonus, Pepitone went right out and bought a Thunderbird and a 14-foot runabout — a tad flashy for the staid, conservative lords of the Bronx.

Pepitone was part of the new breed of ballplayer. Neither deferential to tradition nor veteran ballplayers, they rubbed a few more conservative types the wrong way. In 1962, Pepitone's rookie season, he was sent in to replace Moose Skowron, offering the observation that "Moose, you must have the bad glove," before telling the veteran that he was about to take his job. He did, and after Skowron was traded to the Dodgers, Pepitone cabled him: "DEAR MOOSE: TOLD YOU SO ... JOE PEP."

Mostly, people remember the unfulfilled promise of the free-swinging Pepitone. He played in three World Series with the Yanks, but couldn't help them once the team hit the skids in the late 1960s. In 1969, Pepitone was traded to Houston and later moved to the Cubs and the Braves, ending his major league career in 1973 with a career batting average of .258 and 219 home runs. The title of a Pepitone biography, *Joe, You Could Have Made Us Proud*, is appropriate.

It was still a surprise when, on the evening of March 18, 1985, Pepitone was among a group of three men stopped for running a red light at Rockaway Avenue and Newport Street. Found in the car in which he was riding were nine ounces of cocaine, depressant pills, drug paraphernalia, a loaded .22 caliber Derringer, and $6,300 in cash.

The 46-year-old Pepitone, dressed in a leather jacket and a cowboy hat at his arrest, was later sentenced for two misdemeanor drug convictions to six months in jail. How ironic that sentencing came on the same day that the Mets beat the Red Sox to even up the 1986 World Series at two games apiece, a big day in New York baseball.

In imposing the harsh jail term, acting State Supreme Court Justice Richard A. Brown didn't mince words. Asserting that Pepitone had gone from being a "first-rate baseball player" to a "second-rate drug operator," the judge called the former ballplayer, "a very ordinary Brooklyn criminal."

"I find it particularly sad," the judge continued, launching into clichés, "when someone who graced New York in Yankee pinstripes will now have to serve his time with the New York Department of Corrections in their prison stripes."

Before leaving to serve his term at notorious Rikers Island, Pepitone admitted he was apprehensive. "I've never even been in prison before and this is hard on me," he told reporters outside the Brooklyn Courthouse. "I feel like I shouldn't have got it, but I got it and I'm going to go and do it, come out and maybe see if I can get back into baseball."

Pepitone got his wish, when, two months later, he was hired by the Yankees to work in the team's minor league player development program, as part of a work-release program. For the final two months of his term — he served four months altogether — Pepitone returned to Rikers Island after every Yankee home game.

The compassionate soul responsible for the poignant ending? George Steinbrenner, of all people. "He's been nothing but the best since I've known him," a grateful Pepitone said of the Boss. "He's helped me through a lot of things."

BIRTH OF THE BOX SCORE – THE STORY OF "FATHER" CHADWICK
American Sports Publishing Co.
21 Warren Street

Civilization just wouldn't be as we know it without that time-honored American ritual of opening the newspaper and perusing the box scores. Fortunately, we have Brooklyn's "Father" Henry Chadwick to thank for that.

What Babe Ruth was to the playing side of baseball, "Father" Henry Chadwick was to the writing end. He invented the box score, printed the first rule book and is known as the game's earliest and foremost writer.

Born in Great Britain, where he was weaned on cricket, Chadwick came to the US at the age of 13 in 1837. But it was in 1856, while on his way to cover a cricket match at Elysian Fields in Hoboken, that Chadwick's attention was attracted to a number of young men wearing long pants and long whiskers and playing a game called baseball. He was hooked, and for the next 52 years, was the game's greatest advocate.

Chadwick became a kind of one-man publicity machine, covering the games and turning in his stories to newspapers throughout the area. Coincidentally, Chadwick's new passion coincided with his first newspaper job, in 1856 with *The Times*. The following year, he joined *The New York Clipper*, then *The Tribune*, *The Brooklyn Eagle*, and other publications.

Eventually, Chadwick turned in so much baseball copy that the papers, which once took two or three lines on the sport, expanded their coverage. Chadwick, in turn, talked the ears off city editors — there were no sports editors in those days — in urging them to cover baseball. He also served for a time on rules committees for both the National Association of Baseball Players; and, later, the National Association of Professional Players. In 1894, he became an honorary member of the rules committee for the National League.

Along the way, Chadwick developed the box score and devised the system for scoring games — essentially the same as used today. He also edited a vast array of baseball guides from his

Henry Chadwick at Rest in Green-Wood Cemetery.

American Sports Publishing Company office at 21 Warren Street, beginning in 1860 with *Beadle's Dime Base Ball Player*, and including the well-known *Spalding's Base Ball Guide*, from 1881 to his death in 1908.

Chadwick considered himself a guardian of the developing game's image and well-being. He railed against drinking and rowdiness of the players as well as persistent threats by gamblers to corrupt the game and reduce baseball to a betting pit.

In 1904, Chadwick was awarded the only medal given to a journalist by the St. Louis World's Fair. Four years later, he died at 84 of heart failure at his home, "The Glen," at 840 Halsey Street. How fitting that Chadwick's first question after briefly recovering following his stroke was the outcome of that day's Brooklyn-Giants game.

According to news accounts, Brooklyn won, Chadwick expressed his disappointment and died. With the flag at Washington Park flying at half-staff, Chadwick was buried in Green-Wood Cemetery in a tomb adorned with sculptures of baseballs, a catcher's mask, and interlocking bats.

IN THE SKY, IT'S A BIRD, IT'S A PLANE, IT'S ... THE BUMS
Floyd Bennett Field
Gateway National Recreation Area
Off Flatbush Avenue, Rockaway Inlet

Remember the film clips of the Beatles arriving in America? Off the airplane they stepped at Kennedy Airport — and into the hearts of thousands of screaming teenybops who went to meet them.

It was 1964 and the idea of going to the airport to meet and greet celebrity travelers was fresh. Airplane travel was still exotic, even then. That was more than 30 years ago, an era in which dad liked to load the kids in the station wagon and venture out to the airport to watch the planes come and go.

Go back another 24 years from there and you can only imagine the intense excitement of going to the airport to watch the planes. Throw in a bunch of celebrities and it must have been overwhelming.

There was no Fab Four to meet in those days; but in Brooklyn, there was another set of heroes, the Dodgers. So what were 10,000 "feverish fans," as *The New York Times* described them, doing well past midnight on May 10, 1940 at Floyd Bennett Field? Welcoming the Dodgers back from Chicago in what was the second mass flight of a major league team during the regular season, that's what. Only three days before, on May 7, the team had made the first historic flight, traveling from St. Louis to Chicago.

An oversized sign, "Welcome Home Brooklyn Dodgers," left little doubt what the fuss was about. It hung near the entrance to the airport Administration Building, and there was even a small bandstand for the players and a welcoming committee of borough dignitaries.

There were the obligatory speeches, a lot of noise and 135 policemen to keep back the surging crowd. In the days leading to the trip, local newspapers had predicted a crowd of about 1,000 to greet the two Dodger planes after the team's western swing. They got 10,000, who had expected the team at 10 PM, but, because of traffic in Chicago and a refueling stop in Cleveland, had to wait until 12:40 AM for the first Dodger plane to arrive; the second plane, which held most of the Dodger veterans, came 10 minutes later.

"It was a restless crowd," *The Times* reported, "but once the first plane was sighted it behaved remarkably well." Borough president John Cashmore then made the welcoming speech, which included a plea to team president Larry MacPhail to throw out the first ball at that fall's World Series at Ebbets Field.

After all, it was MacPhail who was responsible for the historic flight. As the father of major league flight, he had in 1934, taken a number of the Cincinnati Reds to Chicago, and again in 1936, from Puerto Rico to Miami during spring training. In 1939, several members of the Boston Red Sox had made the St. Louis-to-Chicago flight as well; others took the train.

Hoopla aside, the flight back to Brooklyn was uneventful. Bounding off the first plane was Dodger manager Leo Durocher who happily endorsed air travel, saying he never wanted to go any other way, providing he had the unanimous consent of his players.

And bounding off airplane number two came Dan Comerford, the veteran Dodger property man, who had traveled with the team for 35 years: "It's the greatest thing that's happened to me since I've been with the Dodgers," he said.

One reason for Comerford's enthusiasm in the air may have been the Dodgers themselves, which hadn't won a pennant for 20 years. The wait, however, wouldn't take that much longer; Brooklyn won the National League the following year, 1941.

BERNARD MALAMUD – BASEBALL WRITER?
Erasmus Hall Evening High School
911 Flatbush Avenue

Bernard Malamud once described his novel's essential character as "someone who fears his fate, is caught up in it, yet manages to outrun it; he's the subject of laughter and pity."

Such a character is Roy Hobbs, the seemingly hayseed ballplayer of few words and a mysterious past, as well as the primary character of Malamud's first book, *The Natural*. Written in 1952 when Malamud was a professor at Oregon State University, the story is the combination of a dark morality play, a Greek tragedy, and a subject born of the city that produced him.

Malamud's Hobbs is a star slugger who takes his team, the New York Knights, to the verge of a World Series, as he struggles to overcome a tragic past. As a young man, Hobbs is the quintessential small-town American boy of the 1920s who can hit a baseball a country mile. Things start unraveling when Hobbs — by then a prospect — is lured to a Chicago hotel room and shot at close range by a disturbed vixen with a violent weakness for ballplayers. The story line is fashioned on the real-life shooting in 1949 of Phillie Eddie Waitkus by an obsessed female admirer and a shooting in the 1930s involving Bill Jurgez of the Cubs.

The son of Russian Jewish immigrants who ran a Brooklyn grocery store, Malamud displays a healthy understanding for the game — clear from Hobbs' homemade bat, "Wonderboy," to colorful scenes of batting practice and the life and habits of Baseball Annies, circa 1930.

"At 33, the Whammer still enjoyed exceptional eyesight," Malmud writes in a chapter in which a young Roy strikes out a veteran Ruthian-clone slugger. "He saw the ball spin off Roy's fingertips and it reminded him of a white pigeon he had kept as a boy, that he would send into flight by flipping it into the air. The ball flew at him and he was conscious of its bird-like form and white flapping wings, until it suddenly disappeared from view. He heard a noise like the bang of a firecracker at his feet and Sam (the catcher) had the ball in his mitt."

The book ends with failure, as Roy strikes out, much like Mighty Casey. But a 1984 film adaptation of *The Natural*, directed by Barry Levinson and starring Robert Redford as Hobbs, ends on a positive note. In the final playoff game — and Roy's final game as well, for his health has declined — Hobbs does it one more time — going downtown against a big Nebraska farmboy-turned-Pirate-southpaw, and a spitting image of his younger self. Unlike the book, Redford's Hollywood Hobbs has once again triggered the triumph of good over evil.

Malamud attended Erasmus Hall High School, which also produced Yankee Hall-of-Famer Waite Hoyt. It was there in the late 1940s, he taught night school, before landing the Oregon university position. It was around then, as Malamud worked on *The Natural*, that he married a gentile woman, Ann de Chiara, and started to absorb the awful truth of the Nazi Holocaust.

Their union and his in-depth study of the the Holocaust encouraged Malamud to devout his scholarship to the exploration of Jewish issues; until then, Malamud said years later, he had not given much thought to what it meant to be Jewish. "The suffering of the Jews is a distinct thing for me," he said. "I for one believe that not enough has been made of the tragedy of the destruction of six million Jews."

Translation: *The Natural* was Malamud's last venture into baseball and non-Jewish issues, before he launched into a career of one of America's greatest writers. Alas, there would be no sequel for Roy Hobbs.

END TO A WILD RIDE
Steve Howe bows out with a bang
John F. Kennedy Airport

How odd, it seemed at first, that Steve Howe bowed out so gracefully.

When the 38-year-old left-handed reliever was released by the Yankees in 1996 after six years with the team and 12 in the majors, he spoke so calmly that he freely dispensed his home telephone to reporters.

"I'm not naive enough to not know what the score is," Howe said after being released while the Yanks were in Cleveland. "It's been a great ride here. There came a point where something had to happen."

Odd words when you consider Howe's career as a whole: a 92-mile-an-hour fastball, combined with an even faster lifestyle that included countless teams and seven suspensions — seven! — from the major leagues for repeated substance abuse violations.

Howe personified the wild, out-of-control ballplayer of the 1980s and '90s. So, it was no surprise really, when a day after his release, he was arrested at John F. Kennedy Airport for carrying a loaded .357 Magnum pistol in his luggage.

At the time, Howe was with his wife, Cynthia, and planning to travel on a Delta flight to his home in Whitefish, Montana. Call it an ironic twist to the end of his Yankee career, during which he had mostly been a model citizen, having been suspended only once — in 1992, because he violated his after-care program.

If cats have nine lives, Steven Howe had twice that. He reached the majors in 1980 with the Dodgers after just 13 games in the minor leagues and took National League Rookie of the Year honors. In 1981, he helped Los Angeles take the World Series, winning game four and saving game six in the Dodgers' win over the Yankees.

There seemed to be two constants in Howe's life: pitching and drugs. Howe had tried cocaine in his student days at the University of Michigan, and also tried a few other drugs along the way: marijuana, LSD, and mescaline, among them. No wonder he titled his autobiography *Between the Lines*.

Eventually, drugs took over his life. Taking LSD, he believed his stereo speakers were breathing. In Chicago, he taped the windows of his hotel room so people couldn't peek inside. Needing a fix back home, he'd tell his wife he was running out to buy milk, and stay away for days.

Still, he played well — pitching 62 games and compiling a sparkling 2.08 ERA in 1982 and an even better 1.44 ERA in 1983. Then, things started unraveling, and Howe spent the next few years in and out of rehab facilities. By then, the Dodgers had grown tired of his behavior, fining him, in 1983, more than $53,000 — his pay for the time he'd been unavailable to pitch.

In 1984, Major League Baseball suspended Howe for the first time. In 1985, the Dodgers had run out of patience and he signed with the Twins. There was a notable drop-off in Howe's performance — and more rehab. Then came more suspensions, more teams (Texas, San Jose Bees, and the Seibu Lions in Japan), along with more rehab and, well, you get the picture. By 1988, Howe had visited six treatment centers in six years.

In 1991, Howe signed with the Yankees, managing to somehow throw some heat after all those years. That he stuck around New York for five more years is testament to both an extraordinary left-arm and ironically, a strong Christian faith. It was early in Howe's career that he became deeply religious, accepting Jesus Christ into his life.

Maybe that's why he was so gracious to reporters after being released. For all his troubles and the angst he caused to his teams, Howe remained a gracious man, popular with fans and generous with an autograph.

In November 1996, Howe was sentenced to three years' probation and 150 hours of community service after pleading guilty to the misdemeanor weapons-possession change. The recipient of his community service: The Presbyterian Church of Astoria, Queens, where Howe performed youth counseling.

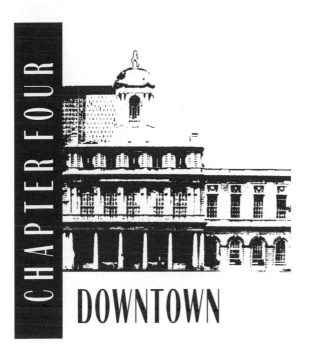

CHAPTER FOUR

DOWNTOWN

"I could never play in New York. The first time I ever came into a game there, I got in the bullpen car and they told me to lock the doors."

— *Mike Flanagan, Orioles' pitcher, 1979*

A GAME IS BORN — HOME OF THE KNICKERBOCKERS
Fijux's Hotel
42 Murray Street

"The young clubs, one and all, with a welcome we will greet,
On their field or festive hall, whenever we may meet;
And their praises we will sing at some future time;
But now we'll pledge their health in a glass of rosy wine."

And so went the quaint verse of one of baseball's first songs. It is courtesy of the Knickerbocker Base Ball Club, baseball's first real team. We owe a late 20th-century tip of the hat to this mid-19th century group, who shaped the game into America's pastime.

The brand of baseball, or "town ball," as it was known, as played by the Knickerbockers, was different than today's game, much different. Not a sand-lot or a semi-pro team in the sense we think of such outfits today, the Knickerbockers were primarily a social club, with a distinctly hierarchical flavor — similar to the role played by country clubs of more recent times.

The Knickerbockers were named for the former fire company of team member, Alexander Cartwright, who fashioned both the team and the rules. Here was a way for genteel young men to play the game, and more impor-tantly, to enjoy the lavish post-game banquets. Indeed, their rules and regu-lations emphasized not so much how to put some pop into the fastball, as it did proper conduct.

In one sense, the Knickerbockers were an exclusive bunch, whose mem-bers constituted a kind of social "jocktocracy." Players couldn't leave the game unless excused by the captain. Those refusing to obey the captain were docked 50¢, and 25¢ for arguing with the umpire. And if the captain left the field before game's end, or neglected his duties in any other way, the fine was a hefty $1.

Profanity was inexcusable. In the Knickerbockers' very first outside match, J. W. Davis swore and paid 6¢ — the game's first fine. Ty Cobb would have gone bankrupt with this lot.

The Knickerbockers started around 1842, playing their version of town ball at 27th Street and 4th Avenue. Three years later, it was Cartwright, a clerk at Union Bank, who suggested they organize formally and adopt rules to thrust some life into a game that was essentially rounders. Cartwright's ideas were revolutionary — he knew that town ball in its current state could be bor-ing for players and spectators alike, so he sought to make some changes.

Cartwright knew that standing in the field waiting to bat while an entire opposing team batted was about as exciting as watching paint dry. He knew that being hit with the ball while on the bases was unnecessary and he knew that positioning a slew of players in the outfield and two catchers behind the plate was too much. His greatest contribution: recognizing that basic simpli-fication could turn this old-fashioned game into something more lively.

For starters, Cartwright approached Billy Tucker, an active member of the rival New York Base Ball Club. One of the city's best players, Tucker agreed to become a Knickerbocker. Just as important, Tucker had a roommate, a law-yer named William Wheaton — a ballplayer and a lawyer, and a good com-bination to assist in the club's formation.

Cartwright's rules were the basis for what became known as the "New

York game," For starters, it meant a player could no longer be deliberately hit by the ball; the danger of injury lessened considerably, which, in turn led to the use of a harder ball. That alone led to profound changes, because a harder ball travels further and more swiftly when struck than does a soft ball, meaning fielders had to develop greater skills and more efficient teamwork to create outs.

The Knickerbockers also decreed the infield be diamond-shaped, rather than square. They set first and third bases 42 paces apart, established foul lines and made pitchers throw the ball underhand, keeping the wrist and elbow straight. And a batter got three missed swings before he was out.

Cartwright's ideas were quickly accepted and a permanent playing field was found across the Hudson River in Hoboken, New Jersey, at a large grassy meadow named "Elysian Fields." Thus marked the historic break from the more primitive game of rounders in which wooden stakes projecting four feet from the ground stood for bases and a player was put out by being struck with the ball.

For the record, the Knickerbockers' rules and club by-laws were formalized in a $2 room at Fijux's Hotel, owned by team member Charles Knickerbocker Fijux, whose mother still took care to collect the rent. The hotel became the place for all team meetings.

It was also at Fujix's that the Knickerbockers voted to limit membership to 40. Of the 50-odd names on their rosters between 1845 and 1860 were 17 merchants, 12 clerks, five brokers, four professionals, two insurance salesmen, several "gentlemen," a hatter, and a US Marshal. The only requisite for admission: some skill in the game and social standing.

That sense of exclusiveness was protected through a system of blackballing still used by fraternal organizations. A demanding schedule played a role as well, since only men of a certain social stature could afford to devote every Monday and Thursday — Knickerbocker "Play Days" — to baseball. Further dues went for uniforms and ballpark rentals.

Led by Cartwright, the Knickerbockers blazed baseball's early trail — the first step of a game that would eventually become commercialized and take the country by storm. With Wheaton, who drew up the team's by-laws and constitution; and Tucker, whose on-the-field know-how helped to fine-tune and formalize this new game, the Knickerbockers were on their way.

Through it all the team maintained their customary post-game habits. It became standard for New York's growing legion of teams to commemorate the off-season by, well, celebrating. In 1854, the Knickerbockers were joined by the Eagle and Gotham clubs in a memorable dinner — at Fujix's (where else?), where "the utmost hilarity prevailed and everything passed off in a happy manner," as one account put it.

But the game that Cartwright and the Knickerbockers had helped to develop was changing. Ask the Knickerbockers and they would have preferred to restrict the game to their own social class. In that regard, they failed, for as the 1850s opened up, baseball spread to all walks, including — horror of horrors — the working classes.

But the die had been cast. By then, Cartwright had moved on, having joined the California Gold Rush in 1849. He later settled in Hawaii, where he started an insurance company and founded Honolulu's fire department. Cartwright died in 1892.

LOU GEHRIG GOES NATIVE
New York City Parole Commission
139 Centre Street

Few stories are equally as tragic and inspiring as the rapid demise of Lou Gehrig. After being diagnosed with ALS and leaving baseball in 1939, the Yankee first baseman known as "The Ironhorse" declined quickly — spending countless months in hospitals and bedridden at home in the Bronx. He died in 1941.

In some ways, Gehrig never really left baseball. He was honored at the famous Yankee Stadium ceremony on July 4, 1940, when he earnestly told a young Yankee announcer of the time, Mel Allen, that it was his broadcasting that kept him going. Yet, for a brief few months, starting January 2, 1940, Gehrig held a desk job — at the invitation of Mayor La Guardia — as one of three members of New York City's Parole Commission.

The mayor, ever the astute politician, thought Gehrig could be an inspiration to troubled youths. And Gehrig took to his new duties seriously, telling reporters at the start that he would not "spout" about his ideas on crime and criminals until he had spent at least a year on the job.

"I hope to be able to do something constructive in the rehabilitation of criminals, most of whom, as we know, are young," Gehrig said. "I've got ideas on crime and the handing of criminals, but I'm not going to talk about them for one year."

Gehrig told La Guardia about a visit he'd once made to New York's Sing Sing Prison in Ossining, for an exhibition game against the inmates. "A lot of those fellows up there kept yelling at me, 'Hello, Lou, how are you,'" he said. "And I thought they were just fans. But when I looked closely, I realized a few of them used to run around with me when were kids."

The Iron Horse signed up for a 10-year term at a salary of $5,700 a year, a fair amount for the day. But it wasn't money that motivated the former Yankee. As Gehrig's wife, Eleanor, said later, "It was a real chance to do something for the old hometown."

The couple felt strongly about moving from Larchmont into New York City to satisfy the mandatory residency law for city employees. They quickly found a white frame house at 5204 Delafield Avenue, on the edge of Fieldston in the Riverdale section of the Bronx, from which they could jump on the just-completed Henry Hudson Parkway for the quick trip downtown.

In his first day on the job, Gehrig was photographed at his desk, while puffing away on his briar pipe. He protested with a plea that would put most modern ballplayers to shame. "I don't want to be shown smoking in pictures because of the possible effect on young boys," he said. "I can't encourage kids to smoke."

Gehrig plunged into his work, keeping almost daily contact with criminals, prostitutes, hoodlums, and vagabonds. One such youngster was 19-year-old Rocco Barbella, who had been imprisoned at The Tombs on a charge of statutory rape. Barbella was a tough street kid from the Lower East Side who straightened out, and, as Rocky Graziano, became the middleweight champ.

Years later, Graziano recalled his curiosity at meeting the great ballplayer with a terminal illness. What he saw shocked him; Gehrig had lost considerable weight and walked by leaning heavily on crutches. It was even difficult to hear his husky voice, because breathing was labored.

On days when Gehrig wasn't visiting Rikers Island or The Tombs, Eleanor drove him downtown to his office. In his last days, she even helped him on the job by holding his trembling fingers as he signed official documents.

Sadly, Gehrig never got a chance to spout his ideas on crime. By December 1940, he could no longer perform his job and Eleanor was forced to asked the mayor to grant her husband a leave of absence. By mid-April 1941, Gehrig wrote his final Parole Commission letter, declining an invitation to attend a Health and Recreation Week function at the Jacob M. Schiff Center. He had always enjoyed such functions, but by then, was virtually bedridden.

On June 2, 1941, Joe DiMaggio got two hits off Bob Feller in Cleveland in the midst of his record 56-game hitting streak. And that evening, back in Riverdale, Gehrig died at home in his sleep, just 17 days from his 38th birthday.

HIP, HIP, HOORAY – HERE'S TO THE JINTS
Academy of Music
2 Irving Place (& 14th Street)

You may know the story of Fred Merkle's base-running mistake and how it cost the Giants the 1908 pennant in the wackiest race of all-time. The reaction of Giants fans: "Never mind," they said, some weeks later, in what became one of the more unusual collective love-ins between fans and players.

"The New York public stood staunchly by its ball players," *The Times* wrote. That was an understatement on the evening of October 18, 1908, as thousands squeezed into the Academy of Music to show their gratitude to the Giants, giving the venerable old palace of culture the feel of the Polo Grounds.

The Times again: "The grand stand crowd filled the boxes and the orchestra, overflowing into the first balcony, while the leather-lunged of the bleachers packed the upper gallaries." Festivities were late in starting; only with the cries of "play ball," did things get moving.

Mike Donlin, accompanied by his wife, the actress Mabel Hite, was the first of the Giants to be recognized.

"Oh, you Mike!" serenaded the crowd.

"Oh, you Mabel, ain't it awful!"

"Play ball!"

Then there was more entertainment and a long-winded speech by US Rep. William Sulzer to the loud cries of "give him the hook." Finally, the players were herded out onto the center of the stage as Sulzer, now the moderator, rambled on. First, catcher Roger Bresnahan and then the others, were presented watch fobs that the Congressman described as solid gold with a real diamond studding.

"This sameness of speech [soon] got on the nerves of the bleachers," *The Times* dutifully reported.

"You're out!" a fan yelled.

"Back to the bench!" bawled another.

Sulzer got the message and the presentations ended. And with it, the wacky, wonderful baseball season of 1908 was quite suddenly over.

BASEBALL GOES PRO
Collier's Rooms, a.k.a. Collier's Cafe
840 Broadway (& 13th Street)

With teams like the Cincinnati Red Stockings and Brooklyn's Atlantics gaining interest and grabbing headlines throughout the 1860s and early 1870s, any pretense that baseball was an amateur endeavor came to an abrupt end on the evening of March 17, 1871 at Collier's Rooms.

That's when representatives of the country's major baseball clubs met to find ways and means of stabilizing their sport. The split was between those bidding to keep it on the gentlemanly level, and the newer brand, as played by the National Association of Professional Base Ball Players. The pros won and baseball was forever changed.

Nine teams joined the new league that night — Harry Wright's latest team, the powerful Boston Red Stockings; the Chicago White Stockings; New York Mutuals; Philadelphia Athletics; Washington Olympics; Troy Haymakers; Fort Wayne Kekiongas; Cleveland Forest Citys; and, the Rockford City Forest Citys. Two Forest Citys? The Kekiongas were replaced midway through that inaugural '71 season by Brooklyn's Eckfords. Got it?

The pros provided order where there'd been chaos. Under the amateurs, the title, "Champions of the United States," was nominal only; here, for the first time, was a bona fide league among member clubs, any of which could compete by applying to a league committee and coughing up a $10 fee.

It seemed simple enough. It wasn't. With no formal schedule, Eastern teams generally made two Western swings and the Western clubs traveled East twice as well. Even so, most games were between clubs in the same geographical area, making the competition haphazard and uneven. Add the expense of traveling and baseball's first pro league, which, at this point, had as many as 13 teams, was a financial failure.

The Athletics took the first championship, beating out second-place Boston and third-place Chicago. The White Stockings performed admirably, considering the Great Chicago Fire destroyed their ballpark in early October 1871, forcing the team to play its last three games on the road. They lost all three.

Then, in the following season — 1872 — Wright's Red Stockings took the first of its four championships. Meanwhile, a parade of teams marched in and out of league competition — of the 25 teams competing in those five years, only the Red Stockings, Athletics, and New York Mutuals made it through intact. Eleven teams survived one season or less.

The problems continued. A bad economy cut into attendance. As smaller franchises folded, disturbing rumors of rowdyism and a practice called "hippodroming" — staging games for gamblers — made things worse. Editorialized *The New York Herald*: "To such a low ebb have the morals of so many professional players descended that no man can now witness game between many of the clubs and be sure that both sides are striving to win."

Then, in 1876, the National League was formed by William A. Hulbert on a business-like basis. Baseball's first savior was ready to roll.

BIRTH OF THE NATIONAL LEAGUE
Grand Central Hotel (later Central Hotel)
2125 3rd Avenue (& Broadway)

The baseball of the early 1870s, as organized by the National Association of Base Ball Players, was an ungainly mess. The enormous turnover of teams, infusion of gamblers, and uneven schedules contributed to a sport that, on a professional level, was fast approaching financial ruin.

Enter William A. Hulbert, owner of the Chicago White Stockings, noted for successfully steering his team through the calamity of the Great Chicago Fire of 1871. The fire cost Hulbert two seasons, after his ballpark burned down — still, he managed to turn a profit, largely through the shrewd acquisitions of players like Al Spalding and Cap Anson, two of the game's early superstars.

Moreover, as a coal baron and a titan in industry, Hulbert knew how organizations should run and had precious little sympathy for his ballplayers and the league they ran. His goal: nothing less than the displacement of the National Association, with a strong new organization, composed of selected clubs and better regional balance, and targeted to exploit the best of intersectional rivalries.

By late 1875, Hulbert went to work on his plan, traveling secretly to St. Louis and Louisville to confer with club owners and draw up the league by-laws and constitution. To a curious public, Hulbert announced that he and his owner-colleagues were reformers, acting to clean up the national pastime. The result: the birth of the aptly-named National League.

When Hulbert, his fellow conspirators and the rest of the league met at the Central Hotel on February 2, 1876, the results were revolutionary. First, Hulbert tightened the discipline among players — forbidding them to drink either on the field or off. He banned beer sales and gambling at parks, set ticket prices at 50¢ and ruled out Sunday games.

The group's true coup was a sea-change of a shift in power to the owners, making players, in effect, employees. "It is ridiculous to pay ballplayers $2,000 a year," Hulbert said, "especially when the $800 boys do just as well." To emphasize their motives, Hulbert's bunch then created the game's first reserve clause for the contracts of each team's top five players. Protesting players were blacklisted; most didn't dare, for times were hard and they needed the work.

"The idea was as old as the hills, but its application to Base Ball had not yet been made," Spalding said. "It was, in effect, the irrepressible conflict between Labor and Capital asserting itself under a new guise."

As head of the *coup d'etat*, Hulbert put himself in charge of the National League. Getting his way required hardball tactics — he is said to have called those hostile to his plan, mainly the Eastern owners, to his suite at the Central Hotel, locked the door and forbade anyone to leave until an agreement was reached.

The story is probably apocryphal. More likely, Hulbert's forceful personality convinced the others to join him. His efforts took some time to be recognized — it took until 1995, more than a century later, for his election to the Hall of Fame.

BASEBALL AGAIN FOR KEN BURNS
Pete's tavern
129 East 18th Street

Like most mortals, filmmaker Ken Burns' dream to make it to the major leagues came to a grinding halt in Little League, where, as he told *USA Baseball Weekly*, his only attribute was speed. That meant his only real chance to get on base was to work the count for a walk and steal bases.

And like a lot of people of his generation, the 40-something Burns was a lapsed baseball fan, who rediscovered it as an adult. Indeed, his nine-part, 19-hour public television epic of baseball history entitled "Baseball" and shown in the fall of 1994, has been heralded by film critics as as documentary masterpiece.

"Baseball" features Burns' distinctive filmmaking style — the same one that created other PBS favorites like "The Civil War" (1990) and "Brooklyn Bridge" (1981). It combines interviews, reel after reel of vintage footage and lyrical odes to the game, read by some of best actors and intellectuals in the land. Among them: Gregory Peck, Garrison Keillor, Doris Kearns Goodwin, Roger Angell, Studs Terkel, and Mario Cuomo, former governor of New York.

Just how Burns found the game again begins on the evening of October 21, 1975. At the time, Burns was a recent graduate of Hampshire College and breaking into the film business in New York, when he joined some friends at Pete's for game six of the World Series.

If you know baseball, you know the game — Red Sox vs. Reds and Carlton Fisk frantically waving his arms and willing his 12th inning shot to stay fair. Result: home run, the Sox take a classic, and Ken Burns is a fan again.

"From that moment on," he has said, "I was back."

Okay, so it wasn't quite O. Henry penning "The Gift of the Magi," as he did at Pete's in 1905. Nor did it match other wacky features of Pete's, opened in 1864, and the oldest continually operating drinking establishment in New York; the place was a favorite meeting place of Tammany Hall politicians, and was a sham florist shop during Prohibition.

But for Burns, it was the place where the baseball spark was reignited. Watching game six at Pete's made him a Red Sox fan, a team he still supports from his home in Walpole, New Hampshire. Accordingly, a major portion of "Baseball's" last episode is devoted to game six and Fisk's home run.

AROUND THE WORLD AND BACK WITH JOHN MCGRAW
Pier 56 and the Hudson River
Foot of 14th Street and the West Side Highway

Baseball in front of Britain's King George V? Baseball in Egypt? In France and Australia? Huh? Why not baseball in the Bronx or at the Polo Grounds, where it's supposed to be?

It all made sense if you were Giants' manager John McGraw on March 6,

1914, and you were just back from a five-month, round-the-world tour that introduced the world to baseball.

McGraw and his all-star group of ballplayers, comprised mostly of Giants and White Sox, sailed into New York Harbor aboard the Lusitania on that snowy March morning (a little more than a year later, the ship was sunk by a German submarine, killing 128 American passengers). On hand to meet them was a delirious throng of 300 baseball fans and officials — egged on by a healthy dose of gushing newspaper headlines.

It was New York's finest nautical baseball celebration. "The tooting of whistles and the shrill blasts of the sirens from every craft in the harbor [heralded] the welcome return of the baseball players," trumpted *The Times*. "[For McGraw, it sounded] better than the thunder of 30,000 fans at the Polo Grounds."

The sirens of the harbor was only the start. Another crowd of 300, many of them Chicago friends of the White Sox, yelled a welcome from the boat, "Niagara." Back on land, ladies waved hankerchiefs and men vigorously pumped their hats in recognition of the 68-person delegation steaming up the Hudson toward home.

As the ship docked, "it could be seen that a change had come over the players," *The Times* said. In short, they had become dudes, using most of their time abroad by dressing for their homecoming in the lastest fashions of Paris and London. "Mike Donlin was nifty in his new scenery, to say nothing of Germany Schaefer who looked as if he had just stepped out of a Bond Street toggery shop," the paper reported. Even Umpire Bill Klem descended the gangplank, sporting a neat mustard-colored coat and walking stick.

They had done well, having romped through 11 innings for King George in London, an audience with the Pope in Rome, and playing before enthusiastic crowds in France, Egypt, Australia, and Japan. It was an old-fashioned demonstration of American diplomacy through sports, the forerunner of ping-pong diplomacy. Said the US ambassador to Great Britain: "This game has accomplished more toward getting the Americans and English together than any other thing."

The homecoming celebration continued on land. The next evening, another 600 admirers paid their respects in a gala banquet at the Biltmore that featured speech after long-winded speech, with guests paying $10 to squeeze their way into the mammoth banquet.

"You have performed a service to the game and your country will bear lasting results," pontificated Governor John Tener. "Wherever the game is

implanted, there will indelibly be associated with it, the word, 'America' —
the American game."

He may have been right — at least for a while. Europeans had other things
on their minds; by the following June, they had plunged into The Great War.

BIRTH OF A BASEBALL ENTREPRENEUR
The rise of Albert Spalding
A. G. Spalding & Bros.
241 Broadway

Albert Spalding wasn't a millionaire, but he came close. Call this
pitcher-turned-entreprenuer the sport's first true player-turned-business-
man, a man whose fastball had pop and manner had genuine old-fashioned capitalistic chutzpah. The evidence — his company's sporting goods
store at 241 Broadway.

"The magnate must be a strong man among strong men," Spalding once
said. "Everything is possible to him who dares." He talked a lot in superlatives:
As the sport's first bona fide tycoon and household name, he could afford to
expound. Wrote *The Boston Herald*, in only slight exaggeration: "Next to
Abraham Lincoln and George Washington, the name of A. G. Spalding is the
most famous in American literature ... It has been blazing forth on the cover
of guides to all sorts of sports, upon bats and gloves ... for many years."

A Byron, Illinois native, Spalding was the pitching wonder of the 1870s
and the first professional to ever chalk up more than 200 victories. Pitching
for the Forest Citys of Illinois and then Harry Wright's Boston Red Stockings,
he led Boston to four straight championships and won 57 games in a single
season. Then, he left Boston for the White Stockings, where he won 46 games
in 1876, hurt his arm, and retired.

Spalding had other ideas anyway. With $800 borrowed from his mother,
he plunged into his lucrative second-career as a promoter and sporting goods
magnate. He manufactured baseballs, paying the National League $1 for
every dozen its teams used so he could promote his product as the "official"
league ball. And he made bats, uniforms, gloves, and every other conceivable
piece of baseball equipment, opening main stores in New York and Chicago,
as well as stores in 22 other cities within a decade.

Carrying his name further into the national conscience was *Spalding's*

Official Baseball Guide, an annual institution of sorts that included a detailed statistical summary of the previous season, in addition to a litany of baseball rules and history, and the inevitable ads for Spalding products.

Spalding's marketing shrewdness did more than create a desire for his products that included some of the game's first fielding gloves and an automatic registering turnstile — "the most reliable, durable and simple Turn Stile made," according to the 1887 *Guide*. His products made players demand better-padded gloves and catcher's masks, which helped them overcome a collective aversion to safety equipment, which they had once thought dandified.

Of Morton's Patent Sliding Pads, made of chamois and strapped outside the hips, Spalding's 1887 *Guide* writes that "its use increases a player's confidence, and renders the act of sliding free from danger." Included are testimonials from Mike Kelly of the White Sox and Charles Comiskey of the St. Louis Browns.

"It is now over a quarter of a century since the game of base ball became popularized as the game of games for American youth," the 1887 *Guide* says elsewhere. "Within that period it has so extended itself in its sphere of operations that it is now the permanently established national field game of America."

Spalding understood baseball's growing hold on the country — "Americans are evolving into fresh-air people," he once said — and it made him rich. Delve into the 1887 *Guide* and you catch the spirit — and almost feel like ordering a pair of those official steel shoe plates.

TRUE HOME A DA BUM
The World-Telegram and Sun
125 Barclay Street

Okay, so Ebbets Field was the spiritual home of the Brooklyn Bum — cartoonist Willard Mullin's daffy, scraggly clown-like creation that symbolized the Dodgers of the 1950s. But the Bum's true home was the office at the late *World-Telegram and Sun*, where Willard Mullin worked.

The Bum started simply enough. Leaving Ebbets Field one day, Mullin hopped in a cab, when the driver asked him, "What did our Bums do today?" A brainstorm appeared, and Mullin got back to the office and created the

Bum — a tramp with a three-day growth of beard, a cigar stub, scruffy old coat, tattered trousers, and oversized shoes held together with tape.

That first Bum was pictured taking a big step — the one into the first division — stumbling a bit, but never quite getting there. And the language: broken and seemingly Brooklynese, with terms like "Ebbets Feel," "Bedford Avenuh," and, for Brooklyn, just plain "Flatbush."

Ironically, the most famous Bum wasn't even Mullin's. It was the one that appeared in *The Daily News* of October 4, 1955 — the day the Dodgers "dood it," beating the Yankees for their only World Series title.

In all the post-Series excitement, Dodger fan and *Daily News* staff cartoonist Leo O'Mealia penned his own toothless bum and took it to his editors, who quickly decided to run him on the cover of that day's *Daily News*. Published under the headline, "Who's A Bum?," it became one of the most popular front pages ever published and wasn't bad for sales either; the paper sold an extra 125,000 copies that day.

In all, Mullin penned more than 2,000 Bums, many after the Dodgers moved to Los Angeles in late 1957. "Member me?," the Bum recalled after the move west. "I used t'reside in a jernt called 'Ebbets Feel' ... ain't there no more."

Neither is *The World-Telegram and Sun*. Beset by a series of strikes and an unusually complex labor structure — pressmen, drivers, and reporters all belonged to different unions — the paper folded in 1966.

STRIKE-ZONE ARBITRATOR
The end of baseball's longest strike
US District Court
500 Pearl Street, Courtroom 1340

"I hope that none of you assumed ... that my lack of knowledge of any of the intimate details of your dispute meant that I was not a baseball fan," said US District Court Judge Sonia Sotomayor on the morning of March 31, 1995. "You can't grow up in the South Bronx without knowing about baseball."

And with that, Judge Sotomayor, the first American of Puerto Rican descent to be appointed to the district's federal bench, took all of 15 minutes — about the length of an average inning — to issue an injunction against major league baseball owners. The ruling ended baseball's and sports' longest strike.

Sotomayor chided baseball owners, saying they had no right to unilaterally eliminate the 20-year-old system of free agents and salary arbitration as the bargaining continued. And just like that, the players agreed to return to work and the ruinous 234-day labor stoppage, which had abruptly ended the 1994 season in mid-August and canceled the World Series for the first time in 90 years, came to an end.

What an irony that it took a 40-year-old judge with what her colleagues said was a mild interest in baseball to end what the two posturing sides, assorted members of Congress, and even President Clinton couldn't accomplish. Along with it went the hideous experiment of union-busting replacement baseball, as the real major leaguers quickly returned to work.

After all, said a colleague, "She does not have much patience for people trying to snow her; you can't do it."

TICKER TAPE FOR PINSTRIPES
City Hall
61 Chambers Street

Crowd estimates varied. Some said 3.5 million, others said more and still others, slightly less. But this much is clear: The 1996 parade in which New York honored its world champion Yankees was a clear signal that the city wasn't quite ready to let go of what *The New York Times* called, "perhaps the most emotional October baseball the city [had] ever seen."

These weren't the Yankees of old, the team about which it was once said that managing is like pushing buttons. These Yankees were different, a group you had to like — overachievers and role players who had defied the odds three days before by taking the World Series in five games against the Braves. How can you not root for new, hard-working, and no-nonsense stars like Derek Jeter, Bernie Williams, and Tino Martinez?

And so, they got their parade. It was vintage New Yawk and included the obligatory ticker tape as players sat in floats that moved north on Broadway from Battery Place to City Hall, where they got keys to the city. "I've never been involved ... never even [come] close to being involved in anything like this parade today and this sea of humanity we see out here," Yankee manager Joe Torre told the masses. "This is absolutely spectacular."

For the record, it was the 25th Broadway parade, the last one coming in

1994 for the Stanley Cup-winning Rangers. The Yankee Parade was the latest in a wonderful tradition of ticker-tape mania that started spontaneously in 1896, when a group of downtown office workers unfurled stock tickers and threw them out the window during a parade that marked the Statue of Liberty dedication. Other ballclubs which got the treatment were the '62 and '78 Yanks and the '69 and '86 Mets.

Leave it to New York mayor Rudolph Giuliani to take the victory a step further, calling it a symbol for a rebounding city. "The Yankees are back and New York City is back," said the mayor, a big-time Pinstripe supporter with an eye to kicking off his re-election campaign. "It is a metaphor for the city that is having a renaissance."

THE MYSTERY ENVELOPE AND THE DOCTOR
35 East 7th Street

Hangers-on aren't new to baseball. How about the shady case of Howard Spira, the New Jersey man whom George Steinbrenner paid off a few years ago for dirt on ex-Yankee Dave Winfield?

But those who think that such modern-day cases have thrown baseball into a new abyss should consider the curious case of Dr. Joseph M. Creamer of 35 East 7th Street. So you think the glorious, olden days of the dead-ball era was a more innocent form of the national pastime? Think again.

Creamer was the Giants' team physician during the early managerial reign of John McGraw. A product of the New York sporting scene of gamblers, ballplayer, and Broadway wise guys, he joined the team at McGraw's request during the 1908 season. And it was in the midst of that memorable season that Creamer rose to a kind of dubious fame, creating a mystery that endures to this day.

Events surrounding Creamer's actions stemmed from the famous afternoon of September 23, 1908, when young Giants' first baseman Fred Merkle failed to touch second base in what he thought was the game's end against the Cubs. Instead, he started in for the clubhouse and was called out in a confused and crazed aftermath. The event, known in baseball lore as "Merkle's Boner," did more than give the young ballplayer an infamous reputation; the National League ruled the game a "tie," and scheduled an October 8 playoff for the pennant at the Polo Grounds.

New Yorkers set the scene early on the afternoon of October 8, by jeering the Cubs as the team emerged at Pennsylvania Station from a 14-hour train trip. Under police escort, the Cubs entered a waiting line of automobiles and went directly to the ballpark.

Waiting for them Uptown was an overflow crowd inside the Polo Grounds and out, filling everything from the grandstand roof to Coogan's Bluff behind the park. Desperate to see the game, some fans charged the gates, while others hung from rafters, and one man fell to his death from the elevated train tracks on which he'd clung.

Down on the field — more chaos. With batting practice canceled because there wasn't enough time, both teams milled around before the first pitch. McGraw and Cubs' second baseman Johnny Evers swore at one another from a distance as "Iron Man" Joe McGinnity and Cubs manager Frank Chance nearly came to blows near home plate.

Meanwhile, "from the stands, there was a steady roar of abuse," recalled Three Finger Brown, the Cubs' starting pitcher. "I never heard anybody or any set of men called as many foul names as the Giant fans called us that day."

Enter Dr. Creamer. With the game's umpires, Bill Klem and Jimmy Johnstone, about to go onto the field, a man they recognized as the Giants' physician approached the pair, showing them the contents of an envelope — $5,000, with $2,500 for each. "You know who is behind me and you needn't be afraid of anything," Klem reported Creamer as saying. The umpire ordered Creamer to leave and never saw him again.

Then, game time: In a memorable pitchers' duel, Brown and the Cubs edged out Christy Mathewson and the Giants to win their third straight pennant. They barely escaped an increasingly venomous crowd at game's end. A cordon of police, with revolvers drawn, pushed the Cubs through the center field clubhouse door and suggested the team dress in street clothes and leave singly or in pairs to escape detection from the mob. The ruse worked; the Chicago players slipped out and later beat the Tigers in the World Series.

Lost in all excitement was the odd case of Dr. Creamer and the mystery envelope. But Klem didn't forget, and he reported his allegation to the National League, which launched an investigation. Curiously, National League president Harry Pulliam formed a three-man commission to look into the matter, headed by, of all people, John T. Brush, owner of the Giants. Even so, they recommended that Creamer be banned from baseball, a decision accepted the following spring by the National Commission, then baseball's overall ruling body.

The Commission never made their findings public. That task was left to
The Chicago Tribune's Harry Woodruff, who reported that McGraw had
hired Creamer the previous year without Brush's knowledge. According to
Woodruff, Brush paid Creamer $2,834 at season's end.

The New York papers jumped into the fray. "Who were the men behind
Doctor Creamer?" asked *The Evening Journal.* But as Charles Alexander relates
in his biography of John McGraw, the newspaper dropped its investigation
after a week or so. "With the pennant races again heating up [the following
spring]," Alexander writes, "the whole business just seemed to evaporate."

The mystery endures 90 years later. Were gamblers behind Creamer? What
was McGraw's role? Some said his drive to win at all costs caused suspicion.
Others argued that the Giants' skipper was too smart for that. Dr. Creamer
certainly wasn't talking; he died 11 years later, his lips sealed to the end.

THROWBACK
Charles A. Stoneham of the Giants
41 Broadway

Upset by the crassness of the unpleasant bunch who pass for today's
major league owners? Take small comfort how history can repeat itself, as in
the case of one Charles A. Stoneham, one-time owner of the late, great Giants
of New York.

Stoneham and the Giants were a baseball traditon of sorts, a family who
made baseball — and not some other product — their business. Along with
minority owners, John McGraw, and a city magistrate named Francis X.
McQuade, he bought the team in 1919.

Stoneham's son, Horace, a Fordham graduate, subsequently ran the Giants into the 1970s. That was well after the team, beset by declining crowds,
left the Polo Grounds in 1957 and pierced the hearts of Giant fans everywhere for the winds of San Francisco. Said Stoneham at the time: "I feel sorry
for the kids, but I haven't seen too many of their fathers recently."

The baseball career of Stoneham the Elder kicked off the morning of January 14, 1919, when the New York press was notified that the Giants had an
important announcement to make at their headquarters, at 5th Avenue and
23rd Street. At the time, it was known that Giants' owner Harry Hempstead
was thinking of selling his team; the general perception was that George Loft,

founder of the New York-based candy company bearing his name, had the inside track.

What New York got was a surprise. It got Stoneham, a 42-year-old who described himself as a "Giant fan all my life," who newspapers called a "Wall Street broker." While Stoneham indeed worked on Wall Street, his firm, with offices at 41 Broadway, was in fact a "bucket shop," or a stock brokerage that took orders to buy and sell stock, but never executed the orders. It was a form of gambling; though perfectly legal until the 1929 crash, "bucket shops" aimed to make good on a client's bad purchase by replacing the stock after it had dropped in value.

When Stoneham's firm went bust in 1921, its books recorded accounts in the millions. To each investor went a form letter thanking them for their patronage and urging that the dissolving firm be allowed to transfer the account to another house. Curiously, at the same time that Stoneham saw to the demise of his brokerage business, he deepened his interest in sports promotion by purchasing a racetrack in Havana. He also bought the Havana Casino, with its gaming tables and developed it into a kind of Cuban Monte Carlo.

The secret to Stoneham's unusual business talent? Clearly, his fortuitous selection of friends, like big-time gambler Arnold Rothstein, and his ties to the dubious morality of Tammany Hall.

Legally, events began to sour for Stoneham and dogged him for the rest of his life. He was indicted August 31, 1923 by a federal grand jury on perjury charges involving the transfer of funds during his business failure. That September, he was indicted for mail fraud, a problem compounded by heavy losses on his Cuban ventures.

The sudden spectacular success of former Polo Grounds' tenants, the Yankees, who moved into their new ballpark, Yankee Stadium, in April 1923, added to Stoneham's financial woes. Fortunately for him, he was acquitted Feb. 26, 1925 in a decision that held up even after a juror charged that he had been intimidated into changing his vote.

More battles were ahead, notably a bitter litigation fight with McQuade, who charged he had been wrongfully ousted as Giants' treasurer. McGraw's death in 1934 left Stoneham as sole owner.

Despite his legal troubles, his Giants were periodic winners, taking the World Series in 1921, 1922, 1933 and 1954. Charles Stoneham died at 59 in 1936, and his 32-year-old son, Horace, took over the team, eventually moving the franchise to San Francisco. The younger Stoneham was 86 when he died in 1990.

RUDE RETURN FOR THE MONK
Russ Meyer is robbed
East 25th Street & Lexington Avenue

Talk about the injustice of it all: Here was onetime Brooklyn Dodger pitching mainstay Russ Meyer back in New York to help promote a quest to bring the team back from Los Angeles.

It was 4 AM on June 3, 1981, when Meyer, out for a night on the town, was held up by two men at gunpoint at the corner of East 25th Street and Lexington Avenue. The former ballplayer was robbed of the two rings he won for his Dodger appearances in the 1953 and 1955 World Series, along with $400 in cash and a watch.

Yikes. At least in didn't happen back in Flatbush.

Known primarily in his playing days for a bad temper, Meyer was a cog for the Dodger dynasty of the early '50s, winning 15 games in 1953, 11 in 1954 and another six for the '55 World Series champions. That temper earned him the moniker, "The Mad Monk," in part for his on-the-field outbursts, and for a former West Point football star he admired named Monk Meyer.

A Peru, Illinois native, Meyer spent 13 years in the big leagues, winning 94 games and losing 73 with the Cubs, Phillies, Dodgers, Reds, Red Sox, and Kansas City A's, in addition to Brooklyn. His best year: 1949 with Philadelphia when he was 17-8.

And Meyer's most infamous moment: May 25, 1953, when pitching for the Dodgers in the fourth inning, he threw a memorable tantrum. Disagreeing with the ball-and-strike calls of home plate umpire Augie Donatelli, Meyer rushed toward homeplate. Shooed back by catcher Roy Campanella, Meyer then flung the rosin bag 30 feet in the air. It landed on his head.

Donatelli ejected Meyer, who then flung a glove into the dugout. Later, he was caught by a television camera, sitting in the dugout and making a rude gesture at the umpire. The Dodgers, however, had the last laugh, scoring 12 runs in the eighth to win 16-2.

Meyer had the last laugh too. Less than a month after his 1981 stick-up, he was named roving minor league pitching instructor by the Yankees. Meyer spent 12 years with the Yanks, serving as the team's bench coach in 1992.

Meyer died in November 1997. He was 74.

TY COBB TAKES ON A FAN
112 Centre Street

You won't find Claude Lueker's name in *The Baseball Encyclopedia*. His only connection to the game is in his presence as a spectator on the otherwise pleasant afternoon of May 15, 1912 at Hilltop Park.

Baseball has long endured the problems of fan abuse by players. But those problems just may have reached a zenith that afternoon with the response to Lueker by Ty Cobb. It was perhaps the ugliest episode of many involving the tempestuous Detroit outfielder.

The incident takes on a particular twist since Lueker was handicapped, having lost a hand and three fingers of his other hand in a printing press accident the previous year. And while Cobb was indeed the subject of torrential abuse that day by rowdy fans, Lueker emphatically claimed he had never heckled Cobb.

Cobb argued otherwise, insisting that Lueker — an assistant in the 112 Centre Street law office of Tammany Hall leader, "Big Tom" Foley, the former sheriff of New York County — had directed a stream of abuse his way for several days, which culminated when Lueker screamed that he was a "half-nigger." That did it, and Cobb charged into the stands during the pugilistic fourth inning.

He did it by vaulting the wall and stalking toward the third row near the dugout, where Lueker was sitting, dressed in a spiffy alpaca coat. Cobb struck him on the forehead above the left eye, knocked him down, and spiked him on the left leg, before kicking him repeatedly in the side. Someone in the crowd shouted, "Don't kick him, he has no hands." Cobb's response: "I don't care if he has no feet."

Cobb insisted that Lueker's taunts had left him no alternative but to attack. "A great injustice has been done," he said. "When a spectator calls me a 'half-nigger,' I think it is about time to fight."

The Times took a bemused view of the festivities. "Everything was very pleasant at the Detroit-Yankee game on the Hilltop," the paper reported, "until Ty Cobb johnnykilbaned a spectator right on the place where he talks ... led with a jab and countered with a right kick to Mr. Spectator's left Weisbach, which made his peeper look as if some one had drawn a curtain over it." Huh?

For Cobb, it was another in a long line of ugly altercations. His brand of baseball was combative and bitter — and he had a personality to match. As a teenager, Cobb endured the tragedy of having his father, a respected educator, shot dead by his mother, when she mistook him for a prowler. Whatever the reason for Cobb's hostility, it just may have been the lingering bitterness from that unfortunate incident that drove baseball's most combative player.

Cobb once pummeled a teammate who had the nerve to jump in the bathtub ahead of him. He beat up a grocery boy and once punched a friend who stuck him with the restaurant check. Cobb reserved particular venom for African-Americans, and got into fights at various times with a black elevator operator and a black night watchman. An early Billy Martin? No. Cobb was worse, having even been arrested after a argument with a female cashier over a glass of water.

After the incident at Hilltop, Lueker's boss, Foley, leapt to the defense of his injured employee. "If a great baseball player like Ty Cobb can't resist the catcalls and ragging of the bleachers without climbing over the rail and assaulting a cripple with one hand gone and three fingers of the other hand missing, then it is time for the public to stay away from the game." Foley called Lueker, a diehard Yankee fan and an "unusually quiet fan," adding he was never known to utter an insulting phrase to anyone.

Surprisingly, Cobb's teammates overlooked their dislike for their spiteful leader and took his side. Cobb was suspended and the incident became an odd baseball footnote when the rest of the Tigers protested by calling the game's first-ever strike.

Three days later in Philadelphia, the Cobb-less Tigers refused to take the field against the world champion Athletics. So manager Hughie Jennings put together a team of college and semipro players, paying them $10 each. With the regulars watching from the stands, the makeshift Tigers lost 24-2, behind the pitching of one Aloysius S. Travers, a St. Joseph's College seminary student who became a Roman Catholic priest.

The strike ended a day later when Cobb thanked his teammates and asked them to return. Cobb himself returned May 26 in a series against the White Sox — two weeks after the incident at Hilltop Park. Nothing more was ever heard from Claude Lueker.

CHAPTER FIVE

MIDTOWN

"It shows what you can accomplish if you stay up all night drinking whiskey."

> *— Toots Shor, restauranteur, on the Hall of Fame induction of Mickey Mantle and Whitey Ford, 1974*

DEATH OF A PRESIDENT
The New York Athletic Club
180 Central Park South

Mention the New York Athletic Club, or NYAC, and most people think of a vigorous game of squash followed by drinks at the bar. But baseball's role in NYAC history accounts for one of the more bizarre, tragic twists of National League history.

Harry Clay Pulliam was National League president in the early years of the century. It was a thankless job requiring steely nerves, iron-fisted negotiating abilities, and resilience in dealing with the squabbling, egomaniacal team owners. Not much has changed, it seems.

Frankly, Harry Pulliam wasn't the man for the job. He liked poetry, nature and flowers. He also suffered from depression over business affairs and just may have been too gentle for such a grinding task. Still, it came as a surprise, when, on the evening of July 28, 1909, Pulliam ended his life at the Club, shooting himself with a revolver through his right temple.

A graduate of the University of Virginia Law School, Pulliam was a Louisville newspaper reporter and a Kentucky state legislator-turned-baseball executive, thanks to his friendship with Louisville Colonels' owner Barney Dreyfuss. When the Colonels moved to Pittsburgh in 1898, to be known forever after as the Pirates, Pulliam went along, working as team secretary. In 1902, he was named National League president, secretary, and treasurer.

That lasted until 1907, when, according to *The New York Times*, Pulliam's health "began to give way under the strain of the multitude of duties." John Heydler took over as league secretary and treasurer; in February 1909, Pulliam's health took an alarming downward spiral when he suffered a breakdown at the National League owners' banquet and the owners gave him an indefinite leave of absence.

Pulliam's job stress had taken a fearful toll. In 1908, he had withstood the slings and arrows in backing the umpires during the infamous "Merkle Affair," in which New York Giant Fred Merkle failed to touch second base, costing the New Yorkers the 1908 pennant. Convinced that National League owners were plotting against him, Pulliam took a long trip west, but even that didn't help. He returned more depressed than ever in mid-June 1909 to his office in the St. James Building.

When he died, Pulliam "had been in a highly nervous state for some time," *The Times* reported, "and some of his friends said ... that his mind had given way under the strain."

A NYAC bellboy found the gravely-wounded Pulliam. He had attracted attention when a club telephone operator noticed that the receiver in his room had been off the hook for quite some time. Dr. J. J. Higgins of 46 West 55th Street was quickly summoned and was working on the body, when the coroner leaned over to ask the baseball executive a question:

"How were you shot?" he asked.

Pulliam moaned and said with considerable pain, "I am not shot," whereupon his head fell back and he lost consciousness. Too severely injured to be transferred to a hospital, the 40-year-old Pulliam died at 7:40 AM the next day. He was buried August 2 in Louisville.

YANKS SNARE STENGEL
21 Club
21 West 52nd Street

Sure, his brilliant gems of twisted linguistics, combined with an offbeat but winning managerial style, made him in hindsight one of baseball's most colorful — and successful — performers.

And sure, he was both enduring — having played, coached and managed for more than half-a-century — and endearing, as he spun his wisdom to an appreciative press corps — a group he called "my writers." Even so, it took every second of those 50 years for Casey Stengel to be properly accepted as a bona fide baseball genius.

"Amazin', amazin', amazin'," said Casey Stengel of the Mets he managed from 1962-1964. And so they became, well, "the Amazins." (National Baseball Hall of Fame Library, Cooperstown, New York)

Nothing captures that curious dilemma more than the signing of Stengel on October 12, 1948 to a two-year contract as Yankee manager. The signing, conducted at the 21 Club before a vintage New York-style crush of reporters and cameras, was captured soberly by newspapers, though most beat writers thought Stengel's hiring was little more than a Yankee publicity move after the team fired the popular Bucky Harris.

Ironically, Stengel's hiring fell on an anniversary — 25 years to the day on which became a local legend by hitting the second of his two game-winning home runs for the Giants against the Yankees in the 1923 World Series. Stengel also played for and managed the Dodgers, making him a well-known, eminently quotable figure for New York fans and writers alike.

Stengel's theatrical blend of pantomime, monologues, and storytelling didn't fit any mold, until he was accused, with some reason, of carrying on to distract the public from less than satisfactory performances by his teams. His patented motor-mouth style of speech came to be known as "Stengelese," once described by *The Times* as "a kind of circuitous double-talk laced with ambiguous antecedents, dangling participles, a lack of proper names and a liberal use of adjectives like 'amazing' and 'terrific.'"

Stengel just didn't fit the Yankee mold. These weren't the daffy Dodgers, but the lordly Bombers of the Bronx. This was the pinstriped team, not only of WASPy co-owners Dan Topping and Del Webb, but of the great Joe DiMaggio, who attended the Stengel press conference to lend his support. You get the idea.

Everyone liked Stengel well enough. "If you didn't, you didn't like anybody," said John Drebinger of *The Times*. But for all his accomplishments as a longtime major league player and manager, Stengel just wasn't considered Yankee material at the start. Said Red Smith: "[The writers] couldn't reconcile their conception of Stengel, the court jester, with the old Yankee tradition of austere and businesslike efficiency."

Things started badly. At the press conference, Stengel called Dan Topping, "Bob," the owner's playboy brother. When somebody asked about his plans for DiMaggio, Stengel, having managed in the National League, said he wasn't that familiar with the Yankee Clipper. Not familiar with DiMaggio? It sounded awkward.

Critics complained that Stengel got the job because he was a friend of Yankee general manager George Weiss, to which the 58-year-old new manager answered, "This is a $5 million business; they don't hand out jobs like this because you're a friend." And up in Boston, Dave Egan of *The Record* wrote that the Yankees "eliminated themselves when they engaged Perfesser Casey Stengel to mismanage them for the next two years."

At the time, as Stengel biographer Robert Creamer wrote, "Stengel had spent almost 40 years in baseball, and it was as if he had done nothing."

Today, baseball fans know better. Despite a season rocked by injury, Stengel engineered a five-game Yankee victory over the Dodgers in the 1949 World Series and kept on winning until they had won five Series in a row. Stengel's overall record in his 12 years as Yankee manager: 10 pennants and seven World Series wins.

Another four years with the early Mets certified Stengel's status as a city legend. It also made him the only man to be associated with all four New York teams. Stengel retired in 1965 and died 10 years later at the age of 85.

GREETING THE CHAMPS — BUMS RULE GRAND CENTRAL
Grand Central Terminal
71-105 East 42nd Street

"WE WIN," screamed the headline in *The Brooklyn Eagle*. "WE" were the Dodgers, which, on September 24, 1941, brought the borough its first National League pennant in 21 years. It was also the first of several flags for the Bums of the Larry MacPhail- and Leo Durocher-era, and it was worth a celebration, the likes of which the baseball-mad borough had not seen in decades.

Brooklyn threw a victory parade for its champions, attended by a crowd of a half-million, many of whom were children given a half-day off from school. And they crammed Ebbets Field for games three, four, and five of the Dodgers' eventual six-game World Series loss to the Yankees. But it was the crowd of 10,000 fans who spontaneously gathered to meet the team at Grand Central Terminal, as it arrived home from clinching the pennant in Boston, that personified the joy that Brooklyn felt that wartime fall of '41.

The grand old masterpiece of Beaux Arts design and architecture has seen its share of events, political speeches, and concerts through the years. So, security at Grand Central was on alert as Brooklynites gathered that Thursday evening for the Dodgers' 11 PM arrival from Boston.

Most of the fans gathered in the main part of the terminal, content to chant and cheer their heroes with an assortment of handmade, vintage Brooklynese-style signs, among them, "The Bums Done It" and "Moider Duh

Grand Central Terminal.

Yanks." Others, looking forward to the World Series, chanted, "Four Straight," a reference to what they hoped would happen to the Yanks. Meanwhile, up in the balcony, stood the Brooklyn Dodgers Band, "The Greenpoint Royal Rooters," also known as the Dodger Sym-phony.

For the Dodgers, speeding back from Boston, the celebration had already started. On the train to New York, the players gulped and sprayed one another with champagne and cut each others' ties with scissors. Mashed potatoes were tossed into the face of Tony Martin, the actor and singer, who, as the guest of manager Leo Durocher, had been superstitiously donning a tan gabardine suit for a week to help bring home the pennant.

Happiest of all may have been Whitlow Wyatt, the Dodger 22-game-winner, who needed only nine pitches to shut down the Boston Braves in a scoreless ninth and nail down the 6-0 victory. The flag was his first after 12 sore-armed seasons of heart-wrenching annual failure. "After being on the verge of quitting the game, I just can't believe what's happened," he said. "I bounced all over the major league and minor league map for years and years and suddenly find myself pitching the game that clinches the pennant."

Trains from Boston usually stopped at the 125th Street station, but this time, Durocher requested they be put straight through to Grand Central. "I don't want anybody getting off at 125th," he said. "There'll be enough at Grand Central."

Bad move. Unbeknownst to Durocher, MacPhail had gone to 125th Street to board the train and ride into Grand Central for the victory party. Outraged to learn that Durocher had issued orders not to stop, he actually fired his manager on the spot. MacPhail relented the next day and assured a nervous Brooklyn that Durocher was indeed the Dodger skipper.

Grand Central WAS packed. At first sight of the Dodgers, who got off their train and descended the staircase into the station lobby, a mighty roar went up.

"The terminal's regular constabulary, accustomed to handling the arrival of presidents, movie stars, and royalty, was obliged to adopt a 'What's the use?' attitude," *The Eagle* reported. "The players themselves aided and abetted their admirers by quickly getting into the swing of things."

For Cookie Lavagetto, that meant kissing every woman in sight. Others were kissed on both cheeks, by women and men alike. Backs were slapped, flashbulbs popped, and people yelled. Up on the balcony, the Royal Rooters launched into performance and Jack Pierce of Brooklyn tossed "Cookie" balloons into the crowd below.

The police tried to form a path for the players but it quickly collapsed. "Talk about being a diplomat," a sweating cop said. "This Brooklyn crowd has them all beaten. There's never been a celebration like this here."

JACKIE ROBINSON LEAVES BASEBALL
Chock Full o' Nuts
425 Lexington Avenue

Most stories have Jackie Robinson leaving baseball in January 1957, shortly after his improbable trade to the cross-town Giants for $30,000 and a left-handed pitcher named Dick Littlefield. Play for the dem hated Jints?, the story goes. Why, a true blue Dodger, a bona fide Bum, would rather be dead.

The real reason for his retirement is something a little closer to a ballplayer's heart — money — a point Robinson made perfectly clear in a press conference a few days after his announcement. "I wouldn't play baseball again for a million dollars," he said.

The immediate reason for Robinson's decision was an article he wrote on his retirement for *Look* magazine, for which he was paid $50,000 — at least

$10,000 more than his annual salary with the Dodgers. The other reason was Robinson's new job as a vice president with the Chock Full o' Nuts Corp.

"My mind had been made up before I knew of the trade," Robinson said at the January 6, 1957 press conference. "On December 12, I went to the *Look* offices to make final arrangements for the story. At five that afternoon, I signed the Chock Full o' Nuts contract. At 5:10, I learned I was traded to the Giants."

Robinson argued he had a moral obligation at the time to keep quiet on his intention to retire until the magazine story came out. The trade was voided and Robinson's spectacular career was suddenly over.

Robinson fit comfortably into his new position at Chock Full o' Nuts, commuting daily to and from the company's Lexington Avenue offices from his home in Stamford, Connecticut. "This is a team operation," he said at the end of his first year on the job. "To gain the confidence of employees, you must be willing to discuss their problems openly with them. Then, when you're looking for their cooperation, you find it working for you."

At Chock Full o' Nuts, a progressive company in which some 80 percent of the employees at the time were black, Robinson had the last word on discharges: "The day when I had the worst butterflies in my stomach, far more than I ever had with the Dodgers, was the day I had to fire an employee," he said of his position. "It was necessary as a last resort."

Robinson's salary with the company was never made public. He traveled occasionally, but usually to the company's various restaurants, a bakery in Harrison, New Jersey and a Brooklyn coffee plant.

Ironically, Robinson's retirement from baseball coincided with the departure from New York of the Dodgers and the Giants for the West Coast and the city's improbable emergence as a one-team town. "I can't believe New York will go on very long as a one-club city," the old Dodger said in a 1958 interview in *The Times*. "People here would be very foolish if they permitted that to happen, because it's the greatest baseball town in the world."

DAILY SNOOZE NO MORE
Dick Young joins *The News*
220 East 42nd Street

New York Times' Columnist George Vecsey wears a wide grin when speaking of Dick Young, the former *Daily News* sportswriter and giant of the press box.

Covering the Mets as a young reporter in 1962, Vecsey was given a pointed piece of advice by Young. "Kid," he said, "Always keep your watch on New York time."

That was Young, the newspaperman's newspaperman, who, with a nod to Howard Cosell, wrote it as he saw it — critically when called for and not giving a damn what anyone thought. Once, when confronted by Duke Snider after writing in *The News* that the Dodger centerfielder was loafing on the field, Young said, "Hit baseballs, Duke, not writers — then I'll be able to write good things about you."

In his time, Young was the king of the press box. Unlike the Rices and the Runyons of the previous generation of sportswriters who became writers and columnists, he considered himself a reporter first and then a writer. For Young, runs batted in were "ribbies" and Carl Furillo, the great Dodger rightfielder who loved the Italian dish of scungilli, was "Scoonge."

At a time when sportswriters covered baseball as if it was chess and rarely talked with the manager or players, Young ventured into the clubhouse before and after the game, regularly scooping his rivals and setting a precedent.

Young joined *The News* in 1937 as a messenger and copyboy, moving five years later to the sports department, which he once called, "one of the few businesses where you can laugh while you work." He stuck to his word — after a 1957 Dodger home game at Roosevelt Stadium in Jersey City, when rumors were rife that the team was moving to Los Angeles, he began his story with the line, "Inching their way westward ..."

Young spent 45 years with *The News*, moving downtown to *The Post* in 1982. He was identified primarily with the Dodgers and baseball, along with pro football and boxing. He ignored sports he disliked like horse racing and tennis; Young attended the US Open for a day and never went back.

Along the way, he could be profane, trivial, and callous, writing his column, in true tabloid fashion, "with all the subtlety of a knee in the groin," as Vecsey puts it. Other writers often disliked him, not for his work ethic that he essentially created, but for his attitude.

Young's biggest failure may have been an inability to change with the times. He never accepted the presence of women in the locker room, television reporters, or drugs in sports. "To me, there's no such thing as a liberal or a conservative," he said in 1965. "It's this case, this case, and this case — whose side deserves to be attacked at a particular time."

Others attacked Young for his column, "My America," in which everybody was employed, owned a house with a white picket fence, had 2.4 kids, and went to church on Sunday. In more recent years, he urged Met fans to boo Dwight Gooden in his first Shea Stadium appearance after drug rehab, insisted players made too much money and is generally considered to have led the push that drove Tom Seaver out of town in 1978 after a salary dispute.

Young tamed his rage long enough to serve as president of the Baseball Writers Association of America and be elected to the writers' wing of the Baseball Hall of Fame in 1978. He died in 1987 at the age of 69.

TRIBUTE TO A GENTLEMAN – BART GIAMATTI IS REMEMBERED
Yale Club
50 Vanderbilt Avenue

"All I ever wanted to be," Bart Giamatti once said, "was president of the American League."

He never got his wish. Instead, this Renaissance-style scholar-and-university-president-turned-baseball-executive fulfilled an egghead's dream, when, in 1988, he was named baseball commissioner. And when this most unusual of baseball executives died less than a year later of a heart attack at 51, the game had lost the man who might have become its greatest leader.

A. Bartlett Giamatti may not have been associated with the game long enough to earn a statue or a Yankee Stadium monument. How appropriate, then, that the only apparent New York tribute to his memory is an understated portrait on the south wall of the lobby at the Yale Club. Giamatti, one of the nation's leading scholars in English and comparative literature, was the youngest person in two centuries to serve as Yale's president; he was all of 40 when when he succeeded Kingman Brewster in the position.

Not as weird as it sounds. As the university's 19th president, Giamatti served from 1978 to 1988, and was anything but the stuffy, blue-stocking stereotype who passes as the leader of most Ivy League universities. Long before leaving academia for baseball, Giamatti, known as "Bart," published widely, writing on subjects as varied as Spenser's *Faerie Queene*, the Renaissance, and Tom Seaver.

Some doubted Giamatti could make the transition from the ivory tower to baseball's gutter warfare. After leaving Yale in 1986 and cutting his teeth as president of the National League for more than two years, Giamatti became baseball commissioner on April 1, 1988, succeeding Peter Ueberroth.

"We wanted the kind of man who could be totally objective," said Avron Fogelman, then a co-owner of the Kansas City Royals. "Whatever decision(s) he makes ... nobody wins except the integrity of the game."

He was tested severely and almost immediately, taking on former Cincinnati Reds' legend-turned-manager Pete Rose for allegedly betting on his team. Stating that "no man is above the game," Giamatti acted decisively, banning Rose for life for conduct detrimental to baseball.

A Massachusetts native and long a frustrated Red Sox fan, Giamatti wrote of his team that, "Mutability had turned the season and translated hope to memory once again." Too bad Giamatti peers out from his 1987 Yale Club painting by Everett R. Kinstler, his neatly-trimmed trademark beard flecked with white, and nary a baseball reference. Instead, there's a background of muses behind Giamatti, who looks very much the Ivy League scholar, wearing his striped tie and holding an important-looking collection of papers.

Could those papers have been gallies of Giamatti's last academic book, *A Free and Ordered Space: The Real World of the University*, published in 1988? Or maybe it was Rose's written confession that yes, he had really gambled. Ah, baseball after all.

GOING TO BAT FOR WAR
Waldorf-Astoria Ballroom
301 Park Avenue (& East 50th Street)

Baseball functions are standard stuff at the Waldorf-Astoria, the scene of countless year-end Baseball Writers Association of America events. But no other baseball ceremony there was as important as the June 8, 1943 luncheon that made a staggering dent on the national drive for war bond pledges — putting to rest forever the claim of some historians that World War II was the national pastime's lost age.

Sponsored by the New York and Brooklyn chapters of the Baseball Writers Association, the luncheon raised an astounding $123 million in war bond pledges. That's $123 million in 1943 dollars — all from a single event in which former mayor Jimmy Walker auctioned off players from the three New York teams of the day.

Here was "The People's Cherse," Dixie Walker of the Dodgers, drawing an $11,250 bid from the Brooklyn Club, a social organization. And here were the Esso Marketers, paying $3.5 million for Carl Hubbell of the Giants, and the National Bronx Bank scooping up the Yanks' Joe Gordon for $3.5 million. Each sponsor had not only to fulfill the pledges but to buy more bonds based on their player's accomplishments the rest of the season, starting at $2,500 for a single to $10,000 for a home run. Pitchers went for $35,000 a victory and $50,000 a shutout.

Then, on August 26, 1943, 26 players from the Dodgers, Giants, and Yankees performed as the War Bond All-Stars against a team of US Army baseball stars, featuring Hank Greenberg of the Tigers and Enos Slaughter of the Cardinals. The game drew 38,000 to the Polo Grounds and raised another $800 million in war bond pledges. By September, New York teams had helped in the sale of enough war bonds to fill nearly a quarter of the city's war bond goal.

What a noble contrast to the stereotype of World War II baseball goofiness. At its most extreme, that stereotype suggests an inferior brand of major league ball, symbolized by the appearance of Pete Gray, the St. Louis Browns' one-armed outfielder and a 15-year-old pitcher, Joe Nuxhall, of the Reds. Interest dipped a lot in those years, with some big league games drawing crowds of 2,000 or less; a 1943 Cubs-Phils game at Wrigley Field drew 314. In 1944, the Browns won the American League pennant but finished last in attendance.

"People have a tendency to downgrade baseball in that era, but it wasn't all pratfalls and humiliation," argues Bill Gilbert in his book, *Baseball Goes to War*. "That's unfair to the men who played, as well as historically inaccurate."

"The war years were four special years in America and in baseball," Gilbert writes. "Just like the entertainers, the ballplayers helped military and civilian morale. In that way, it was one of baseball's finest hours."

THE MAN, THE MYTH, THE MICK – AWAY FROM THE PARK
St. Moritz Hotel, 50 Central Park South;
Mickey Mantle's Restaurant Sports Bar, 42 Central Park South

A story made the rounds after Mickey Mantle died in August 1995: It seemed an old sportswriter ran into Mantle one late evening in the pinnacle of the great slugger's career, finding him slobbering drunk and passed out on a bathroom floor of a midtown nightclub.

Mickey Mantle at bat — the pose that launched a thousand relief pitchers. (National Baseball Hall of Fame Library, Cooperstown, New York)

"Quick," the sportswriter thought to himself, "call my bookie and bet the house on the Senators," the following day's Yankee doubleheader opponents. No way Mantle was in any condition to play. A can't-miss bet.

You can guess the rest. The sportswriter bet the house. Mantle, meanwhile, hit four home runs — two in each game, two from each side — and the Bombers ruled the roost.

That was Mantle, baseball's last great player on its last dynasty. He wasn't the greatest player who ever lived, perhaps not even of his era, next to Willie Mays. But for a generation of men who came of age in the 1950s, he was THE MAN — more than just a centerfielder of stunning quickness and a switch hitter of prodigious power, tamed somewhat by a lot of injuries and a periodic lack of focus. In the long run, it didn't matter — Mantle was a national icon, a true legend whose death prompted magazines to run his photo on their covers without caption or an identification. None were needed — everyone knew the Mick.

But did they? Death for Mantle at 63 was particularly hard, his body ravaged by 40 years of alcohol abuse, and, in his last days, by a particularly aggressive form of cancer. His death triggered an emotional outpouring of grief for a superstar whose character as the shy Oklahoma country boy re-

mained essentially intact through the years. But it did more than that — it exposed how little we really knew of the private Mantle.

As the story with the sportswriter shows, the public Mantle hit tape measure shots during the day and partied all night. Early in his career, he lived at the Grand Concourse Hotel, a stone's throw from Yankee Stadium. Then, with the big paychecks, he moved to the swanky St. Moritz, living on bourbon and room service, and running with the Yankee "Rat Pack" — Whitey Ford, Billy Martin, Hank Bauer, and Moose Skowron, all of them teammates, Mantle said, as close as brothers.

Many a late night did Mickey Mantle pass through this entrance at the St. Moritz.

Living on Central Park South was tony stuff for this onetime coal miner. The St. Moritz, which opened in 1931 and billed itself as the "biggest little hotel in town," attracted a dose of notoriety when columnist Walter Winchell, a hotel resident for years, threatened to leave after it offered gangster Lucky Luciano an apartment. Luciano went to the Waldorf-Astoria instead and Winchell stayed. After all, he had a good deal, living at the St. Moritz rent-free in return for frequent hotel mentions in his *Daily Mirror* column.

Mantle liked the St. Moritz too. These were the Fabulous '50s and he and his Yankee buddies were the toast of New York. Within a 30-block radius, their thirst could be quenched at Toots Shor's, The Stork, The Plantation Room, Mama Leone's, and Jack Dempsey's joint, where the old champ enjoyed decorating the window by sitting at a nearby booth.

Mickey, Billy, and Whitey were all welcome regulars at these places, seldom having to pay for a drink. Their presence brought in women, who brought in the men and, well, you get the picture.

Maybe it was Mantle's familiarity with the neighborhood around Central Park South that prompted him in 1988 to open the restaurant that bears his name and in which he was a full partner. It was there that Mantle, in his last years, sewed up his status as an American icon.

A slice of New Yawk: Mickey Mantle's Restaurant Sports Bar.

Whereas sportswriters had found him uncooperative and wary of their intentions during his playing days, the elder Mantle, holding court at a booth in his restaurant, had, by then, mellowed considerably. By then, he enjoyed nothing more than signing an autograph for a youngster and telling stories from the baseball wars to an appreciative audience.

"Casey (Stengel) said, 'This guy's going to be better than DiMaggio,'" Mantle said of himself in a 1994 *Sports Illustrated* interview. "It didn't happen. God gave me a great body and I didn't take care of it." Regrets aside, he had a lot of fun trying — and became an icon in the process.

BAD NIGHT FOR "MR. BANKROLL"
Arnold Rothstein meets his match
Park Central Hotel
870 7th Avenue (between West 55th and West 56th Streets)

Remember the last scene in the film, *Eight Men Out*, the story of the 1919 World Series fix? It shows Arnold Rothstein, underworld hotshot and baseball money man, sailing from New York Harbor and peering back toward Manhattan, before gruffly muttering to himself in a Hollywood-style, parting-shot kind of way: "See you later, suckers," he says.

Poetic fiction perhaps, but there was a time when Arnold Rothstein could say things like that. As the numbers king of New York and the bankroller for the 1919 World Series fix, he didn't even like baseball and knew little about the game that helped to make him rich. Yet, Rothstein in his prime may have been worth $10 million, thanks, in part, to the national pastime.

Rothstein was an enigma. He dressed in the conservative threads of a Wall Street banker, lived frugally and alone in a hotel, never chased women, and received most of his visitors at Lindy's over coffee (see pages 130-131).

On the other hand, he liked action — betting vast amounts at the race track and in card games. And he was known to walk the streets around Broadway with as much as $100,000 in $1,000 notes stuffed in his pockets. His pals: fellow gamblers and colorful wise guys like "The St. Louis Kid" and "Titantic Thompson."

Rothstein's life reads like a Damon Runyon story. It was a high-stakes game of stud poker and spades at the Park Central Hotel in which the gambler, known as "Mr. Bankroll," was shot. Rothstein, who died a week later from his wounds, was killed by an unknown assailant after refusing to pay $300,000 from a bet because he thought he had been cheated.

How appropriate it was the Park Central, later the scene of another sensational murder. In 1957, Brooklyn mob boss Albert Anastasia, a steaming hot towel wrapped around his head, was shot dead while getting a hair cut at the hotel barber shop — chair number four — just inside the front door. As with Rothstein, the assailants escaped. The hotel, now the Omni Park Central, and known for a time as the Park Sheraton, was also home to a widowed Eleanor Roosevelt, director D. W. Griffith, and boxer Joe Louis.

For Rothstein, the shooting was the end to an improbable life. Rothstein's father, Abraham, was a devout man, an Orthodox Jew from the Lower East Side, who wanted nothing more for his family beyond giving them a good life. Abraham ran a dry-goods store, then a cotton-converting business and was known as a generous, pious man.

In fact, in 1919, the same year his son was bankrolling crooked Chicago ballplayers to throw the Series, Abraham was honored by New York governor Al Smith and US Supreme Court Justice Louis Brandeis at a testimonial dinner for his arbitration of a garment industry dispute.

The son was different, much different. When Arnold was three, Abraham was awakened one night by a noise and went to the boy's room to discover Arnold standing over his older brother, Henry, holding a knife and screaming, "I hate him." A poor student in everything but arithmetic, Arnold cut school for the action in street crap games. Before long, Arnold was financing the games with change stolen from his father. The boy would steal the money on Friday, the day his father removed it on observance of the Sabbath, and amass a profit in gambling — always careful to return his father's portion by late Saturday.

Rothstein's unusual acumen in picking winners soon gained the attention of Tammany Hall. While still in his 20s, he became rich, accumulating a tidy fortune at two gambling dens in the West 40s, both protected by Tammany-friendly police.

So, Rothstein became a powerful presence in the New York underworld, lending his name and considerable wad to a collection of illegal and marginally legal operations, including a share in a downtown pool hall with Giants' Skipper John McGraw. Bigger action was had at the track and roulette wheels of Saratoga, where Rothstein bought a mansion and spent $100,000 converting it to a gambling joint and cabaret. Along the way came "Titanic Thompson" and others in his stable of colorful hangers-on, enforcers, and cronies from the sometimes interchangeable world of gambling and sports.

The complete story of Rothstein's role in the 1919 World Series is hazy.

He wasn't as much the idea man behind the fix as the money man who pushed it through. Approached only 10 days before the Series by former featherweight boxing champion Abe Attell, Rothstein refused to get involved, saying it would never work.

Asked again days later by a Boston gambler named Sport Sullivan, Rothstein thought it over and changed his mind, contributing $100,000 and another $100,000 on the Series' first day. So great was Rothstein's power in the underworld that the expectation of his involvement was enough to make it work.

Sure, Rothstein's line of work was profitable, but it could get sticky. For all his friends, the gambler had just as many enemies. Indeed, Rothstein's extraordinary streak finally ran out late on the evening of November 4, 1928 when he used the telephone at Lindy's to call Room 349 at the Park Central to discuss his poker debt. Convinced he had been cheated the day before, Rothstein refused to pay up — a few hours later, he was gunned down by a single shot to the groin. Papers labeled the culprit a "hot-headed creditor."

Rothstein lingered for two days in a coma and died on November 6 — Election Day, when he would have collected $570,000 for his correct pick of Herbert Hoover over Al Smith in the Presidential Election. His alleged assassin was tried but never convicted.

BASEBALL COLUMNIST FOR THE TIMES
Red Smith sets the standard
The New York Times
229 West 43rd Street

"Writing is easy," New York Times sports columnist Red Smith once explained. "I just open a vein and bleed."

He didn't have to. Simply put, Smith was the best sportswriter ever. "Of all those who have written sports for a living, nobody else ever had the command of the language, turn of the phrase, the subtlety of the skewer as he did," wrote Dave Anderson, a Times colleague. "And perhaps nobody else ever enjoyed it more. All he ever wanted to be was a 'newspaper stiff,' as he often identified himself."

Humility aside, Smith was a giant of his field, a writer who plied his trade as a New York sports columnist for 37 years, both at *The Times* and earlier at *The Herald Tribune*. When he won the Pulitzer Prize for distinguished commentary, in 1976, Smith became only the second sports columnist to be honored with that award; Arthur Daley, also of *The Times*, was the first, in 1956.

Some argued that a sportswriter had no business winning something as solemn as a Pulitzer. But Smith had no illusions, remaining as self-effacing as ever. "This may sound defensive — I don't think it is," he said, "but I'm aware that games are a part of every culture we know anything about. And often taken seriously."

Smith wrote with a wry sense of timing that put the games and the people behind the games into perspective — most of it on a tight deadline. "Now it is done, now the story ends," he wrote after Bobby Thomson hit his 1951 playoff home run to beat the Dodgers. "And there is no way to tell it. The art of fiction is dead. Reality has strangled invention. Only the utterly impossible, the inexpressibly fantastic, can ever be plausible again."

In 1956, when the Brooklyn Dodgers went to Jersey City to play some home games, Smith wrote of Dodger president Walter O'Malley that "[He] shares with other persuasive men a gift for supporting an argument with figures that can't easily be checked."

And about Reggie Jackson's three home runs on three swings in game six of the 1977 World Series that won it for the Yankees, he wrote, "it had to happen this way."

"It had been predestined since November 29, 1976, when Reginald Martinez Jackson sat down on a gilded chair in New York's Americana Hotel and wrote his name on a Yankee contract," Smith wrote. "That day, he became an instant millionaire, the big honcho on the best team money could buy, the richest, least inhibited, most glamorous exhibit in Billy Martin's pinstriped zoo."

Smith's three-to-four weekly columns for *The Times* were syndicated by the paper's News Service to 275 newspapers in the US and another 225 in about 30 foreign countries. Although he was 66 when he joined *The Times* in 1971, Smith continued to believe that his responsibility as a sportswriter was "to add to the joy of the reader interested in the games and to capture the grace and drama and beauty and humor."

On January 11, 1982, Smith wrote in his regular column of his plans to cut back to three columns a week. He recalled years past when he had written a daily column, adding, "Between those jousts with the mother tongue, there was always a fight or football match or ball game or horse race that had to be covered after the column was done; I loved it."

Poetic irony was at work; four days later, Smith was dead of heart failure. He was 76.

GLADYS GOODING AT THE KEYS
Belvedere Hotel
319 West 48th Street

Pop quiz: Who is the only person to play for the Brooklyn Dodgers and the New York Rangers? Why, Gladys Gooding, the organist. Okay, trick question. Sorry.

When Gladys Gooding pushed her keys on the Hammond organ, people listened. That goes for her serenading of the umpires at Ebbets Field with "Three Blind Mice." It includes the aftermath of the 1952 World Series, when the Dodger crowd, having just seen their team lose yet again to the Yankees, were comforted by Gooding's rendition of "What Can I Say Dear, After I Say I'm Sorry?"

And it doesn't include the Brooklyn man living near Ebbets Field who took her to court for disturbing his sleep. The case was thrown out when the complainant — moderately deaf — had to cup his ear to catch the judge's remarks.

In her Ebbets Field "organ loft," a glass enclosure high atop the diamond, Gooding entertained a legion of baseball fans for 16 years with her gentle and whimsical riffs. Her seemingly innocent renditions at appropriate moments were gentle jabs at umpires and opponents, and another colorful offshoot of wacky, everyday life at Ebbets Field. Gooding was an occasional singer of the national anthem as well.

"Mine was a wonderful relationship with the players and the fans," Gooding recalled years later. "Before the games, I would serenade the players on their birthdays, play their state songs, and their favorite popular numbers."

Gooding even managed to inject a slice of Mexican culture to her Brooklyn repertoire. Her organ rendition of "Chianpenecas" became a standard part of the Ebbets Field seventh inning stretch in which fans clapped rhythmically to the music.

A Belvedere Hotel resident, Gooding directed both amateur shows and music for the Major Bowes amateur talent unit, when not playing the organ at Ebbets Field.

Gooding played at Ebbets Field until the Dodgers left for Los Angeles in 1957. She continued to play at Madison Square Garden hockey games and boxing matches until her death in 1963 at the age of 70.

KIDS, GRAB YOUR PENS
The Grand Hyatt
109 East 42nd Street (just east of Grand Central Terminal)

Those kids — and adults, for that matter — armed with pens, paper, baseballs, and bats, and prowling the 42nd Street sidewalk outside the Grand Hyatt these days are there for a reason: The hotel serves the same role as in the days when it was the Commodore, that is major league teams' New York home-away-from-home.

Both National and American League teams stay at the glitzy, glass-covered Grand Hyatt, a very New York kind of place with the hustle and bustle of 42nd Street and Grand Central Terminal right there. And they stayed there back when it was the Commodore, also home for a short time in 1920 to F. Scott and Zelda Fitzgerald who were soon kicked out for disturbing other guests.

As for all those kids, do each of them really need 14 signatures from each weak-hitting utility infielder? A signed Christy Mathewson ball is enough to put anyone through a year of college. But multiple Paul Wagner cards? Come on.

WACKY BASEBALL OWNER PERSONIFIED — ANDREW FREEDMAN
Democratic Club of the City of New York
617 5th Avenue

If, at times the questionable behavior of today's owners is enough to test the patience of even the most loyal baseball fans, their collective self-righteousness barely holds a candle to the fiery, cantankerous, turn-of-the-century Andrew Freedman, who never met a man he wouldn't sue.

A real estate operator who studied law at City College of New York,

Freedman became a force in Tammany Hall, using his political ties to make numerous choice real estate and government bonding deals, including the bonding for construction of New York's subway. In 1895, he purchased controlling interest of the Giants for $48,000 from local Republican politicians and promptly drove this proud team from contenders to cellar-dwellers.

The Sporting News called Freedman, "vain, arrogant, ruthless — and cheap." Another paper said that "whenever a man's work didn't suit him, it was off with his head." The irascible Freedman knew so little about baseball that he couldn't tell where the bases were, but ran the team like a Tammany fiefdom, feuding with players, managers, sportswriters, policemen, rival club owners, and city officials. In other words, downright Steinbrennerian.

When Giant pitcher William "Dad" Clarke, short of funds one winter, wrote Freedman and asked for an advance of $200 on his salary. Freedman sent him $100, with a note that read, "Since $20 is not enough to live on until the season opens, I am sending you $100." Managers were hired and fired for no conceivable cause, rowdyism on the field was encouraged, and both players and sportswriters were bullied and barred from the ballpark.

During Freedman's "Reign of Terror," as his tenure was known, 13 managers passed in and out of the Polo Grounds' Giant dugout. Among them: Cap Anson and Buck Ewing, future Hall of Famers who didn't last because they couldn't stand Freedman's second guessing. Another manager, one Harvey L. Watkins, was hired in 1895 from P. T. Barnum's Circus, where he'd been business manager.

Also in 1895, Freedman picked a fight with the finest pitcher of the day, Amos Rusie, who was fined $200 after a 22-win season, causing the so-called "Hoosier Thunderbolt" to sit out the following season in protest. When sportswriter Sam Crane wrote a series of stories critical of Freedman's management style, he was banned from the Polo Grounds.

Freedman's policy of talent depletion drove the Giants into the cellar. But it was his continual feuding with fellow team owners that proved his ultimate undoing. When Freedman sought to establish a national baseball trust to operate the sport on sound business principles, including tight control over wages and shifting franchises to the most profitable sites, his scheme of pooling profits was turned down.

In 1902, Freedman sold the Giants because it didn't meet anticipated profits. John T. Brush bought most of Freedman's stock for $200,000 after selling the Cincinnati Reds. But following the sale, Freedman continued to exert his influence by using his position as a director of the Interborough Rapid

Transit to block the subway from subsidizing a new American League team in New York. The AL was then forced to find investors with personal political clout in Tammany Hall capable of overcoming Freedman's opposition and breaking into the lucrative big city market.

Freedman, a lifelong bachelor, accumulated an estimated $7 million fortune and lived, courtesy of his Tammany connections, at the Democratic Club of the City of New York and at a Red Bank, New Jersey estate. He belonged to 14 clubs, and owned yachts and race horses. After his death in 1915 at the age of 55, the bulk of his estate was used to construct a home for the aged in the Bronx.

THE GAME ROY CAMPANELLA COULDN'T WIN
Rusk Institute of Physical Medicine and Rehabilitation
New York University-Bellevue Medical Center
400 East 34th Street

The news hit the front pages with the force of a freight train — early on the icy morning of January 28, 1958, Dodgers' catcher Roy Campanella broke his neck when the car he was driving went out of control on a winding S-curve on Dosoris Lane in Glen Cove, Long Island.

The three-time National League Most Valuable Player and Brooklyn folk hero was paralyzed. The accident occured as Campanella returned alone from a television appearance to his home, "Salt Spray," a 10-room ranch on Eastland Drive in Glen Cove.

From the accident scene, Campanella was taken to Community Hospital in Glen Cove for a more than four-hour operation to repair the two fractured vertebrae in his neck. And some weeks later — May 5 — it was on to the Institute of Physical Medicine and Rehabilitation at New York University-Bellevue Medical Center, the Rusk Institute, where he spent the next six months in an intensive therapy program.

Doctors said the extent of his injuries would have killed a man in less than Campanella's peak physical condition. Even so, the accident left him a quadriplegic. That Campanella became as revered in his baseball afterlife for his remarkable courage and grace as he was when he was pounding the ball in Flatbush is the stuff of legend.

At NYU, Campanella spent more than three hours a day lifting weights, pulling sandbags and exercising, all in an effort to learn the living skills of a wheelchair-bound man. It's there he started to demonstrate the extraordinary optimism that earned him the enduring admiration of the world.

"There is a gallantry about Roy Campanella ... that is almost beyond understanding," wrote an admirer. "It is the very humanity ... that makes us see that he and others who have gone through what he has gone through create the highest standards of the human spirit."

Campanella's doctors agreed. "He is an amazing man," said Dr. Howard Rusk, founder and director of the Institute that bears his name. "He is a great spirtual force, a very strong character. He has worked so hard to accomplish the things he has that he has been an inspiration to us all. I honestly believe that Roy's contribution to this life has been far greater than anything he could possibly contribute to it through baseball."

Rusk said that the way Campanella was able to combat his misfortune "has given hope to so many, many thousands of disabled people [and has made him] a symbol."

Indeed, the severity of Campanella's injury would have made limited functioning hopeless even a decade before, Rusk said. But of the 400 or so similar cases in the dozen or so years after World War II, up to 75 percent were able to get around in a wheelchair.

Still, there were times when Campanella wanted to chuck it all and just give up, he admitted in *It's Good To Be Alive*, his candid, heartfelt memoir, published in 1959. He credited his faith, family, and friends with making him face up to his condition and get on with living.

"I compared it to baseball," Campanella wrote of his disability. "When you're in a slump, you don't feel sorry for yourself. That's when you have to try harder. You don't quit. You have to have the faith, hope and conviction that you can lick it."

By November 1958, Campanella had progressed enough to go home, continuing his outpatient rehabiliation at Rusk three times a week. A brace still strapped to his head, and confined to the wheelchair, he went home to his wife, Ruth, and the couple's six children, bursting with the optimism that had so impressed his doctors.

"I feel very good mentally and physically," he told reporters on his discharge. "I'm not going to lose what I've gained and I plan to work as hard as ever on my rehabilitation program."

In some respects, Campanella's attitude harkens back to his playing days when he was known as baseball's greatest catcher, and as one who loved the game. "In order to be a good ballplayer," he once said, "you gotta have a lotta kid in you. I mean you gotta be like a small boy. I'm still a kid."

Further insight into Campanella's remarkable character is revealed in the book. He writes movingly of meeting a young Dodger fan of 11 or 12 who asked for his autograph, to which Campanella replied, "I can't hold a pen in my hand yet."

"That's all right, Mr. Campanella," the boy said. "I can't see."

He writes of a visit by several of his Dodger teammates, rained out of a game in Philadelphia. "You know how players gripe," Campanella says. "I told them, 'Fellas, don't ever gripe about nothing. If you've got to live like this, there's nothing else to gripe about.'"

Campanella writes of Rusk that, "I think if I told that man I wanted to ride a horse tomorrow, he'd say, 'Go right ahead, Campy. And while you're at it, have a real good ride!' In Dr. Rusk's book, there's no such thing as 'can't.'"

Campanella eventually returned to the Dodgers — as a coach and an advisor for the rest of his life. Wheelchair-bound but always upbeat, he was often photographed imparting his wisdom to Dodger prospects at spring training in Vero Beach, Florida. He died in 1993 at 71.

NYU MEDICAL CENTER – PART TWO
Better than the roar of the crowd
Gil McDougald can hear again

For ex-Yankee Gil McDougald, a veteran of eight World Series in his 10 big league seasons, the sounds of cheering began to wane in the summer of 1955, when he was hit in the head by a ball in a freakish batting practice accident. Struck just above the right ear while standing near second base, the versatile infielder started to experience a gradual loss of hearing.

The injury lead in part to McDougald's retirement from the game in 1961. He then entered the building business, but the hearing loss grew steadily worse, causing him to leave that business too. Before long, McDougald was virtually deaf — able to hear some tones, but not words. Indeed, for most of the last quarter-century, the 70-year-old Spring Lake, New Jersey resident got by with a combination of a hearing aid, lip reading, and written notes.

But in November 1994, a miracle happened. Thanks to a newspaper story publicizing his condition, McDougald discovered an extraordinary medical breakthrough that involved the insertion of a tiny microchip into the inner ear, thus restoring hearing to a considerable degree.

The microchip, called the cochlear implant, was surgically installed by Dr. Noel Cohen, an acknowledged Brooklyn Dodgers fan, at NYU Hospital, allowing McDougald to hear his first words in 25 years. His wife, Lucille, summed up the impact: "Unbelievable."

The surgery involves insertion of an electrode, which stimulates the cochlea, an organ in the inner ear. The implant cannot restore normal hearing because it does not amplify sound, instead converting sounds into electronic signals. And with the aid of a small microphone behind his ear, the old Yankee paused to consider his new-found fortune: "It's great," he told Ira Berkow of *The New York Times*. "But I have a problem: My voice, gee, it sounds terrible."

Voices in a crowded room or on the telephone can be difficult for cochlear implant recipients. But McDougald, who has since become a sought-after spokesperson around the oral deaf community, wasn't complaining. "I really didn't expect (this)," he told *The Times*. "They've turned the music on."

IN THE CATBIRD SEAT — RED BARBER RULES THE AIRWAVES
WOR Radio
1440 Broadway (& West 38th Street)

Walk the streets of residential Brooklyn on a soft summer evening in the 1940s and early '50s and the voice would come at you from a thousand radios. You didn't need a radio yourself, mind you, to appreciate it — all you had to do, it was said, was listen up and follow along.

The voice belonged to Walter Lanier "Red" Barber, the Mississippi-born broadcaster whose melodious Southern twang is as much a part of Dodger folklore as Ebbets Field and Carl Furillo. Barber, known as "the Ol' Redhead," broadcast Dodger games on WOR for 15 years, from 1939 through 1953. Along the way, he combined his distinctive Southern charm with a thorough reportorial style, making the game enjoyable for generations of fans and leaving his mark on sports broadcasting forever.

Barber's baseball diamond was the "pea patch." A game in the bag was "tied up in the crocus sack." Similarly, a team in control was "in the catbird seat" and an argument with the umpire was "a rhubarb." A really dazzling event, like a grand slam or a miraculous catch: "Oh-ho-Doctor!"

In between such distinctive idioms was an eloquent linguist. On Barber's death in 1992, current Dodger broadcaster Vin Scully recalled his mentor as, "perhaps the most literate sports announcer I ever met."

Barber wasn't an outrageous personality in the spirit of a Harry Caray. He just called the action with thoroughness and quiet objectivity. He never openly rooted for the Dodgers and is said to have described a home run by Ralph Kiner with exactly the same objectivity as one by Duke Snider.

It was just that objectivity that cost Barber several dream broadcasting jobs. He left the Dodgers in 1953, unable to continue after Walter O'Malley had taken over and pushed him to make his style more supportive of the team. In 1966, while broadcasting Yankee games with Mel Allen, he was fired after revealing that the last-place Bombers had drawn a crowd of 413 — that's right, 413 — to a meaningless late September game.

"His soft Southern voice and his meticulous intellect conveyed baseball as a rural game being played outdoors by men who should not be taken too seriously," wrote George Vecsey in a tribute that appeared in *The New York Times* after Barber's death in 1992. "When Gil Hodges would be shackled by Ewell "the Whip" Blackwell, Barber could convey the flawed moment without making the Dodgers sound like the forces of good beset by the forces of evil."

No slouch in retirement, Barber wrote seven books and countless magazine articles, while serving as a lay minister with the Episcopal church, after leaving the broadcast booth. In those last years, he was also a regular contributor to National Public Radio, and gathered up a gaggle of honors, including a George Polk Award, and, with Allen, one of the first two places in the Broadcaster's Wing of the Baseball Hall of Fame.

BENCHWARMER, BRAIN, SPY — MOE BERG
NBC Studios
711 5th Avenue (& Rockefeller Center)

His career was anything but memorable:

- Lifetime batting average: .243;
- Career home runs: six;
- Total teams: five (Dodgers, White Sox, Senators, Indians, Red Sox).

Yet, more than a half-century after the end of his mediocre 15-year big-league career, Morris "Moe" Berg remains one of the most quoted, written-about, talked-about players in major league history. At card shows, his autograph commands top dollar. And, in 1994, a major biography of Berg reached the best-seller list.

So, what on earth is it about Berg that continues to fascinate? Raw intelligence, a splash of eccentricity and a dose of bona fide swashbuckling old-fashioned espionage, that's what. Simply put, Berg was a man of extraordinary intellect, arguably the smartest man to don a major league uniform.

A graduate of Princeton and the Columbia Law School, Berg was a linguist-turned-attorney and World War II US spy who just happened to play major league baseball. It was said he could speak a dozen languages but couldn't hit in any of them. And he just may have been the only player of his generation to regularly keep a tuxedo in his locker; a gregarious storyteller in his younger days, Berg was a sought-after guest at parties, particularly among the Washington, DC diplomatic crowd when he was playing for the Senators.

Berg didn't play much and may have been best known among teammates for the quality of his bullpen stories. "He'd tell you about something in Latvia and then the next minute it was something in China or Japan," ex-Red Sox pitcher Jack Wilson told Nicholas Dawidoff in *The Catcher Was A Spy*, the scholarly 1994 biography of Berg. When *New York Times'* columnist Ira Berkow asked Berg if he'd ever published anything, the old catcher replied, "Only a treatise on Sanskrit."

But perhaps nothing demonstrated the depth of Berg's intellect like his triumphant appearance on February 21, 1939 at NBC Studios as a contestant on "Information Please," a popular radio quiz show of the era. Berg dazzled, flawlessly and steadily identifying the bordereau, an important document from the Dreyfuss affair; Haley's as the most visible comet; "loy" as the ancient French spelling of law; and the "Dear Willy/Nicky" as part of the correspondence between Czar Nicholas II and Kaiser Wilhelm.

Berg plowed ahead in the show's American-presidents-as-athletes' segment, identifying Warren Harding as a former sportswriter; Theodore Roosevelt as a one-time boxer; and, Woodrow Wilson, like himself, as a Princeton baseball alumnus. And just like that, his half-hour was up, as the host Clifton Fadiman, a *New Yorker* book critic, thanked Berg "for catching them so neatly ... You've been brilliant."

Others thought so too. NBC received stacks and stacks of letters — 24,000 of them, Berg said later — asking for a return appearance. So, he went back, twice in fact, in October and November, answering another round of questions on everything from political history to geography and cognates.

But for how smooth Berg was with the questions themselves, he proved testy about other things, sounding tense on quick introductory questions from Fadiman about his personal life and his absolute refusal to answer anything about the law. (Fadiman: "Mr. Berg, you were once a lawyer among your spare extra vocations, weren't you?" Berg: "I refuse to answer.") "He was not very forthcoming," Fadiman said later. "We didn't get to know him at all."

But the aloofness that cost him on the radio may have been an advantage in spy work. The following year, 1939, was Berg's last in the big leagues; in 14 games with the Red Sox, he hit .273, had a home run, and that was that for baseball. The European theater of World War II was next, and Berg performed with distinction, working as an OSS (Office of Strategic Services) spy to help determine Germany's atomic bomb capability.

Heady stuff for a man still in his early '40s. The problem was afterwards, when Berg, back home and restless, never really readjusted to civilian life. Berg's spy work was his last job, which gave him ample time to read a lot of newspapers, sit at lunch counters and hang around the press boxes of New York baseball parks. There, it was noted, he was the only former major leaguer to habitually show up with the latest copy of *The Times Literary Supplement.* Berg's last years are marked by a descent into eccentricity and odd behavior; he died in 1972 at the age of 70.

BASEBALL 'TIL THE END
Gotham Hotel
5th Avenue (& 55th Street, SW Corner)

A magnesium flare cast an eerie light on the street as thousands looked up, oblivious to traffic, and watched the scene unfold. In their sight was an urban scene of true horror: a young man straddling the 17th-floor window ledge of the Gotham Hotel and threatening to jump at any minute.

It was July 26, 1938, and through the long summer day, the smartly dressed, distraught young man, John Warde, 24, kept both an army of police and firefighters, as well as thousands of curiosity seekers, at bay as he clung to the 18-inch ledge, 160 feet above the ground. Then, at 10:38 PM, after 11 hours on the ledge, it was over, as Warde jumped to his death, just as police with lifebelts were preparing to grab him.

The tragedy was complete. Scores in the crowd fainted. The next day, it was revealed that members of the New York Police Department had tried just about every method they knew in an effort to talk the young Southampton, Long Island resident out of suicide. They had brought up his sister, Katherine, to talk him out of it. They discussed ping pong and picnics to get friendly. They passed him coffee and cigarettes and even sent up a patrolman, Charles Giasco, in the guise of a bellboy, who argued he could lose his job if Warde jumped.

But in the end, not even Giasco's efforts to connect with Warde through — you guessed it, baseball — was enough to avert the tragedy. It turns out that Warde, an ardent Chicago Cubs' fan, was skeptical of the chances of the Brooklyn Dodgers, then fifth in the eight-team National League, of finishing in the first division. There was method to the madness: Patrolman Giasco thought he had found an opening and tried to develop it by offering to get tickets and accompany Warde to a game at Ebbets Field.

"I'll have to think that over," Warde told him. Moments before jumping, Giasco, his right leg roped to a bed in room 1714 as a precaution, said he thought that the baseball talk was key to helping turn the corner. Several times, Giasco said later, he thought he had convinced Warde to give up talk of suicide and go inside.

But dark forces were at work. Warde, neatly dressed that day in white shirt, blue necktie, pressed gray trousers and polished black dress shoes, had tried suicide the previous year by slitting his throat with a knife. A graduate of Southampton High School, he had last been employed until mid-1937 by the Southampton Bank.

Giasco was not at the window when Warde jumped. It was when he heard the roar of the crowd outside that he knew it was over. Warde's last audible words: "I'd rather jump than watch those Dodgers."

It was a case of baseball 'til the end. Ironically, earlier that day, the Cubs beat the Dodgers 10-8 at Ebbets Field.

BIG FAN
Helen Dauvray makes her mark
40 Park Avenue

Today, there are BIG FANS — the Vinnies from Brooklyn and Als from Staten Island, the ones who call sports radio talk shows at 3 AM in December to discuss Joe Torre's five o'clock shadow or Todd Hundley's bad throw the previous June that may have cost the Mets a chance at fourth place.

A century ago, the equivalent was Helen Dauvray. She was a fan, a BIG FAN and a fixture at Giants' games at the Polo Grounds at a time when women didn't venture much to ballparks. But Helen Dauvray was the Vinnie from Brooklyn and Jack Nicholson-at-courtside BIG FAN rolled into one: a name actress of her day and celebrity fan who left a little-known, but indelible stamp on the game.

Her mark was a sterling silver cup in her name that she generously offered to award to the winner of the annual World Series between the champions of the National League and American Association. The cup, which showed a right-handed hitter at bat with pennants to either side, a catcher's mask over the hitter's head, and crossed bats as the handles, became the symbol of late-19th century baseball supremacy.

First awarded in 1887 — 16 years prior to the start of the formal National vs. American League World Series — the Dauvray Cup continued its run through the 1891 collapse of the Association and was awarded for two more years to the National League champion.

Born in San Francisco, Dauvray made her stage name early, playing a series of child roles in California, before arriving in New York at age 11 to pursue fame and fortune under the stage name, "Little Nell, the California Diamond." By 1885, she was a bona fide star, appearing in the Lyceum's Theatre's comedy, *One of Our Girls*, which *The New York Times* called her greatest acting triumph.

Along the way, Dauvray, who lived at 40 Park Avenue, acquired a passion for baseball, nurtured by her 1887 marriage to John Montgomery Ward, the dashing Giant star. Armed with a steady bat and a law degree from Columbia, Ward earned lasting fame as a founder of the Brotherhood of Professional Base Ball Players, a forerunner to the Players' League.

The cup outlasted the marriage. Within a year, Dauvray and Ward were feuding, it was said, because of Dauvray's desire to return to the stage. At the time of their marriage, she had announced publicly that she was leaving the theater.

Their dispute is thought to have started in St. Louis, where the Giants were playing the Browns in the 1888 Series. After the Giants won, Ward left on Al Spalding's extended world tour and was away for months. The couple later tried a reconciliation but divorced in 1893. Three years later, Dauvray married a US Naval officer, Albert Gustavus Winterhalter, and moved to Washington, DC. By then, she was acting again and all but forgot about baseball.

And the Dauvray Cup? In 1893, the Boston Beaneaters were awarded the cup for the third time and given permanent possession. The cup, however, has been lost to history.

The following year, William Chase Temple, owner of the Pittsburgh Pirates, donated a cup to be awarded to the champion. Called the Temple Cup, it was awarded to the winner of a series between the NL pennant winners and the second place finishers. The rival AA had folded after 1891. The cup is on display at the Baseball Hall of Fame in Cooperstown, New York.

Dauvray died in 1923. Although obituaries mentioned her stage career, nothing at all was said about her brief but intense love affair with baseball.

"I GOT DA HORSE RIGHT HERE"
Damon Runyon rules Broadway
Lindy's Restaurant
1655 Broadway

Okay, so what does Damon Runyon have to do with the national pastime? The chronicler of Broadway whose contribution to literature were wonderful characters like "Sky Masterson" and "Harry the Horse," isn't generally known as having very much to do with baseball.

The characters around Broadway were Runyon's true beat. His forte was incorporating the characters he met along the way — the actors, race-track bookies, dancers, agents, promoters, and wise-guys — and turning them into memorable short stories and plays. Baseball, particularly the Giants of John McGraw and all the action around the Polo Grounds, was an integral part of his storytelling.

Take Runyon's story, *Baseball Hattie*: "It comes on springtime, and the little birdies are singing in the trees in Central Park, and the grass is green all around and about, and I am at the Polo Grounds on the opening day of the baseball season, when who do I behold but Baseball Hattie?" the story begins.

Turns out Hattie, a groupie or "Baseball Annie" of sorts, falls for and marries a hot lefthander of a prospect named Haystack Duggeler, who falls in with a bad crowd led by a gambler named Armand Fibleman. After that, things get real complicated, real fast. Downright Runyonesque too, which means baseball, betting, race tracks, and all the familiar flourishes.

Runyon's joint was Lindy's, the well-known restaurant he immortalized as "Mindy's" in many of his stories. It was there that many of his enticing characters met, only to find themselves worked into a short story sometime later. Never a drinker, Runyon would occupy a seat at Lindy's for long hours, consuming quarts of coffee, as he hosted a steady stream of characters. Said one regular, after reading a Runyon piece: "It ain't hard to spot the guys in the stories."

Runyon's men were "guys." Women were "dolls" and money, "potatoes." Complimentary show tickets were "Chinee," in those politically incorrect times. His reference was to the holes punched in the tickets that he thought resembled a Chinese coin. Even the names of his plays were classics: *Guys and Dolls, Blue Plate Special* and *A Slight Case of Murder.*

A native of Kansas and raised in Colorado, Runyon arrived in New York in 1911 as a sportswriter at *The American.* From baseball, he soon moved to cover murder trials, political conventions, the Mexican Revolution led by Pancho Villa, and World War I. His plays were done on the side, as was his later work as a Hollywood scriptwriter.

In his nearly 40 years in New York, Runyon lived in a number of Manhattan locations — in the early 1920s, in the Hotel Gotham at 2 West 55th Street and 5th Avenue; and then, starting in the mid-1920s, with his first wife, Ellen, on the Upper West Side at 251 West 95th Street and Broadway. In the 1930s, after separating from Ellen, he moved to the Hotel Forrest at 224 West 49th Street, between Broadway and 8th Avenue.

Runyon's final address was a residential hotel called the Buckingham at 101 West 57th Street and 6th Avenue, northwest corner. He moved there in 1944, after separating from his second wife, Patrice — and it was there he died in 1946 of cancer at 62.

Columnist Walter Winchell created the Damon Runyon Cancer Fund to memorialize his close associate and friend.

NO SERIES THIS YEAR – JOHN BRUSH RULES BASEBALL
St. James Building, 1133 Broadway (& 28th Street)
Home: Lambs Club, 130 West 44th Street

A gaunt man with a crooked nose and a perpetual frown on his face, John T. Brush did not resemble a New York baseball magnate.

Anything but a bombastic type, Brush suffered from locomotor ataxia, a progressive disease of the nervous system, was thin to emaciation and walked with a cane. But leave it to this unusual baseball executive to bring excitement and a dash of glamour — not to mention John McGraw and Christy Mathewson — to his New York Giants and the ballpark he built by Coogan's Bluff.

The ballpark, originally called Brush Stadium, was later called the Polo Grounds. Under Brush, who bought the team from the penny-pinching Andrew Freedman in 1903, it was home to the Giants as the team became a winner. And it was from Giant headquarters at the St. James Building that Brush, perhaps the least-known baseball immortal, set to work building his empire and throwing away the 1904 World Series in the process.

An Indianapolis clothing store owner, Brush took to baseball as a means of promoting his sale of "ready made" suits for men and boys. He had already built a diamond and organized a semi-pro team when, in 1886, he learned that the St. Louis club of the National League was for sale. Brush promptly bought the team and moved them to Indianapolis.

In 1890, the league dropped Indianapolis and Brush sold some of his players to the New York Giants for cash and stock. In 1891, while holding on to his portion of the Giants, Brush bought the Cincinnati Reds. That arrangement continued for more than a decade until he sold the Reds in 1902 and took over majority ownership of the Giants the following year.

As a transplanted New Yorker, Brush lived at the Lambs Club, the city's oldest theatrical club and the meeting place and temporary residence to a generation of entertainers and actors, among them, W.C. Fields, John Barrymore, Al Jolson, and Spencer Tracy.

Unlike Freedman, Brush poured money into the Giants and made them a winner. He also brought a showman's touch to the Polo Grounds, bringing in brass bands at least once a series, leather cushions for women and thousands of cardboard fans bearing an ad for his clothing company.

But a funny thing happened on the way to immortality: With Brush's Giants of 1904 racing to the National League pennant, the city's other team, the upstart Highlanders did the same in the American League.

As the season headed toward a climax, New York faced the alluring prospect of its first intra-city World Series, the forerunner of the Subway Series. The Series had started only a year before, when the American League Boston Pilgrims, later the Red Sox, defeated the Pittsburgh Pirates.

Boston's Series victory was an upset. Baseball's upstart American League had only been operating for a couple of years when a former Cincinnati sports editor named Ban Johnson took over the old Western League, aggressively pursued more than 100 National Leaguers and labeled his new venture, "baseball's second major league."

For the more established National League owners, Johnson's move was utter insolence. Even with the 1903 Series in the history books, men like Brush and McGraw were not inclined to dignify the upstart league any further. That point was brought home to Brush in 1904 as the Highlanders played well, theoretically stealing Giant fans away.

Some suggested that McGraw's refusal to play was motivated more by an intense dislike of Johnson, stemming from the Giant manager's rough-and-tumble days as a player and a manager of the Baltimore Orioles. Among Johnson's goals was a new league free of the rowdyism and assaults on umpires that characterized the game of that era.

But the ultimate refusal in playing the Series belonged to Brush. Taking on the Highlanders would only legitimize the new team in the city he once monopolized. Granted there was money to be made with the Series, but Brush was thinking of the long range competition.

It didn't matter anyway because the Highlanders failed to get their pennant. They had entered the season's final week neck-and-neck with Boston, when, on the final day, the Highlanders' Jack Chesbro, uncorked a wild pitch to let in the winning run and hand the pennant to the Pilgrims.

The night they won the American League, Boston sent a note to McGraw, challenging the Giants, "to play for the championship of the world ... if you refuse to play, we get the title by default." Even the Giant players petitioned the team to play, and the press and fans alike pushed for a Series.

It didn't work. "Regret we can't meet you in any such series," Brush replied. Later, he said that the Giants didn't "desire any greater glory than to win the pennant in the National League."

And so ends the story of the World Series that wasn't — the last such interruption before a player's strike canned the 1994 Series. Ironically, Brush's refusal prompted owners to set some standards. The result: as of 1905, the Series in its current form, as in a recognizable best-of-seven series with set percentages of the receipts going to the winners and losers.

Brush had the last laugh. His 1905 Giants went to the Series, becoming the first to play under what became known as "The Brush Rules," and defeated the Philadelphia A's behind three shutouts, courtesy of their ace Mathewson.

Those shutouts came on top of Mathewson's 31 wins in the regular season. His feats are legendary. And John T. Brush? His ultimate contribution to the World Series looms large, but is virtually unknown.

BIG HIT FOR "CASEY AT BAT"
Wallack's Theatre
1224 Broadway

A challenge, trivia buffs — who wrote the famed baseball poem, "Casey at Bat?" As most red-blooded lovers of baseball esoterica can tell you, it was a San Francisco newspaperman named Ernest Thayer.

Thayer may have written it, but who made it famous? An actor with the intriguing name of De Wolf Hopper.

Hopper, a giant of his day in Thespian circles, estimated he may have performed the well-known poem as many as 10,000 times. Audiences loved it, and before long, Hopper, a versatile actor who played roles from Gilbert and Sullivan operettas to Shakespeare's Falstaff, became the man who made Casey a household name.

How it all happened rests with Hopper's whimsical but profound love of baseball. "Casey" debuted on the evening of May 13, 1888 at Wallack's Theatre as Jim Mutrie's Giants hosted Cap Anson's Chicago White Sox at the old Polo Grounds, 5th Avenue and 100th Street.

Hopper, a fan for years, spent most free afternoons taking in the Giant games. It was at the ballpark that the actor developed the idea of hosting a gala baseball night at Wallack's, complete with the different teams glaring at each other from opposite rows of the theater boxes. The idea was quickly accepted.

Up stepped one Archibald Clavering Gunter, author of several theatrical successes of the day. "I've got just the thing for your baseball night," he told Wallack's empasario Colonel McCaull. "It's a baseball poem I cut out of a 'Frisco paper when I was out on coast last winter. I've been carrying it around ever since. It's a lulu and young Hopper could do it a turn."

Gunter produced the clip, McCaull slapped his knee in delight when he read it and turned it over to Hopper. The actor was a quick study, so he put the crumpled poem in his pocket and forgot about it. The next day, Hopper went to the ballpark and that night learned that his 20-month-old son, John, had a diphtheritic sore throat and was nearing a crisis.

Afterwards, he told McCaull that he couldn't go on. "Surely, surely," sympathized his employer. "Forget all about it, my boy." But when the news from sickroom came back, it was good and Hopper's young son was better. He burst into McCaull's office, telling him that the show must go on.

"I'll study it now," the revived actor said. "Just give me the office to myself for awhile." McCaull left, and in less than an hour, Hopper had engraved the story of Casey on his mind.

That night at Wallack's, Hopper performed "Casey," roaring through the suspense of the first stanzas and building to a stunning climax, before plunging the wide-eyed throng, as one account put it, "into salvos of applause with the swish of the third strike." A legend was born.

In time, Hopper was receiving constant requests to recite "Casey," which he did on command and usually dressed in a baseball uniform. The story behind "The Mighty Casey" — the one about his son — was a tale he never tired of telling either. His son recovered completely and grew up to be a Chemical Bank vice president.

Hopper once said he expected to be "repeating the lines on resurrection morn." He almost did, dying of a heart attack in 1935 at the age of 77 as he sat perusing the box scores in a Kansas City hospital. Baseball was in his blood until the very end. His last words, as directed to his doctor: "Run along while I see what the Cards did."

GET YOUR RED HOTS – HARRY M. STEVENS, INC.
320 5th Avenue; Then 524 5th Avenue

"Hey hot dogs here!" Baseball just wouldn't be baseball without them. So why hot dogs? The hot dog king, Harry M. Stevens, that's why.

Legend has it that the story of Harry M. Stevens started at the Polo Grounds on a cold April day in 1900, when Stevens, the ballpark's head caterer, wasn't selling too much ice cream and soda water.

Calling his vendors together, Stevens told them to go to neighborhood markets and buy all the dachshund sausages they could find and an equal number of long rolls. Frankfurters — so named for their Frankfurt, Germany birthplace — were called "dachshund sausages" because of their shape. Stevens heated the sausages, placed them in the rolls and sent his vendors through the stands with a cry, "Get your red hot dachshunds!" The verdict: an immediate hit.

Legend, act two: Sitting in the press box that day was Tad Dorgan, America's most successful cartoonist, searching for an idea to meet a deadline. Seeing the vendors roaming through the stands, he sketched them selling "red hots" ... then stopped because he couldn't spell, "dachshunds." The next day, Dorgan's cartoon appeared showing the dachshund sausages in rolls, barking at one another. And for "hot dachshunds," the lousy-spelling Dorgan had substituted, "hot dogs."

It was just the beginning for the Hot Dog King. In time, Stevens expanded his food selection to include not just hot dogs, but soft drinks and scorecards at sporting events. A new industry was born.

Years later, Stevens told a slightly different story. Actually, the King said, it was his son, Frank — get it? — who developed the idea of hawking hot dogs at sporting events. In the case of young Stevens, it was at the then-popular six-day bicycle races at Madison Square Garden that the idea took hold.

"At the time, we had been selling mostly beer and sandwiches," the elder Stevens said, "but I told Frank that the bike fans preferred ham and cheese. He insisted we try it out for a few days." They did and the hot dog was a hit, or so he said.

An English immigrant, Stevens came to the US in 1882 and found work in an Ohio steel factory. One day, while watching a baseball game, he hit on the idea of selling scorecards. He sought and obtained the concession, first in the Tri-State League and then among big league teams in Boston, Brooklyn, Pittsburgh, Washington, and Milwaukee.

Stevens didn't actually create the scorecard; his genius was in perfecting it by accurately printing the players' names. "I made it a business to find out just how the teams batted and gave fans a card on which they could keep score," he said. "It was a selling campaign. I had to convince them that a game could not be really enjoyed without a scorecard."

Stevens' unusual marketing aptitude was already evident — as in his profitable idea to sell scorecards printed in German in Milwaukee. It was also there that he met John Montgomery Ward, manager of the New York Giants, who advised him to go to New York for a shot at a truly big market. Stevens did, arriving there around 1894 with exactly $8.40 in his pocket.

His first New York catering job were bicycle races at the Garden and baseball at the Polo Grounds. In time, he was selling sandwiches and lemonade and hit it big with hot dogs, peanuts, and soft drinks. Stevens soon had concessions at all three major league parks in New York, as well as Belmont Park and Aqueduct racetracks, and the polo matches at Westbury, Long Island.

Stevens' gentle charm, prodigious work habits and energy — he kept offices first at 320 5th Avenue, before the company moved to 521 5th Avenue, and ultimately to its current locale in New Jersey — masked a surprising breadth of education and erudition. Much was made of Stevens' knowledge of Shakespeare, and it is said he could quote almost any line from the bard's plays.

Stevens' four sons followed their father into the business. Today, the thousands of vendors selling those "red hots" would do well to raise a ceremonial toast — make that a jumbo hot dog with relish and mustard, no ketchup — to Harry M. Stevens.

BIG SIX WRITES A BIG BOOK
Christy Mathewson, matinee idol, author
G. P. Putnam & Sons Publishers
2 West 45th Street

In 1912, Christy Mathewson could have run for mayor of New York and won hands-down. As the pitching mainstay of the Giants, he had star quality — charisma, brains, and looks. It didn't hurt that he also had the talent to win 373 games in a distinguished 16-year career. No wonder sportswriters called him, "Big Six," because he doused enemy fires as well as New York's finest fire company.

At a time when baseball was a rowdy game populated largely by hard-drinking, skirt-chasing men, a step removed from a life in the mines or on the farm, Mathewson came straight from central casting. Here was a flesh-and-blood version of the Frank Merriwell model, a fictional, clean-living hero whose serialized exploits thrilled millions of boys.

Those boys idolized Mathewson and he courted a brand of fame that cut across social classes. His picture adorned ads of all kinds. His presence on a train was often broadcast by the host railway, to which Mathewson played along, delighting in speaking to the assembled passengers. Even his walk on pitching days from the center field clubhouse in the Polo Grounds to the dugout came with a sense of high drama.

Fellow Hall-of-Famer Three Finger Brown remembered that walk. Typically, Mathewson would wait until about 10 minutes before game time, Brown said, "then he'd come from the clubhouse across the field in a long linen duster like auto drivers wore in those days, and at every step, the crowd would yell louder and louder."

How fitting that Mathewson was among baseball's first big ball-playing authors. His 1912 book, *Pitching in a Pinch*, was a forefather of sorts to *Ball Four* and a long line of tell-all books by players about the inside game. Based on a series of interviews with John N. Wheeler of *The New York Herald*, the book's roots are a series of Wheeler's ghost-written *Herald* newspaper columns with Mathewson's by-line during the 1911 Giants-Philadelphia World Series.

That Series was a precedent — the first in which Mathewson and other baseball stars supplemented their income by telling their version of events to sportswriters as columns. Already a veteran in such endeavors, Wheeler had written similar sorts of columns for, of all people, Mexican revolutionary Pancho Villa. Also in 1911, he founded the North American Newspaper Alliance.

Pitching in a Pinch was published by G. P. Putnam & Sons in three editions, including a special Boy Scout edition. While it doesn't provide much "inside" baseball, most of which today is rather obvious, it is nonetheless worthwhile reading as a timepiece and for the stilted phraseology of a bygone era.

"In most big league ball games, there comes an inning on which hangs victory or defeat," Mathewson and Wheeler write in the title chapter, *Pitching in a Pinch*, republished in 1994 by the University of Nebraska's Bison Books. "Certain intellectual fans call it the crisis; college professors, interested in the sport, have named it the psychological moment; big league managers mention it as 'the break,' and pitchers speak of the 'pinch.'"

Red Smith once declared that *Pitching in a Pinch* was the first book he ever borrowed. It came from the North Side Branch of the Kellogg Public Library in Green Bay, Wisconsin, where he grew up.

Critics still were disappointed. Writes Ray Robinson, author of the superb 1993 biography, *Matty: An American Hero:* "Nothing in *Pitching in a Pinch* was designed to offend even Mattie's worst enemies, if he had them."

BILLIARDS ANYONE?
John McGraw and friends run a pool hall
149 West 41st Street, then 1328 Broadway

For all his genius on the baseball diamond, John McGraw was the kind of person, as his biographer Charles Alexander observed, "who could always make plenty of money, but ... never seemed to have much of a plan for doing anything with it — except to spend it."

A case in point: The Little Napoleon's continual investments in a series of Midtown and Downtown pool halls that he certainly hoped would do better financially than his other dismal ventures, like Florida real estate and Western US mining stocks.

By 1906, McGraw's position as the feisty manager of the world champion Giants meant he was well-paid and the toast of New York. Accordingly, he surrounded himself with a steady stream of acquaintances from show biz, racetrack, and gambling circles, many of whom shared a penchant for action with money to burn.

How fitting then, McGraw should turn to the manly pursuit of pool. That February, he opened his first in a series of New York billiard halls at 149 West 41st Street, a 15-table establishment that debuted with the young pool champ Willie Hoppe among the guests. It was McGraw's second effort at starting a pool hall; he and Wilbert Robinson ran "The Diamond Cafe" during their years in Baltimore.

When his first New York pool hall failed to turn a profit, McGraw, in October 1908, invested in still another establishment, this one at 1328 Broadway, in the Marbridge Building on Herald Square. This time he took some precautions — taking in the young Hoppe as an associate, along with a silent partner named Arnold Rothstein.

Rothstein's interest wasn't generally known. Only 26-years-old at the time, Rothstein was still a small-town gambler, pool shark, and part-time cigar salesman, with a burning ambition to have a $100,000 bankroll in his pocket. Some years later, he got his wish, but, as we have learned, met an ignoble end following a poker game gone bad.

McGraw's second pool hall venture was slightly more profitable than the first. Standing out was a legendary 34-hour game — that's right, 34 hours — between Rothstein and Jack Conway of Philadelphia that only stopped when McGraw sent everyone home to get some sleep. Still, it survived, despite the average monthly police "protection" supplement forked over by McGraw and the city's other 400 or so pool hall operators to the police.

The message, if any? John McGraw, baseball legend and American icon, was no businessman.

MANLY PORTIONS ... MANLY PLACE
Rusty Staub's on Fifth
575 5th Avenue (& 47th Street)

In his 23-year career with five teams, Rusty Staub had a reputation for big home runs and a big appetite.

No wonder: The New Orleans native was a popular player, as known for his unusual off-the-field passion for cuisine as for knocking the ball out of the park. This wasn't a Babe Ruth "inhale-the-entire-contents-of-the-refrigerator" kind of interest in food — this was the genuine thing. Indeed, the feature writers of the 1970s stayed busy with the requisite stories about Rusty Staub, ballplayer and gourmand.

It didn't hurt that Staub played in Montreal for several years, adding a whiff of cosmopolitan mystique as "Le Grand Orange," the red-headed star of the expansion Expos. It was in Montreal that Staub dated a restaurant manager, who taught him something about the business.

It didn't hurt either that Staub was from New Orleans, where food is taken pretty seriously — both of Staub's parents were good amateur cooks — or that, as he later said, his first few minor league paychecks were so meager that it forced him to stay at home and learn his way around the kitchen.

By 1972 — when Staub came to New York for his first of two Mets tours of duty — he was a full-fledged baseball-playing, cuisine-head. From New York, he went to Detroit, briefly back to Montreal and then to the Texas Rangers, before returning to New York in 1981 and ending his career with the Mets in 1985.

Staub did well in baseball. He hit the first of his 292 home runs for Houston in his teens, and his last in his 40s, the only person, along with Ty Cobb, to do so. He made six All-Star teams and achieved permanent status as a Met deity by batting a hefty .423 in the 1973 World Series against Oakland.

So, who better than Staub to run a restaurant? The first Rusty's, at 3rd Avenue & 73rd Street, opened in 1977 while Staub was with the Tigers. Reports *Zagat New York City Restaurant Survey* of the current Rusty's: "A great original for manly portions, sports memorabilia and good wine ... This Midtowner is a hit, especially if Rusty is around."

You'll know if Rusty is around. Like we said, big home runs, big appetite, and a BIG guy.

DING ... DONG ... THE KING IS GONE
Helmsley Palace Hotel
455 Madison Avenue (& East 50th Street)

It was the bottom of the third with the Yanks ahead by a run as Roberto

Kelly stepped to the plate at Yankee Stadium against Detroit. It was 8:21 PM on July 30, 1990, a time and date forever etched into the minds of Yankee fans everywhere.

First came some smatterings of cheers. Then, a spontaneous, emotional, only-in-New York crescendo of sound, as many in the crowd of 24,037 stood and celebrated about something that had nothing to do with the game itself. Said Yankee pitcher Dave LaPoint: "I actually thought people were running on the field from the third-base line, the noise was so loud."

What was happening? New York baseball fans had just received some extraordinary news: George Steinbrenner was gone, banished from baseball for his three-year association with a man that Baseball Commissioner Fay Vincent called a "known gambler." And just like that, the man they call the "Boss," the most depised person in baseball, was gone, wiped from the base-ball landscape. For Yankee fans, it was Christmas in July.

Okay, so church bells around New York didn't exactly herald the news, but they nearly did. "I can't believe it," said one Yankee fan. "It's about time. Now maybe we can turn this whole damn thing around." Wrote *Time Maga-zine*: "July 30 may become a patriotic holiday in New York City and wherever the proud traditions of baseball are honored."

And so ended — for a time anyway — the 17-plus year association of George M. Steinbrenner III, the "Boss," as managing partner of the Yankees. Steinbrenner, a millionaire shipbuilder from Cleveland, bought the team in 1973 for $10 million and promptly bullied, blundered, and bludgeoned his way to his undeniable position as the man who embarrassed the once-proud Yanks.

But Steinbrenner wasn't kicked out of baseball for being mean. Vincent's big announcement at the Helmsley Palace Hotel, now the New York Palace Hotel, was punishment for not acting, "in the best interests of baseball," as the commissioner put it at the press conference. In doing so, Vincent invoked a clause originated by Commissioner Kenesaw Mountain Landis following the Black Sox Scandal in the 1919 World Series.

Specifically, the decision was in response to Steinbrenner's involvement with a 31-year-old small-time gambler from the Bronx named Howard Spira. Steinbrenner had paid Spira $40,000 for what he thought was incriminating information about star Yankee outfielder Dave Winfield. "In essence," ruled Vincent in his 11-page report, "he heard no internal warnings because none went off."

Steinbrenner seemed to have it in for Winfield from the minute the ballplayer signed a 10-year, almost $20 million Yankee contract in 1980. It's not that Winfield had done anything wrong; he, in fact, was a model citizen and managed to average 25 home runs a year in his eight years as a Bomber. Observers said the Boss felt cheated that Winfield just wasn't the kind of impact player that Reggie Jackson had been as a Yankee.

Things got ugly after Steinbrenner had contractually agreed to make a donation to Winfield's New Jersey-based charitable foundation for disadvantaged youths. Steinbrenner promised $300,000, but in January 1989, the foundation sued him for the third time, asking for $450,000 it said the Yankee boss owed.

Steinbrenner then filed his own suit, stating that Winfield had failed to make his own contributions and charging him with misuse of funds. The suit also charged the ballplayer with making loans to Spira.

Spira had worked as a gofer for the Winfield Foundation from 1981 to 1983. When Winfield broke off their relationship, Spira contacted the Boss. The two met in Tampa in 1986 and again in 1987, where Spira told Steinbrenner that the foundation had indeed misused funds and that Winfield had loaned him $15,000, before demanding it back by threatening him with a gun.

In 1990, Steinbrenner paid Spira the $40,000, but contacted authorities when the gambler demanded $110,000 more. Either way, what the Boss did was wrong, particularly in baseball, which has been downright skittish about gambling since Black Sox days. Spira was later convicted of extortion.

That's not sports; that's a soap opera. On the other hand, it's typical of the kind of legacy Steinbrenner created in his years with the Yanks: After all, this wasn't *any* franchise, the logic went ... these were the Yankees, the most famous and successful franchise in American sporting history. Destroy them and you're destroying, well, an institution. You don't go to Rome and mess with the Vatican, do you? Okay, a stretch perhaps, but point made.

Indeed, they don't typically run newspaper agate on owners, except in Steinbrenner's case, that is. The numbers please:

- Managerial switches ... 18;
- General manager hires ... 14;
- Team presidents ... 10; and,
- Pitching coach changes, random examples of an ego-gone-berzerk and situations involving offensive behavior ... too numerous to name.

Sure, Steinbrenner's Yanks won the World Series a few times — for starters in 1977 and 1978 — but he helped them lead the league in embarrassments too. He hired Billy Martin, fired him and hired him again, driving him to the bottle in the process. He promised team captain Thurman Munson that he would be the team's highest paid player, before paying Reggie Jackson more. He humiliated players in the press, demanded lineup changes with dugout phone calls and basically ran the franchise like a bully, skipping through "front-office people and [public relations] men," as Red Smith put it, "the way the rest of us go through pistachio nuts."

The low point? Several are in contention for the honors. But perhaps the lowest of all was Steinbrenner's dismissal of manager Dick Howser after the 1980 season, in which the Yankees won 103 games, but not the pennant. Steinbrenner's reason: Howser had an "unbelievable" real estate deal in Florida. Right, and the moon really is made of cheese.

As for the most enduring low point, it may have been that the Yankees, once the sport's best franchise, had to wait until 1996 — that's 18 years — between World Series titles. By then, Fay Vincent had himself been drummed out of baseball and Steinbrenner was back, having been reinstated in 1993.

Are more Boss-related fun and games ahead? Judging by his mid-1997 stunt re-arranging the Yankee players' parking lot, you bet. And the most recent Boss-related news? January 3, 1998 marked his 25th anniversary as Yankee majority owner, making him the longest-tenured owner of the team. Jacob Ruppert had owned the Bombers for 24 years when he died in 1939.

JACKIE ROBINSON GETS HIS BEARINGS
McAlpin Hotel
Broadway & West 34th Street

The inside scoop of Jackie Robinson's major league debut wasn't much covered in the 1940s. While the extraordinary story of his April 1947 debut with the Brooklyn Dodgers is common knowledge today, details behind Robinson's ordeal still merit attention.

Robinson never talked much about the abuse he took in those first grueling days as a major leaguer. Sure, he was met by appreciative crowds in Brooklyn and sure he was spectacular those first few weeks — establishing a pattern of all-round excellence for which he was elected to the Baseball Hall of Fame. Indeed, Robinson may just have been one of the best complete players in baseball history, from hitting to fielding and unnerving pitchers by dancing around the bases. And he started quickly: In 1947, Robinson was Rookie of the Year and practically willed the Dodgers to that season's National League pennant.

But as Brooklyn celebrated, racists burned. In a sport populated at the time by southern rural white men, many were not happy. The St. Louis Cardinals threatened to boycott, and Robinson's Dodger teammate, Alabamian Dixie Walker, asked to be traded rather than play with Robinson (he later amended his demand and became Robinson's hitting mentor). Add to the barrage hate mail, death threats, and a constant stream of verbal abuse from rival dugouts.

That abuse reached a culmination in an April series against Philadelphia at Ebbets Field. Leading the lowly Phillies that year was another Alabama native named Ben Chapman, a former Yankee with a vicious, racist temper — booed by Yankee fans one day, he turned to the grandstand and yelled, "F—ing Jew bastards."

Chapman disliked Jews and he hated "nigras." So, as the April 22 Dodger-Phillies game, the first of a three game series, started, his distinctive drawl could be heard from the visiting Ebbets Field dugout.

"Hey you, there — snowflake," Chapman started. "Yeah, you ... When did they let you outta the jungle?"

And on it went. While baseball banter in those days contained the odd nasty reference or two, none were forthcoming this day. The Dodger players were shocked, as were some of the Phillies, including Lee Handley, the third baseman, who sought Robinson out, saying Chapman's team didn't share their manager's sentiments.

For a proud, fiercely competitive man like Robinson, it was almost too much to bear. Sure, he had promised Dodger general manager Branch Rickey to never fight back. This, however, was almost too much. As he told Roger Kahn years later in a conversation related by the superb book, *The Era*, that game was almost the end of what has become known as baseball's great experiment.

"So, I play ball, but they don't stop," Robinson told Kahn. "'Jungle bunny.' 'Snowflake.' I start breathing hard. I'm just playing ball. I'm doing my job. I'm a good ballplayer. Deep down, I've been thinking, people will see I'm a good ballplayer and they'll see I'm black and they'll put that together. A black guy's a good ballplayer. A black guy can be a good guy."

As Robinson said later, that day against the Phillies may have been the hardest time of all. On one hand, he wanted to ignore the insults; at the same time, he felt like reaching into the Philadelphia dugout, smashing Chapman's head and walking away from baseball. JUST WALKING AWAY. Said Robinson: "Standing on that ballfield in Brooklyn, standing still, I had come to a crossroads."

How did he take the pressure? Robinson played hard, winning some games almost single-handedly — the best tonic. He took comfort in the friendship expressed by teammates like Pee Wee Reese, the Dodger captain. And most of all, he turned to the quiet strength of his wife, Rachel, and baby son, Jack Jr., living at the time at the McAlpin Hotel, where the family lived those few lonely months while looking for a house. For Robinson, eating a dinner cooked on an electric hot plate, it was a refuge of sorts. At the time, Ebbets Field was a world away on the subway.

Robinson also realized the power of his own talent. "But wait ... Am I gonna give Ben Chapman the satisfaction [of responding]?," he remembered himself thinking in that Phillies' game, as related to Kahn. In the eighth inning of the scoreless game against the Phillies, Robinson singled up the middle, stole second, took third on an error and scored on Gene Hermanski's single. The final: Brooklyn 1, Philadelphia 0. Winning was Jackie Robinson's best revenge.

The death threats continued. Chapman kept up the insults, but Robinson's courage and extraordinary talent started to outweigh the abuse of those first terrible days. He would survive and become both the on-the-field and spiritual leader of the Dodgers. And he, Rachel, and baby Jack didn't stay long on 34th Street, moving shortly to a comfortable tree-lined street in St. Albans, Queens.

WILL THE REAL MRS. ARTHUR IRWIN, STAND UP?
Grand Hotel
Broadway & West 31st Street (SE Corner)

Okay, so the baseball talents of Arthur Irwin, an 1890s' era manager of the Phillies, Giants, and others, will never be confused with the demonstrated genius of Connie Mack or John McGraw.

Suffice to say that Irwin, the quintessential journeyman manager who skippered six teams in eight years, had misplaced talent. For him, just getting to the ballpark everyday was an accomplishment.

Cooperstown recognition isn't given for Irwin's unusual extracurricular talents. Away from the park, the former shortstop and 13-year major league veteran, had a wife, Edna, who he had married in 1883 while playing for Providence of the National League. Edna and the couple's two daughters and son lived in Boston. So?

Irwin's story gets interesting around 1890, when he became a bigamist — this time, marrying a New York woman, with whom he had a son, all the while managing in Philadelphia. Neither woman was aware of the other, although for a time, Edna and the couple's three children from family number one lived with him at the Grand Hotel. Meanwhile, wife number two and their son, whose names are lost to history, resided nearby. Both wives considered Irwin a devoted husband and family man.

Irwin lasted only two years with the Phillies, before managing the Giants in 1896 and the Washington Nationals for two years after that. Then, his undistinguished major league managing career ended.

Maybe it all did catch up to him after all. Irwin died in 1921 at the age of 63, an assumed suicide. *The Baseball Encyclopedia*, says he died in the Atlantic Ocean, bringing an odd close to an odd life. No further word on Edna.

MAKING THE METS — WILLIAM A. SHEA GETS BUSY
Manning, Hollinger & Shea, Attorneys
41 East 42nd Street

The story of William A. Shea's efforts in spearheading the return of National League baseball to New York in 1962 actually begins years earlier and gives credence to the philosophy that if you fail once or twice, don't fret and try again.

It was just after the 1957 announcement of the departure from New York of the Dodgers and Giants that Shea got busy. First, the corporate lawyer, named by Mayor Robert Wagner as chairman of the city's baseball committee, tried to get existing National League teams to move to New York. That failed, and he and Branch Rickey organized the Continental League as baseball's third major league. That didn't work either, so it was on to Plan B — a new major league franchise for New York.

Eureka! He got the team. Too bad they were the bumbling Mets, who lost 231 games in their first two seasons at the Polo Grounds. Then, in 1964, lovable but still terrible, the Mets moved into a new stadium in Queens, heralding the facility with a traffic jam and an obligatory loss to the Pirates. Its name: Shea Stadium, a tribute to the 56-year-old lifelong Brooklynite who willed the National League back to New York.

Shea said he would have preferred another name. His 24-year-old son, Bill, Jr., on learning of his father's honor, quickly put things in perspective: "Now dad, with a token and a ticket," he said, "you'll be able to get into the ballpark."

"I worry," Shea said in modest explanation of how he did it. "Why, I'm the worst worrier in the whole world. But I have no ulcers, don't take pills. You see, I don't worry from the stomach out. I just worry and get it done."

Shea made his remarks on April 17, 1964, the day he threw out the ceremonial first pitch to christen the new ballpark. At the time, he was well on his way to worrying about another mission — attracting The Olympic Games to New York. It didn't work, but he worried about it all the same.

SALOONKEEPER TO THE STARS – TOOTS SHOR
51 West 51st Street

"I'm not like Will Rogers," Toots Shor, confidante to the stars, once said. "I've met plenty of guys I don't like. I don't mean to hate guys, but if I don't like a guy, I wouldn't do nothing for him. If I like him, there's nothin' I wouldn't do. I ain't braggin' but I got something. Maybe it's how to be a friend."

And so went the blustery homespun philosophy of New York's preeminent saloonkeeper and pal of the city's baseball stars of the 1940s and '50s. A garrulous, outgoing bear of a man, Shor ran Manhattan's best-known watering hole, which symbolized the boozing, macho, big-city sports world of the era, and served as a Mecca for the famous and infamous alike. "Show me a man that don't drink," he was fond of saying, "and I'll show you somebody I don't want to be with."

Shor's famous circular bar was the epicenter of a vanished age in New York — a city of lunch counters, automats, hotel bars, nightclub singers, men in fedoras, and taxi drivers who called you "chief" or "ace." Frank Sinatra and Jackie Gleason were regulars at Shor's. But Toots reserved his most lasting praise for athletes; Joe DiMaggio ate up to three meals a week at Shor's, one of the few places where the most intensely private of all Yankee greats felt comfortable.

Indeed, it was the close friendship with Shor that served to bring the solemn DiMaggio out of his shell. In turn, Shor became DiMaggio's biggest booster, a kind of unofficial press agent to the New York baseball beat writers.

When DiMaggio was suffering from painful bone spurs in 1949, Shor visited him regularly, and even had his meals delivered to his hotel, never charging a dime. DiMaggio was a frequent visitor to Shor's house in Deal, New Jersey — the restaurateur also kept a 12-room duplex at 480 Park Avenue — and once actually referred to the Yankee Clipper as "among the 10 most important living men."

For all his bluster, Shor's sports and entertainment friends always came first. His barometer was what he called "class," a concept that could be difficult considering Shor's occasional feuds mixed with bombast. When Dodgers owner Larry MacPhail was arguing with Shor, he made certain the saloonkeeper had his usual allotment of World Series tickets anyway, earning Shor's enduring gratitude.

When sitting with Sir Alexander Fleming, the discoverer of penicillin, Shor was told Mel Ott, who had hit the 500th home run of his Giant career earlier that day, had arrived at the bar. "Excuse me, Sir Fleming," Shor said, leaving his guest, "but somebody important just came in."

Shor was a product of a tough neighborhood in South Philadelphia, raised above the candy store founded by his German Jewish immigrant father. When Toots was 15, his mother was killed in a car accident; five years later, his father committed suicide and Shor headed to New York.

Before long, Shor parlayed his considerable size — he stood 6'3" and weighed about 270 pounds — into a job as a bouncer at the Five O' Clock Club, one of the city's hottest nightclubs. He moved to the Napoleon Club, then to Billy LaHiff's, the Ball and Chain, and Leon and Eddie's — all of them noted speakeasies of an earlier generation.

"I was learning how to live," Shor said of his early, Depression-era years in New York. "I learned how important it was to be a spender, to buy a drink for people." Around 1940, he went into business for himself, actually owning at his peak, several "Toots Shor" restaurants, all within a few blocks of one another — at 51 West 51st Street; 33 West 52nd Street; 5 East 54th Street; and, in later years, 1 Penn Plaza, across from Madison Square Garden.

No wonder Shor was eulogized as, "the world's greatest saloonkeeper." He was the subject of a 1970 biography by Bob Considine, a Hearst columnist, who spoke philosophically of his subject: "I spent 30 years on Toots and Gibbon spent only 20 on *Decline and Fall of the Roman Empire*," he said. "There must be a lesson in there somewhere."

At the time, Shor was facing a decline of sorts himself. In 1971, his 52nd Street restaurant was padlocked for non-payment of taxes. By then, much of his clientele had left or died, while others had moved to the suburbs or found new watering holes closer to the current Garden on West 34th Street.

In a larger sense, Shor was staring full-flush at a trend — the decline of a boozing era. By the mid-1970s, he had lost his restaurants, reduced to working as a figurehead at other people's places. A big benefit for Toots was held that drew all the old-timers and raised $200,000, all of which was gobbled up by the IRS. In 1977, Shor died at 73 of cancer.

It was still a good ride, admitted Toots, late in life. "It's been like New Year's Eve every night all these years," he said. "Except when some wonderful pal has gone away."

CHAPTER SIX

THE THEATER DISTRICT

"There is much less drinking now than there was before 1927, because I quit drinking on May 24, 1927."

— *Rabbit Maranville, 1928*

CUBS HIT GOTHAM
Times Square Hotel
West 43rd Street & 8th Avenue

Most managers begin their tenures with the usual cliches: If they're not "taking it one game at a time," they're "staying the course" or conducting "business as usual."

But it was never business as usual for Walter J. "Rabbit" Maranville. A Hall of Fame shortstop with the Braves, Cubs, Pirates, Dodgers, and Cards, Maranville was a smooth-fielding, fast-talking, bona fide baseball personality whose managerial debut, as usual, defied the norm.

There are all kinds of comparisons that describe the wiry, 5'5" Maranville. On the field, he was the Ozzie Smith of his day, a cat-like shortstop who broke into the majors with the Boston Braves in 1912. Before his 24-year career was finished, he had played more games at short than anyone else in National League history.

Off the field, Maranville was, as baseball writer John Holway puts it, "the Joe Garagiola of Grandpa's day," a raconteur of uncertain diction and non-stop, wacky behavior. Everyone, it seems, had a favorite Rabbit story, which usually involved a speakeasy or two, a brawl, and good times.

No wonder Maranville's short stint as player-manager of the Cubs was mostly unhappy; he was too much a partier to discipline his players. Named as player-manager of the seventh place Cubs in July 1925, he resigned from the position two months later, with the Cubs still in seventh, and went back to playing full-time.

Named manager while the Cubs were in Brooklyn, Maranville had promptly gone out during a rain day with a group of his players and in Rabbit-like fashion, brawled and ended up in jail. Not a good beginning.

It all happened July 10, 1925. With no game to play that day, Maranville piled into a taxicab along Broadway with four of his Cub players and headed off. Their destination was the Times Square Hotel and when the tab came — 30¢ — the players thought the fee was excessive.

The players — infielders Mandy Brooks and Pinky Pittinger, and pitcher Jim Brett — refused to pay. One thing led to another and, as Maranville puts in his memoirs, Brett took a punch at the cab driver, the cab driver punched back and Pittinger tried to kick him in the stomach.

The cabbie then went after Maranville, seated in the back seat of the cab, he writes in his memoirs. So Maranville jumped out and joined the fray, discovering some disturbing information. The cabbie, George Werner of 416 Grand Street, was, of all things, a retired fighter.

"We went at it tooth and nail and where all the people came from, I don't know," Maranville writes. "Then the cops came and all I saw was cops using their nightsticks on our heads."

Many of those "people" were commuters rushing for the nearby subway. The fight took place just after 6 PM, the peak of the rush hour, making this brawl only slightly less crowded than the paying ones taking place less than 10 blocks north at Madison Square Garden.

Maranville, Brett, Pittinger, and Werner were arrested and charged with disorderly conduct at the West 13th Street Police Station. All charges against the ballplayers were dropped by a judge who was a ball fan and a confidante of Giants' manager John McGraw, Maranville later said. Werner, the cabbie and ex-fighter, was fined $5.

NO ROOM AT THE INN (THE POLO GROUNDS, ACTUALLY)
Watching the big game
The (old) *Times* Building
Broadway & West 42nd Street

Few pennant races were as exciting as the final weeks of the 1908 National League season, which featured a fierce battle between the Giants, Cubs, and Pirates.

Every game, every inning, and every pitch was important. What excitement for Giant fans when the New Yorkers met the Cubs, with the pennant at stake, at the Polo Grounds on the afternoon of September 23; that's when Giants' manager John McGraw made his famous last-minute lineup change that would decide the pennant. With first baseman Giant mainstay Fred Tenney laid up with a sore back, a 19-year-old rookie named Fred Merkle came in as a substitute.

Nothing to worry about, McGraw assured: Merkle was a bona fide star-in-the-making. But it was in a critical spot that day that Merkle made the base-running miscue that went down in the lore as "Merkle's Boner," essentially handing the pennant to the Cubs in baseball's weirdest ending and marring his otherwise splendid career.

The score was knotted at one in the ninth, with runners on the corners and two out. When Giant shortstop Al Bridwell hit a single, Moose McCormick ran home from third and the Giants had clinched the game and most likely the pennant. Or, so it seemed; as jubilant Giant fans ran onto the field, Merkle, the first base runner, was on his way to second, when, alarmed by the onrushing crowd and convinced the game had ended, he headed for the clubhouse.

But Cubs' second baseman Johnny Evers saw that Merkle hadn't touched second and figured if he could somehow get the ball and touch the base himself, McCormick's winning run would be canceled by the force-out to put the Cubs right back in the game. Result: mayhem. Evers, searching for the ball, finally found it in the stands in the hands of a fan trying to take it home.

Two Cubs chased the man through the mob, knocked him down when he resisted and grabbed the ball and tossed it to Joe Tinker who threw it to Evers, who made the tag at second and jumped up and down at the bag to make certain the umpire had seen what had happened.

Mayhem intensified: The Cubs said Merkle was out and the score was tied. The Giants said they'd won and the game was over. It took National League president Harry Pulliam a full week to disallow the Giant run and declare the game a tie — to be replayed as a playoff at season's end. It was — and in the October 8, 1908 playoff, the Cubs beat Christy Mathewson and the Giants, 4-2, for the NL flag.

So what does this have to do with Times Square? Plenty. Old photos tell part of the story of the feverish excitement that accompanied the game. With the Polo Grounds filled to the rafters, fans lined the outfield, the ballpark roof and nearby Coogan's Bluff in trying to catch a glimpse of the big game. When Chicago won, disappointed Giant fans hurled bottles at Cub players who were driven back to the hotel in a paddy wagon guarded by six armed officers.

Better, much better then, to have kept track of the proceedings some five miles downtown before the big window bulletins in the relative safety of Times Square. There, 1,500 fans gathered before the automated scoreboard linked to the distant ballpark by telegraph. The play-by-play results were posted over the second-story window of the north side of the unusual triangle-shaped *New York Times* Building.

It was the start of a New York tradition of sorts. Watching the progress of the game on the electronic scoreboard in Times Square evolved into a pastime for all big games and the World Series. No records are kept on how long the custom endured, but a panoramic shot of the action around the big board during the 1919 World Series reveals a crowd so big that it hindered Broadway traffic.

The '08 crowd was estimated at 1,500. It disrupted traffic too and required six policemen to keep them, according to one account, "from bulging out over the Broadway car tracks or pressing in against *The Times'* windows and blocking pedestrians."

A *Times'* staffer named Massey kept score on the big board, periodically climbing through the window to post the numbers and joking with the crowd that grew increasingly good-natured when the Giants took an early lead and held off the Cubs behind Mathewson's pitching.

Unlike the unruly scene at the Polo Grounds, the crowd maintained its composure even after the Cubs knocked around Mathewson with four runs in the third. And Massey deserves credit for sticking to his reports after a rumor swept the audience that the Giants scored, not one run in the seventh, but 11.

Massey stuck to his guns, earned the respect of the crowd and even got a farewell cheer when he finally posted the crushing news: "Chicago Wins."

DOWN AND OUT IN TIMES SQUARE
Grover Cleveland Alexander joins the flea circus
Hubert's Museum
228 West 42nd Street (between 7th & 8th Avenues)

There are all kinds of stories about Hall-of-Famer Grover Cleveland Alexander that go beyond his 373 lifetime wins. Unfortunately, most of the tales of this hard-throwing, hard-living, righthander don't involve baseball.

"Ol' Pete," as he was affectionately called, never played for a New York team, although he did have perhaps his greatest moment as a ballplayer in the 1926 World Series at Yankee Stadium, where he pitched the Cardinals to a dramatic upset win over the Yankees in game seven. And no, he wasn't a native — he grew up and died far from New York in St. Paul, Nebraska.

Ranked among the sport's immortals, Alexander broke in with the Phillies in 1911, winning 28 games. For the next 19 years, he pitched brilliantly for the Phillies, Cubs, and Cardinals, winning 30 games three years in a row and compiling 90 shutouts. Asked his opinion of the game's greatest pitcher, Walter Johnson had a one-word answer: "Pete."

Old-timers point to Alexander's razor-sharp control. More remarkable is that he maintained such astounding consistency, suffering from alcoholism, made worse by seizures due to epilepsy. Everyone liked Pete; teammates could always count on him for a handout and to be a pleasant companion in an age when most ballplayers were underpaid and could use the cash.

But Alexander couldn't handle his liquor on the days when he wasn't playing and would disappear, usually showing up only on pitching days, when he would go out and win the game. No wonder then that Alexander's inability to curb his alcohol consumption took on desperate proportions after the Phillies released him in 1930.

Alexander's baseball afterlife was hard, taking on a kind of roaming quality as lived by countless Depression-era itinerants. Hard times meant odd jobs for Alexander; among them, selling tickets at a Midwest race track, working at a Washington hotel, as a guard in an Indiana munitions factory, and as a greeter at a Springfield, Illinois saloon.

But perhaps Alexander's strangest, and perhaps saddest, post-baseball turn was the time he spent in 1939 and 1940 as the opening act at a 42nd Street flea circus museum. Even so, hundreds of people flocked to the see and hear one of baseball's greats on exhibit at Hubert's Museum, a honky-tonk between 7th & 8th avenues.

Sandwiched on a platform amongst a snake charmer, the penny slot machines, the nickel games, and the freak shows, Alexander just talked baseball. Hundreds flocked to see his dozen or so daily performances — consisting of baseball reminiscences about everything from striking out Tony Lazzeri to win the '26 Series on a sidearm "slider" as he told the crowd, to "monologues on fast balls, curves, fadeaways, and sinkers, along with actual demonstrations of the same," as one scribe put it.

"If the sob stories stung a little, Pete shook them off, the way you shake off a catcher's signal that you know wouldn't send a man down swinging," another account said. The job paid $100 a week, not bad for a Depression-era job, Alexander said. He liked the lively questions tossed up from the crowd, young and old, and packed a lot of humor and drama into the stories he told in each 30-minute session.

From Hubert's, Alexander drifted out to Indiana, then to Washington, and back to St. Louis, the scene of his glory years with the Cardinals, where he worked as a sandlot baseball coach.

Then, Alexander just disappeared. He got back for a time with his wife, Aimee, whom he eventually divorced, took off again, and resurfaced at a veteran's hospital in the Bronx before heading to California. In Los Angeles, Alexander was scraped unconscious from an alley and taken to a hospital, where he was identified only after an intern stripped off his ring and saw the inscription — "St. Louis Cardinals, World Champions, 1926."

The end came mercifully back home, in Nebraska, in 1950 at the age of 63. Admirers described him as the kind of man who always faced each moment as it came along and let tomorrow take care of itself. Found in his typewriter at the time of his death — an unfinished letter to his former wife, Aimee, whom he was planning to visit — again.

(Read more about Alexander in Jack Kavanagh's biography, *Ol' Pete: The Grover Cleveland Alexander Story*, from Diamond Communications.)

CRUSH THE YANKS! *DAMN YANKEES* HITS BROADWAY
46th Street Theatre – 126 West 46th Street (1955)
Marriot Marquis Theatre – 1535 Broadway and West 45th Street (1994)

There was a story making the rounds when *Damn Yankees*, the exuberant

Eisenhower-era fable of how the then-invincible Yankees finally lost the pennant, hit Broadway in 1955. It was said that Dodger fans should see it.

The reason: They would have had a blast. A sporting twist on the "Faust" legend, *Damn Yankees* is the story of middle-aged Joe Boyd, a perpetually frustrated fan of the lowly Washington Senators, who loses his soul to the Devil. He becomes Joe Hardy, the 22-year-old slugger, who will finally lead his team to the promised land of the American League flag.

Hardy swings for the fences, winds up on a Wheaties box, and becomes a hero. But he catches himself pining for his previous life as Joe Boyd with wife, Meg, and the pink- and pale-green kitchen of '50s-style domestic tranquilty. As he is busy transforming the Senators into winners, Hardy, played by Robert Shafer in '55 and Jarrod Emick in '94, meets and spends much of his time trying to avoid a she-witch of a femme fatale named Lola.

The hijinks lead to a generous serving of Bob Fosse's swivel-jointed choreography and roisterous anthems like "Heart" and "Shoeless Joe from Hannibal, Mo." Performing the memorable "Whatever Lola Wants, Lola Gets" were two alluring Lolas, played in 1955 by Gwen Verdon, and in 1994 by Bebe Neuwirth.

Those Brooklyn fans had the last laugh. Ironically, the year that *Damn Yankees* hit Broadway, the real-life Yankees, which had won five of the previous six World Series, finally lost the Series — to the Dodgers.

VAUDEVILLE AND JOHN MCGRAW — PERFECT TOGETHER
Colonial Theatre
1887 Broadway

No wonder Congress has a hard time making up its mind about the antitrust matter of whether baseball is a business. It may be today, but there was a time when it was strictly entertainment, the best evidence being the sport's interchangeable links to vaudeville.

Most recognize John McGraw as the surly, successful one-time manager of the New York Giants. But McGraw was more than a manager; of him, it was said, "He took baseball off the Bowery and placed it in the glittering old Waldorf-Astoria." A master showman, he is credited, along with Babe Ruth, for leading the national pastime to new heights of popularity in the early part of the century.

How fitting that McGraw found vaudeville. If, during the winter, he couldn't manage, he did the next best thing — taking it to Broadway. McGraw hit the stage at the Colonial Theatre on November 8, 1912, shortly after winning his fourth National League pennant. His show for the B. F. Keith circuit — a monologue called "Inside Base Ball" — was "the most exciting and most humorous experiences of his career on the diamond," a reviewer wrote. "And with the aid of a diagram, [McGraw] revealed the hitherto carefully guarded secrets of inside base ball as perfected by the Giants."

Crowds flocked to the show. Critics raved. McGraw's performance, said another, showed he "can be as cool and collected on the stage as on the diamond when the bases are full. It was John J's first experience as an actor, and he got away with it."

He did so by moving along quickly, not sticking to a script and praising his team that the previous month had lost a tough eight-game World Series to Boston. Christy Mathewson, along with Fred Snodgrass, who dropped a flyball in the eighth game of the World Series that paved the way for the Boston win, came in for particular praise.

"I do not blame Fred Snodgrass in the least for his failure to catch that flyball," McGraw said during the show. "Snodgrass is a valuable and conscientious player and he will be a member of the Giants next season. His failure to make the catch is something that would happen but once in a thousand cases."

McGraw kept his word, but benched Snodgrass the following year, in the 1913 World Series. The Giants lost that one too — to Philadelphia, four games to one.

STAR COUPLE GOES SPLITSVILLE
Lexington Avenue & East 52nd Street (NW Corner)

Know anything about movies and you've seen it — Marilyn Monroe's signature scene, in which a gust of wind from a subway grate sends her white skirt billowing up over her bare thighs.

The film was the 1954 Hollywood classic, *The Seven Year Itch*, in which Monroe is Tom Ewell's voluptuous neighbor who lives upstairs. Its relevance to baseball? At the time, Monroe was married to Joe DiMaggio and the scene — actually, the whistling and catcalls from the crowd watching it — just may have spelled the end of their largely unhappy nine-month union.

DiMaggio retired after the 1951 season and married Monroe on January 14, 1954 in San Francisco City Hall. Jimmy Cannon called them "America's sweethearts," comparing them to Mary Pickford and Douglas Fairbanks. The country gushed and the tabloids covered every move of this unlikely star couple.

Why was the Clipper so grumpy on the movie set? One reason may have been that his storybook career was finished, while that of his new wife was very much on the rise. With devastating beauty and a surprising comic touch, Monroe was already a veteran of 16 films, including the 1950 Bette Davis classic, *All About Eve.*

But beneath the surface, the marriage had deep flaws. DiMaggio, long a celebrity, was actually painfully shy, craved privacy, and had a particular loathing of Hollywood. Contrast that to Monroe, who could work a crowd, enjoyed the attention and came with a heavy load of emotional baggage from her troubled past. Throw in the kind of reception Monroe routinely received — catcalls and hoots with every slinky, wiggling song, and dance routine — and doom was inevitable.

"Oh Joe, you've never heard such cheers," she told DiMaggio after a trip to Korea, entertaining American GIs. "Yes, I have," came the terse reply. For a possessive, traditional man like DiMaggio, the idea of his wife being mobbed by young soldiers must have been galling. The same goes for the famous *Seven Year Itch* scene, shot in front of the old Trans Lux movie theater at midnight on a balmy September night in 1954, to avoid the crowds and congestion of midtown Manhattan.

A big crowd showed up anyway, cheering every take of the skirt-flying scene, shot over a subway grate that is still there. DiMaggio stood off to the side, watching and privately seething.

He still was angry when he arrived at Toots Shor's some time later, wrote Joe Durso in his biography of DiMaggio, *The Last American Knight.* And he was even more pissed off after reaching the St. Regis Hotel, where the couple was staying, and got into a loud argument with Monroe that other guests overheard.

It was the nail in the coffin for the storybook marriage; the next morning, DiMaggio flew back to their home in Beverly Hills. Two weeks later, Monroe announced she was filing for divorce.

What, ultimately, went wrong? A combination of things probably. "Whatever it was," writes Durso, "a test of willpower, a conflict of careers, a clash of personalities, it came unraveled with electrifying speed." At the divorce trial, Monroe, sounding a lot like DiMaggio's first wife, Dorothy Arnold, some 13 years before, testified that DiMaggio was cold, distant, and uncommunicative.

They were divorced October 27, 1954. Final nuptial box score: a marriage that lasted nine months, two weeks — slightly longer than the baseball season.

CHAPTER SEVEN

UPPER EAST SIDE

"In the building I live in on Park Avenue, there are 10 people who could buy the Yankees, but none of them could hit the ball out of Yankee Stadium."

— *Reggie Jackson, Yankees outfielder, 1981*

A HUMBLE START FOR LOU GEHRIG
1994 2nd Avenue (& East 103rd Street)

There is nothing romantic about the birth and formative years of Lou Gehrig. The future Yankee great entered the lineup June 19, 1903 at 1994 2nd Avenue, in the hardscrabble lower-middle class section of Yorkville, then home to many of New York's first-generation German and Hungarian immigrants.

Gehrig's family had little, living perilously close to the poverty level. When Gehrig became a famous ballplayer, legend had it that he was a product of the slums. Not so, protested his protective mother, Christina, acknowledging that sure, the family was hard up, but hardly destitute.

Christina and her husband, Heinrich, were German Lutherans with four children, only one of whom, Lou — who weighed a hefty 14 pounds at birth

A nursery, next door to a fried chicken restaurant, stands today where Lou Gehrig was born.

— survived past infancy. Heinrich was an art-metal mechanic by trade, but took more to beer and pinochle. Quite an irony considering Lou hated to miss a game, played 2,130 straight games, and was celebrated for his work ethic.

The circumstances meant Christina, the true rock of the family, had to go to work as a cook, a maid, and a laundress. Her reputation as a cook who specialized in authentic German dishes like roast pig, roast geese and duck, pickled eel, and sauerbraten, is said to have kept the family going in tough times.

"I don't know if the Gehrigs looked back cheerfully and looked ahead fearfully, the way other people might have done," recalled Lou's widow, Eleanor in her memoirs. "There, life was basic and there was nothing cheerful about the way they lumbered through it. And if fear grew into foreboding in Lou's mind 30 years later, this was where it all began."

Today, Gehrig's onetime building is the site of a nursery, next door to a fried chicken restaurant.

BILLY MARTIN — ANOTHER DAY, ANOTHER BRAWL
The Copacabana
10 East 60th Street

New York is famous for taking people from the hinterlands and turning them into, well, New Yorkers.

If there is any New York baseball figure of recent years with that reputation, it's Billy Martin. A native of Oakland, California, the former Yankee player and manager was as renowned for his fists as he was for his considerable skills in managing good Yankee teams of the 1970s and '80s. "Everybody looks up to Billy," it was said, "because he probably just knocked them down."

After an 11-year career as an infielder, spent mostly with the Yankees, Martin managed a succession of American League teams before landing back with the Yanks, arguably as the game's best manager. Along the way, he fought — everyone from opposing players like Boston's Jimmy Piersall, St. Louis' Clint Courtney, and the Cubs' Jim Brewer to Minnesota's traveling secretary, and several of his own players, like Twins' pitcher Dave Boswell and Reggie Jackson.

Other opponents included the obligatory umpire, a Las Vegas reporter, a California real estate investor, a marshmallow salesman from Texas, and a Cleveland Municipal Stadium clubhouse urinal. Demographically, Martin covered most of the country in his brawling.

But few of Martin's fights attracted the kind of attention as the celebrated Yankee brawl of May 16, 1957 at the Copacabana. It happened as several Yanks, including Mickey Mantle, Yogi Berra, Hank Bauer, Gil McDougald, and Johnny Kucks celebrated Billy's 29th birthday at the Sammy Davis, Jr. 2 AM show.

Seated nearby was Edwin Jones, a delicatessen owner and his 19-member New Jersey bowling team, "the Republicans," and their wives. What happened next was a tabloid headline writer's dream as Yankees and bowlers fell scuffling and fighting to the floor in front of the stage.

A body flew into the coat room and policemen flooded the club in front of the Yankee's table #11. Afterwards, the accusations flew: The Yanks charged they were defending Davis' honor, when the bowling team called the entertainer a "little black sambo." They said when Bauer had asked them to stop, the racial insults only grew worse. Yelled Davis above the noise: "I wish you people would either keep quiet or leave. I'm trying to entertain."

Jones paid for his alleged remark, ending up with a broken nose, a fractured jaw and a concussion. Bauer, hitting .203 at the time, took most of the heat for striking Jones, but denied it. "Hit him?," he asked. "I haven't hit anybody all year." The ballplayers claimed it was the nightclub bouncer who inflicted most of the damage.

Headlines the next morning trumpeted the news — "YANKS IN BRAWL AT THE COPA" — and Bauer was arrested for assault. Mantle, not noted for his grasp of modern European history, compared the ensuing grand jury appearance to the Nuremburg Trial. Sure, Mick.

Charges against Bauer were quickly dropped. But things weren't forgotten. Each Yankee at the club that night was fined $1,000 by the team, except for Kucks, who was fined $500. And Martin? He took the brunt of the blame, due to his reputation as a short-tempered brawler. A month later, he was banished — traded to Kansas City.

Martin died in 1989 from injuries sustained while driving intoxicated in upstate New York. He is buried in Gate of Heaven Cemetery in Hawthorne, an infield-peg of a distance from the grave of Babe Ruth.

Only in death is Billy Martin finally at rest.

A BIG BREAK FOR MR. HARMONICA
Mr. Laff's nightclub
1185 1st Avenue (& 64th Street)

In the great scheme of things, it was quite a break.

Here was Phil Linz, the Yankees' light-hitting utility infielder, on board the team bus after a devastating doubleheader loss to the White Sox late in the 1964 season.

And here was Linz, of all things, in a jubilant mood — laughing, playing his harmonica, and making manager Yogi Berra very angry in the process.

Berra: "Cut it out (or something to that effect)."

Linz: "Huh?"

Mickey Mantle (seated nearby): "Yogi said to play it louder."

So Linz did, got fined, and became a legend in the process. In what became the August '64 tabloid sensation of the month, Linz became known as "Mr. Harmonica," parlaying his unusual celebrity into a steady off-season gig and eventually, a nightclub and restaurant, "Mr. Laff's." The club, an Upper East Side fixture for 23 years, closed in 1988.

There were other harmonica-related gigs. Linz endorsed the Hohner Harmonica Co. He did the winter banquet circuit, and to this day, happily signs autographs, Phil "Harmonica" Linz, when asked. And yes, he still owns harmonicas and really enjoys playing them.

A Baltimore native, Linz was a Yankee bonus baby, debuting in 1962. He spent four years with the Bombers, even contributing a pair of home runs in the 1964 World Series against St. Louis, perhaps making up a tad for his impromptu harmonica solo on the bus.

Linz played two years with the Phillies and another two back in New York with the Mets, where he closed out his harmonica-playing, banjo-hitting eight-year major league career in 1968. His lifetime batting average: .235.

THE LIP GETS SOME ... WELL, LIP
46 East 61st Street

The most hated Giant of all time? Easy. John McGraw. No debate there. The most hated Dodger? Take a minute or two, because the team was so laughable for so many years that it was hard for them to inspire much loathing.

But with the late 1930s came a new Dodger front office led by Larry MacPhail and the Bums got good. And MacPhail's choice for manager: a feisty St. Louis Cardinal "Gashouse Gang" member-turned-Hollywood groupie named Leo Ernest Durocher.

Durocher joined the Dodgers in 1939, and, in 1941, directed them to their first World Series in more than two decades. An eager cologne user and a wearer of expensive suits, inspired perhaps by his close friend, the actor George Raft, Durocher was decidedly un-Brooklyn. Indeed, he didn't even live in the borough, but in a tony Upper East Side apartment at 41 East 61st Street and in Beverly Hills during the off-season. But he helped turn the Dodgers into winners and all was forgiven.

Make that almost forgiven. In one of the stranger court cases of New York's baseball history, Durocher was indicted in early 1946 on charges of assaulting a 22-year-old Brooklyn veteran in an altercation under the Ebbets Field grandstand.

The incident took place June 9, 1945 when the Dodger manager became aware of insults hurled his way by the veteran, John Christian. Admitting at the trial that baseball fans "have a right to holler at the game," Durocher claimed that Christian had crossed the line: He was "very noisy and using profane language" in heckling the Dodgers.

That's when things heated up. Hearing Christian's abuse, Durocher then asked Joseph Moore, an Ebbets Field policeman and a co-defendant in the trial, to bring him under the grandstand after the game. Christian said Durocher then attacked him and fractured his jaw. The manager disagreed, saying he admonished him for his behavior, but that Christian had slipped on a wet walkway and hurt himself in the fall.

The jury agreed, and on April 25, 1946 in a noisy ballpark-like atmosphere, a Kings County jury took only 38 minutes to acquit both Durocher and Moore. The decision brought a burst of applause from the more than 200 fans and well-wishers who crowded the sixth-floor of the Central Courts Building, Brooklyn.

Durocher's reply on the proceedings: a terse "no comment." He offered a more symbolic opinion two years later on July 16, 1948, when he was fired by the Dodgers in his ninth season as Brooklyn manager. After the firing, his wife, the actress Laraine Day, removed the rugs and photographs from his tastefully-decorated Ebbets Field office, all except for a single item: an autographed picture of the man who fired Durocher, Branch Rickey. It remained, hanging over the toilet.

How surprising then that it was the Giants, of all teams, which then called Durocher to see if he was interested in heading uptown to manage at the Polo Grounds. Lending further irony was the fact that both teams were tied for fourth place at the time.

So Durocher became a Giant, a truth hard to stomach for its fans. Earlier that spring, Durocher had chimed in with his famous comment that then-Giant manager Mel Ott was a great man — but "nice guys finish last." That said of a Giant hero and future Hall of Famer, who, in 1926, as a 16-year-old phenom, had been regarded as "John McGraw's baby."

Dodger fans adjusted accordingly, turning their admiration for Durocher to venom. He became, in official Brooklynese as "Da-ROACH-a." But he made the Giants a winner too — helped by a young Alabamian named Willie

Mays — and managed them, in his seven-and-a-half years at the helm, to two National League pennants and the 1954 World Championship.

Years later, he would manage both the Cubs and the Astros. There were no more pennants, but as usual, Durocher had the last laugh: In 1994, he was posthumously elected to the Baseball Hall of Fame.

SPORTS WRITING GETS RESPECT
The life and times of Grantland Rice
1158 5th Avenue (& East 97th Street)

"When the great scorer comes to mark against your name," the august sportswriter Grantland Rice once wrote. "He'll write not 'won' or 'lost,' but how you played the game."

Rice played it with elegance and eloquence, distinguishing a profession that many consider slightly below pond scum in the great food chain of life. Although not generally known as a baseball writer, Rice considered all sports his beat, giving the profession a scholarly shot in the arm.

Born in Tennessee and a Vanderbilt graduate, Rice hit New York in 1911 as a reporter with *The Evening Mail* after spending several years on papers in Nashville, Atlanta, and Cleveland. National fame came later, as a reporter for *The New York Herald* and finally, with syndication.

Rice was a writer of extraordinary range. At a time when many reporters called in their reports to the newsroom, preferring to have somebody else write the story, Rice typed a syndicated column, wrote books, published poetry, and collaborated in a series of one-reel sports films, including one on boxing, which won a 1943 Academy Award.

Golf was Rice's acknowledged favorite sport. Yet, he is perhaps best known for a piece of football reporting — a 1924 description of Knute Rockne's Notre Dame backfield as "The Four Horsemen," a nickname that caught America's fancy.

Rice's favorite athlete of all the thousands he saw? A toss-up between Babe Ruth and Ty Cobb. He couldn't decide. And he was convinced beyond a doubt that Ruth had pointed to the flagpole in right field during the "called shot" game of the 1932 World Series in Chicago, a moment he called his greatest thrill in more than 50 years as a reporter.

To mark those 50 years, an anonymous donor established a Grantland

Rice Fellowship in journalism at Columbia University. Rice died in 1954 at the age of 73.

BASEBALL AS LITERATURE
The short, eventful life of Ring Lardner
25 East End Avenue (& East 80th Street)

When Ring Lardner was a young man, he wrote down the three consuming ambitions of his life:

- Write stories for magazines and get paid for it;
- Get a play produced; and,
- Watch a lot of baseball.

His was an abbreviated life marked by journalistic and literary triumph. Lardner accomplished all three, banging out short stories and plays, his long face adorned with a trademark skimmer on his head and a cigarette dangling from his lips. And each step of the way, there was a lot of baseball to watch, report on for Chicago papers, and to write about in what became a part of popular early 20th-century American literature.

Baseball was the link. A Michigan native, Lardner covered baseball as a reporter in South Bend, Indiana, Chicago, St. Louis, and Boston; so much for ambition number three. That encouraged him to write short stories on baseball for magazines, and publish them as collections under titles such as *The Love Nest*, *You Know Me Al* and *How To Write Short Stories*.

Take the latter, which included a story called "Alibi Ike" and offered an insight into Lardner's success. It stemmed in part from the pressure of turning out a daily column for *The Chicago Tribune*. Sitting in hotel lobbies, trains, and dugouts, Lardner took in the banter and chatter of ballplayers and penned a fictional story, complete with period slang, double negatives, and other intentionally ungrammatical flourishes, about the conversation between two teammates in a Pullman Car poker game.

Skillfully presented, it was the natural language of the generally uneducated ballplayers of the era and it was a big success. Take this, from "Alibi Ike," published in 1915:

"What do you think of Alibi Ike?" ast Carey.

"Who's that," I says.

"This here Farrell in the outfield," says Carey.

"He looks like he could hit," I says.

"Yes," says Carey, "but he can't hit near as good as he can apologize."

Once, for the World Series, Lardner invented a Giants' pitcher who narrated the action in this distinctive style. He did the same for *The Saturday Evening Post* and other magazines, after moving, in 1919, to Great Neck, Long Island. That took care of ambition number one.

Moving east led to the completion of Lardner's second ambition — producing plays. Baseball to the rescue again — in 1922, the Ziegfeld Follies featured none other than Will Rogers as Lardner's thick-headed pitcher. Then, in 1928, Walter Huston appeared in Lardner's *Elmer the Great*. And Elmer? Yup, a dim-witted pitcher. And when talkies came in, Joe E. Brown starred in both *Elmer the Great* and *Alibi Ike* — which became his signature roles.

But by then, Lardner was a sick man, suffering from a heart ailment. Choosing city living, he and his wife, Ellis, took an apartment in September 1931 at the 15-story "Yorkgate" at 25 East End Avenue. Just out of the hospital, Lardner experienced a further decline and moved back to the hospital after only six months. He died in 1933 at 48.

Lardner's legacy endures. In the preface to *The American Language*, George Jean Nathan and H. L. Mencken, a man not noted for plaudits to others, wrote:

> "Its discovery (the speech of the masses) had to wait until Ring W. Lardner, a Chicago newspaper reporter ... In his grotesque tales of baseball players, so immediately and so deservedly successful, Lardner reports the common speech not only with humor, but with the utmost accuracy. His writings are a mine of authentic Americana; his services to etymology incomparable."

YANKEE ARCHITECT — COLONEL JACOB RUPPERT
1116 5th Avenue (& East 93rd Street) ... then 1120 5th Avenue

Hard to believe, but there was a time when the baseball lords were, for the most part, cerebral, elegant men of the moneyed, sporting set. Such a man was Colonel Jacob Ruppert, the beer baron whose shrewd business acumen and wealth turned the Yankees from laughingstocks of the American League to the nation's most storied, professional sports franchise.

Ruppert, the aristocratic New York gentleman of leisure and business, would be out of fashion today. In his 20s, he became manager of the Ruppert Brewing Company (1693 3rd Avenue and 93rd Street), founded in 1851 by his father. Within a few years, he tripled production.

Later, he served in the National Guard, where he was named colonel. At 32, Ruppert was elected to the first of his four terms in Congress, where he served as a Tammany Democrat on the silk-stocking Republican Upper East Side.

Ruppert was a lifelong bachelor, directing a staff of servants that included a butler, maid, valet, cook, and laundress in a 12-room mansion on the northwest side of 5th Avenue and 93rd Street. Built at the turn of the century, the mansion was among the first such grand houses in a neighborhood of small farms and houses.

It came with large grounds in the back that featured peach and apple orchards. They were protected by two watchdogs and an iron-spoked fence. Among those regularly braving the fence and dogs was a young Harpo Marx, who grew up a few blocks away, at 179 East 93rd Street, between Lexington and 3rd avenues.

Ruppert was introduced to baseball in 1915, when he and another colonel, the resoundingly-named Tillinghast L'Hommedieu Huston, bought the Yankees, then the Highlanders, for $450,000. At the time, the team was a pathetic stepchild to its landlords, the lordly Giants, the toast of New York, with whom they shared the Polo Grounds and were nearing the end of a costly talent war with the upstart Federal League. "For $450,000," the colonel said years later, "we got an orphan ballclub, without a home of its own, without players of outstanding ability, without prestige."

Actually, Ruppert's efforts to secure a ballclub had started just after the turn of the century, when he had tried to buy the Giants, but gave up when Andrew Freedman rejected his offer and sold the team, in 1903, to John T. Brush. In 1912, the colonel considered buying the Chicago Cubs, but turned the offer down. "I wasn't interested in anything so far from Broadway," he said.

Ruppert said that the idea of buying New York's American League franchise had never been a long-term obsession. When he took over, he had seen them play only a few games — and then, "only because Walter Johnson pitched or Ty Cobb was a participant."

He and Huston bought the team anyway and wasted little time in making them winners. Cementing their success was the arrival, in 1920, of a young slugger named Ruth; and the opening, in 1923, of baseball's grandest palace, Yankee Stadium.

By then, the colonel was the Yankees' sole owner, having bought out Huston in 1922. And while Ruppert always had many interests, the Yankees became his consuming passion. That interest was personal and profound; at the same time, Ruppert expected big things from his "boys," as he called them.

As he told Lefty Gomez when the star pitcher signed with the Yanks in 1937: "Now, go out and win 30 games." (Gomez would win a paltry 21 games, which led the AL that year.)

Ruppert still managed to squeeze in those other passions. He yachted, and, in 1933, sponsored the second Byrd Antarctic Expedition. At his country estate in the Dutchess County hamlet of Garrison along the Hudson River, Ruppert raised St. Bernards and Boston terriers, kept a racing stable, and even a score of monkeys.

The colonel's death in 1939 at the age of 71 prompted a heartfelt outpouring of affection. Some 15,000 people lined the streets around St. Patrick's Cathedral, where a Mass was held. Mourners ranged from celebrities to the rank-and-file, lending what newspapers of the day described as the kind of crowd who belonged at the ballpark.

As a man with a distinct love of life, Ruppert would probably have approved. He is buried near Lou Gehrig in Kensico Cemetery, Westchester County.

HELP FOR FALLEN HEROES
Smithers Center
56 East 93rd Street (& Madison Avenue)

In Toots Shor's day, ballplayers drank a lot, lost control, and well, that was part of being a ballplayer. Drinking too much was not only socially acceptable; it was part of the game's machismo.

Back then, the 45-room limestone Renaissance Revival mansion on East 93rd Street was the scene of some raucous parties as the home of theatrical producer Billy Rose, who lived there from 1956 to his death in 1965.

Ah, how times change: In more recent years, the mansion has served as the Smithers Alcoholism and Rehabilitation Center. Quite a contrast to a time when nobody realized the price people can pay for alcoholism.

Darryl Strawberry and Dwight Gooden paid the price. These two Met stars of the 1980s, along with Joan Kennedy and Truman Capote, were among a star-studded lineup to check into Smithers to get their lives back on track. Strawberry's standard 28-day stay at Smithers in February 1990 came as a thunderbolt, giving the Center untold publicity on the sports pages and searing it into the nation's conscience.

In Strawberry's case, the telltale signs of addiction were there — games missed because of dubious injuries, lackluster performances, and run-ins with teammates. No question that Strawberry, while the Mets' most talented player of the 1980s, never reached the greatness predicted for him on arriving in New York in 1983. The same went for Gooden, who followed the spectacular success of his 1984 Cy Young year at age 20 with arm problems, troubles with the law, and similar tales of substance abuse.

None of that mattered at Smithers: "It's being able to see yourself reflected in someone very different that helps bring home the disease," the Center's director, Dr. Anne Geller, said in the wake of the Strawberry/Gooden publicity.

The Smithers' treatment was modeled on group therapy and the principles of Alcoholics Anonymous. Anyone viewed as less than forthcoming was upbraided by other members of the group in what Strawberry and Gooden called a strict, uncompromising course of treatment.

Both players emerged from treatment and returned to baseball. Sadly, they suffered relapses, with Strawberry later treated at the Betty Ford Clinic and both men suspended for further violations of the major league drug policy. Neither ever came close to matching their earlier success.

Smithers had problems too, but of the financial kind. In 1995, it was transferred by its owner, St. Luke's-Roosevelt Hospital, to the hospital's Roosevelt Division, at 58th Street and West 10th Avenue.

COLUMNIST FOR THE AGES — JIMMY CANNON SPEAKS
440 East 56th Street

"The people who write the pieces up front in the paper consider this a wasted life," Jimmy Cannon once said of his long career as New York sports columnist for the ages. "It's true that I have solved little of my country's dilemmas, but the statesmen also have failed. I function in glad places."

So spoke the most memorable New York tabloid sports columnist of all. Jimmy Cannon's prose wasn't elegant like Red Smith or Grantland Rice. As a longtime columnist for *The New York Post, The Daily News,* and *The American,* he was Damon Runyon with a splash of the poet.

Cannon's men were guys. Women were dames. His heroes were men's men like Joe DiMaggio and Mickey Mantle. And his language was that of the working man, for whom his periodically-titled columns entitled "Nobody Asked Me, But ... " were geared. Those columns — one-or two-line bursts of opinion about baseball, life, the pursuit of happiness and anything else that came to his charmingly-insightful mind — were Cannon's trademark. Some samples:

- "Ballplayers who are first into the dining room are usually last in the averages."
- "Guys who fiddle with the knot in their necktie are bad listeners."
- "I haven't the courage to smoke in bed."
- "Nothing improves an actress's diction more than marrying money."
- "I never met a man from Sandusky, Ohio."

Cannon covered all sports, focusing on baseball and boxing. Never married, his world was a macho one of athletes, actors, and bartenders, of nights that stretched into dawn, cigars, and club hopping. His great friends were DiMaggio and Frank Sinatra, with whom he often prowled nightclubs like the Stork Club and shared meals at Toots Shor.

"I like my life as a columnist," Cannon once said, "because a columnist is always permitted to get off his chest whatever is bothering him. Because of that, I have no need for a psychiatrist."

Born in Greenwich Village and the son of a Tammany Hall politician, Cannon enjoyed writing of the ballplayers and horse-players of his youth. In his early career, Cannon covered news, ranging from the Lindbergh kidnapping case to the Korean War; it was during the Lindbergh trial that he caught the eye of Runyon himself, the Hearst columnist, and became a sports columnist at *The American.*

By the 1950s, he was king of New York tabloid sports columnists, believed to be the country's highest paid, as well. So, Cannon changed his lifestyle and moved from the Edison Hotel, where he lived for many years, to the high rent district — an apartment on Central Park West, then to another near Sutton Place, and finally to East 56th Street, where he died in 1973 at the age of 63.

"You're Mickey Mantle," Jimmy Cannon wrote in 1953. "You're a bubble-gum kid in a chew-tobacco league. The climate of your youth varies as though all the seasons of existence pass through your life in a single week. On how many hot summer days have you shivered with the wonder of being Mickey Mantle? But often the sun sets before noon."

Yup, Cannon could be eloquent. On the other hand, "I burn," he once wrote, "when I buy a bartender a drink and he takes a cigar."

BROADWAY JOE BEDS DOWN
370 East 76th Street (near 1st Avenue)

Broadway Joe? As in Namath? We know; he played quarterback for the Jets. Just seeing if you're paying attention.

Namath, the playboy football star — well, he did play baseball in high school back in Beaver Falls, Pennsylvania, okay? — lived in this modern high-rise apartment building called "Newport East" in the groovy, late-1960s. A real chick pad. Bet he even he had a lava lamp, which he may have shared with Joe Pepitone. Peace, man.

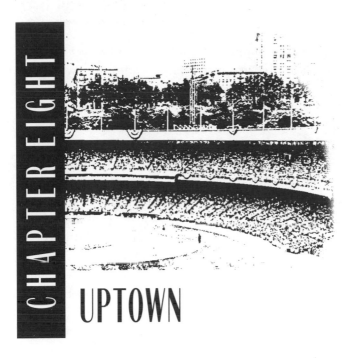

CHAPTER EIGHT

UPTOWN

"Just when my fellows learn to hit in this ballpark, they're going to tear it down."

— Casey Stengel, Mets manager, on the Polo Grounds, 1965

FIRE AND BRIMSTONE
Billy Sunday preaches the gospel
Fairgrounds, West 168th Street & Broadway

So what does a foot-stomping, hair-raising, fire-and-brimstone preacher have to do with baseball? Plenty, in the case of Billy Sunday, whose evangelical routines included winding up like a pitcher and slamming a fist into his other hand to demonstrate what he called a "fastball to the devil."

William A. Sunday was the most prominent evangelist of his day — a former big-leaguer who became the Billy Graham and Oral Roberts of the teens, '20s, and '30s. Sunday's crowning achievement in a long career as a man of the cloth just may have been when he is said to have converted 68,000 believers one spring evening at an Upper Manhattan tabernacle.

Sunday found The Lord in the summer of 1886 while sitting on the curb of State and Van Buren streets in Chicago, in the midst of carousing with three fellow members of his Chicago White Stockings. After hopping in and out of State Street saloons most of the day, Sunday was captivated by a gospel wagon that drove up and held a service.

As Sunday related in his autobiography, he was so moved by the same hymns he used to hear his mother sing in his hometown of Ames, Iowa that he turned to his teammates and said, "Boys, I bid the old life good-bye." And just like that, his life took a new direction.

Sunday kept on playing, compiling a modest .248 average and a reputation as a base stealer in an eight-year career as a part-timer with the White Stockings and the Pirates that ended in 1891. Then, after apprenticing with the eminent evangelist J. Wilbur Chapman, he became a full-time preacher and hit the road — winning converts and condemning everything from "whiskey kings" to suffragettes, slackers, and Sunday baseball.

Sunday's most memorable night in New York was perhaps the most significant of a more than lucrative, 40-year career of spreading the Gospel. It happened April 1, 1917 as Sunday preached to thousands in a low, rambling structure of brick and wood at grounds just off 168th Street. It's where Hilltop Park once stood and Columbia University Presbyterian Hospital Medical Center now stands.

In its first incarnation as Hilltop Park, or the Hilltop, the grounds housed the late, nearly-great New York Highlanders, starting in 1903, the team's debut year. The park was also home for six weeks in 1911 to the Giants, who played there after a fire at the Polo Grounds. When the Polo Grounds were rebuilt, the Giants left, taking the Highlanders with them after 1912. The Hilltop was demolished in 1914.

A few details on Hilltop Park: It was a wooden stadium carved out of solid rock on the ramparts of Washington Heights. It offered a commanding view of the Hudson River and the New Jersey Palisades to the west and a swamp along Broadway to the east that shortened the 400-foot right-field line. However, center field was a hefty 542 feet from the plate, while right field, a more reachable 400 feet, was notable only for a huge sign advertising "Bull Durham" tobacco; shaped like, well, a bull, the sign was twice the height of the rest of the fence.

For the record, the American League Highlanders arrived at the Hilltop in 1902 after a mysterious case of intrigue and skullduggery that brought them from Baltimore. Ostensibly under the auspices of one Joe Gordon, the future Yankees were really the property of two gamblers and political fixers, "Big" Bill Devery and his partner, Frank Ferrell, who was reputed to own 250 pool halls and almost as many politicians.

But it was only with Sunday that real crowds ventured to these northern confines of Manhattan. "Measured in terms of claimed converts and net profits ... Billy Sunday was the greatest high-pressure and mass-conversion Christian evangel that America, or the world, has ever known," *The Times* wrote.

His exhortations usually lasted an hour and borrowed liberally from baseball. At times, he posed like a pitcher winding up. To illustrate a sinner coming home for salvation, Sunday would slide headfirst on the stage, groping with his hands for home plate — perhaps forgetting for a moment that he had struck out his first 13 times at bat in the majors.

The converts came and Sunday became a millionaire. His 1917 appearance in New York marked the pinnacle of his success, wrote *The Times*. "Although a wave of revivalism has swept the country on the heels of every economic depression in its history," the paper theorized, "there has not yet ever been any indication of a evangelist to even approach the records by the old-time ballplayer."

Sunday stayed away from New York for 16 years after his 1917 revival, choosing to spread his message in smaller cities. He returned in January 1934 for four weeks of "real preaching," as he called it, divided equally between Calvary Baptist Church (123 West 57th Street) and Cornell Memorial Methodist Church (281 West 76th Street).

And although Sunday disliked baseball on the Sabbath, he was a fan 'til the end. In 1934, a year before his death, he was asked for his all-time all stars. After considerable thought, he produced the following:

    1B: Hal Chase or Lou Gehrig;
    2B: Tony Lazzeri;
    SS: Honus Wagner;
    3B: can't think of one;
     C: Buck Ewing;
    OF: Babe Ruth, Ty Cobb, Tris Speaker, and Chuck Klein; and,
     P: Christy Mathewson, John Clarkson, and Rube Waddell.

Sunday died November 6, 1935 at the age of 72 of a heart attack in Chicago. Meanwhile, the grounds where he had held forth on that spring evening years before had become the hospital in 1925. In 1993, a bronze plaque marking the exact spot — more or less — of the Hilltop's home plate was placed in the hospital garden.

ROY CAMPANELLA — BUSINESSMAN
Roy Campanella Liquors
198 West 134th Street (& 7th Avenue)

Baseball players worry constantly of injury — tear a rotor cuff, lose some pop off the fastball, and faster than you can say "Herb Score," the phenom has vanished from The Show and is back home running the car wash.

Roy Campanella felt that way — not about the tragic 1958 car accident that left him a quadriplegic — but at least when he was playing, about things like hamstring pulls, painful foul balls off the foot, swollen joints and other hazards of life behind the plate. In fact, it was an eye injury that prompted Campanella to find a business to give his large family some security beyond baseball. The business: Roy Campanella Liquors at West 134th Street and 7th Avenue in Harlem.

As a catcher, Campanella suffered his share of injuries that made him think of work beyond baseball, he admits in his 1959 memoir, *It's Good To Be Alive*. Actually, the Dodger catcher got the eye injury during the winter of 1951 when he was burned and temporarily blinded by a malfunctioning water heater at home in St. Albans, Queens.

At Jamaica Hospital, Campanella's eyes were covered with black patches and his face was bandaged. "The Doc said my eyes would be all right, but suppose he was wrong," Campanella writes. "Or even if I didn't go blind, would my eyes be good enough for baseball? Gee, what else could I do?"

At that point, Campanella says, he prayed, making a solemn promise, "…that if He allowed me to see again, I'd do my best to get into some kind of business that would give my family some security after my baseball days were over … And I kept that promise."

Campanella recovered quickly from the eye injury, and the following season, 1951, won the first of his three NL Most Valuable Player awards. Even so, the injury had jarred him into preparing for life beyond baseball; within a month or two, thanks to an advance from Dodger owner Walter O'Malley, Campanella opened a package liquor store in Flushing, Queens.

On September 6, 1951, Campanella moved the store to Harlem. With his name in big neon lights, four clerks, and three gleaming new cash registers, he kicked off the store with a gala opening that was attended by Jackie Robinson, Don Newcombe, Nat King Cole, Sugar Ray Robinson, and Archie Moore, all friends.

Ironically, it was after leaving the store on the snowy evening of January 27, 1958 that Campanella was involved in the horrible car crash that left him paralyzed. He sold the store a short time later, eventually moving to Los Angeles as a Dodger coach.

REST IN PEACE, RAY CHAPMAN
St. Lawrence Hospital
457 West 163rd Street

"In the course of an average nine-inning baseball game, there are approximately 200 to 250 balls thrown by the pitchers," writes Mike Sowell in his superb 1985 book, *The Pitch That Killed.*

"There have been roughly 1,200 baseball games played each season for more than 100 years since big-league baseball began in 1871," he writes. "That adds up to about $1/4$ of a million balls hurled toward the plate annually. All told, there have been more than 25 million pitches thrown to batters. Only one of them killed a man."

The dead man was Ray Chapman, the Cleveland Indians' star shortstop, who crumpled to the ground August 26, 1920 after being struck in the head by a pitched ball in the fifth inning of a tense game against the Yankees at the Polo Grounds. Chapman's death at St. Lawrence Hospital from a fractured skull at 4:40 AM, August 27, some 12 hours after the accident, made him the first and only casualty on a major-league diamond.

Chapman's beaning took place, according to the papers, as "he was leaning over in a crouching position," when Carl Mays let go with one of his patented underhanded pitches that rose high and tight. The ball struck Chapman on the left side of his skull, with the awful sound of the impact heard throughout the park.

Mays called the ball, a "sailer." At the plate, Chapman, who had stood motionless for a brief moment after being struck, sunk slowly to the ground, his features twisted in pain. Behind the plate, umpire Thomas Connolly looked at the ballplayer, blood rushing from his left ear, and took off toward the Polo Grounds' grandstand, yelling for a doctor.

Players from both teams rushed toward the plate, where Chapman, not yet unconscious, struggled to his feet. Enter Dr. Joseph Cascio of St. Lawrence Hospital, a spectator who rushed to the field at the urging of Connolly. First, Cascio called for ice to be applied to Chapman's head. The still-conscious Chapman begged off efforts at assistance and began walking across the infield toward the center-field clubhouse. Helped by several of his Cleveland team-mates, Chapman approached second base, before his knees buckled and he was carried the rest of the way.

Inside the clubhouse, Cascio and others quickly determined that Chapman should undergo an immediate operation to relieve the pressure on his brain. An ambulance was already en route from St. Lawrence Hospital, less than a half-mile away. With Cleveland players gathered around, Cascio assured them that the injury was serious, but probably not fatal.

Before losing consciousness, Chapman tried to speak but couldn't. Arriving at St. Lawrence, he turned to a friend, John Henry, who had accompanied him in the ambulance. "For God's sake," he said, "don't call Kate. But if you do, tell her I'm all right."

Those were the last words Ray Chapman ever spoke. Kate was Kathleen Daly, Chapman's wife of less than a year and the daughter of a wealthy Toledo building company owner who was grooming the ballplayer to one day enter the business.

The 29-year-old Chapman was more than a good player at his peak. His gentle humor and pleasant demeanor made him popular with his teammates and would have been a tremendous business asset. The accident came amidst the Indians' finest season in years; with Chapman hitting .303, his best average ever, and the team in first place, percentage points ahead of the Yankees and White Sox. With future Hall-of-Famer Joe Sewell replacing Chapman, Cleveland went on that year to win the pennant and defeat the Dodgers in the World Series.

Back at St. Lawrence, emergency surgery on Chapman started at 10 PM, as his anxious teammates prowled the lobby of the Ansonia Hotel, where they were staying. X-rays confirmed the accident was more serious than originally thought. Chapman had sustained a two-armed fracture extending 3 1/2 inches to the base of his skull on the left side, leaving a piece of bone pressing the brain. More ominously, his pulse was dropping rapidly.

The operating team consisted of Drs. M. J. Horan and T. D. Merrigan of the St. Lawrence staff, with Cascio, and Drs. A. A. White and J. E. Quinn as attendants. It was no use — symptoms of paralysis and blood clots began forming. In its entirety, the operation took 75 minutes; Chapman died several hours later.

The news hit the baseball world like a sledgehammer. The next day's game was canceled and thousands of fans, unaware that Chapman had died, were turned away from the park by league officials and detectives, who told them what had happened. Instinctively, hundreds of the fans went to James McGowan's nearby funeral home at 1879 Amsterdam Avenue (and West 153rd Street), where Chapman's body had been taken.

Mays took the news hard, but not on the surface. Several Indian players took exception to his seeming indifference to Chapman's plight in the moments after the beaning; they said he just came down off the mound, not joining the gathering around home plate, and yelled to the umpire to throw him the ball for the next batter.

In fact, Mays had considered contacting Chapman's widow to express his condolences, but was advised against it. Similarly, he decided against a visit to see the body at McGowan's Funeral Home, saying that "the sight of his silent form would haunt me as long as I live." It did, and Mays, never popular with the teammates to start with, died a broken and lonely man in 1971, bitter to the end that despite his 207 big-league wins, all he was remembered for was throwing the pitch that killed a man.

In Cleveland, Chapman received a hero's funeral and was buried in Lake View Cemetery, resting spot for the city's elite. The following February, Chapman's daughter, Rae Marie, was born, her birth receiving a eight-column, 72-point headline across the top of the front page of *The Cleveland News*. Despite the heralded start, her life and that of her mother would not be easy.

Rae Marie was 2-years-old when Kate remarried. Her second husband was California oil executive, Joseph P. McMahon, and the couple had a son as well. But in 1928, Kate died unexpectedly in California at 34; the reasons given ranged from suicide to complications from a nervous breakdown.

Rae Marie died almost a year later, from measles at the age of eight. Call it the final chapter in one of baseball's most tragic stories.

BASEBALL'S FIRST TELECAST
Baker Field
West 215th Street & Broadway

The history books tell us that major league baseball made its television debut August 26, 1939. It was at Ebbets Field, where the "two prying electric 'eyes,'"as *The Times* put it, of NBC station, W2XBS, broadcast the double-header split between the Dodgers and Reds.

But it was more than a year before that, on May 17, 1938, in the improbable setting of a Columbia-Princeton game at Baker Field, that baseball made its official television debut. At the time, "radio camera" as it was called then, was spanking new, having made a sizable stir just days before with the televised opening of President Franklin Roosevelt at the World's Fair in Flushing, Queens.

NBC station W2XBS broadcast that first game as well, using a lone camera and a $150,000 mobile van behind first base that bounced the signal to a transmitter atop the Empire State Building, from where the game was beamed to viewers in a 50-mile radius. Veteran NBC announcer Bill Stern brought the few hundred viewers the action of the second game of a doubleheader, won by Princeton, 2-1, in 10 innings.

It wasn't memorable. The single camera gave off a constant image of fuzzy white and showed no more than three players at once. Typically, the camera followed the pitcher's windup, quickly swiveling to the plate and the batter, as he ran the bases. "Too often when the specklike ball was struck," sniffed Orrin E. Dunlap, Jr. in *The Times*, "it ne'er was found, like a white pinpoint it sailed off the screen."

But even Dunlap realized the potential reach of the new medium. "This photographic art is too young to expect it to 'paint' electrically ... a panoramic view, although there is little doubt that the future will bring the complete picture." NBC program manager Thomas Hutchinson already recognized the potential, saying the telecast game "signal[ed] the beginning of an important development in the art of pictures through the air, for outdoor sports will furnish much of the most interesting material we could televise."

Dunlap urged NBC to use several cameras to help viewers follow the action. Evidently, NBC was listening, and for the Dodgers-Reds game, used two cameras this time — one near the third-base dugout for closeups of the batter, and the other in a second-tier behind home, giving an expansive view of the field.

This time, the newspapers were impressed — sort of. "At times, it was possible to catch a fleeting glimpse of the ball," a critic wrote. Like the earlier game, the signal was relayed to the Empire State Building transmitter to the 50-mile service area. Only three commercials were shown — for Ivory Soap, Mobil Oil, and Wheaties.

And that game's broadcaster? Red Barber, the regular Dodger radio broadcaster and member of the Broadcaster's Wing at the Hall of Fame.

HOME AWAY FROM HOME FOR THE NEGRO LEAGUES
The Woodside Hotel
2424 7th Avenue (& West 141st Street)

Much is made of the long bus rides by teams of the Negro Leagues — how they barnstormed, slept in the bus and stayed away from restaurants that wouldn't serve them, particularly in the Jim Crow South.

Not so in Harlem, the spiritual and cultural capital of Black America through the 1920s, '30s, and '40s, and home, for at least a time, to the era's most influential black writers, intellectuals, and musicians. And not so at the Woodside Hotel, Uptown's home-away-from-home to storied Negro League teams like the Pittsburgh Crawfords, Homestead Grays, Kansas City Monarchs, and Baltimore Elite Giants.

The Woodside was central for Negro League teams, which played in Yankee Stadium, the Polo Grounds, and Ebbets Field when the major leaguers were on the road. And, like most hotels with visiting baseball teams, the Woodside's lobby became a kind of unofficial gathering spot for people associated with baseball. That was particularly so with Negro Leagues, when both teams often stayed at the hotel.

And that was certainly the case one summer day in 1945, when Roy Campanella of the Elite Giants called on Jackie Robinson, a rookie shortstop with the Kansas City Monarchs and better known at the time as a former UCLA running back. As Campanella related in his 1959 memoir, *It's Good To Be Alive*, it was in a chance meeting with Robinson in the Woodside lobby when he first learned of the plan to integrate the major leagues.

Already that summer, Campanella had paid a visit to Dodger general manager Branch Rickey to talk contract. At the time, an unwritten rule prohibited blacks from the major leagues, keeping big-league baseball lily-white.

Unknown to Campanella, Rickey had already met with Robinson. But unlike his meeting with Robinson, Rickey hadn't quite leveled with Campanella, telling the Elite Giant catcher that he was interested in signing him for a prospective team called the Brooklyn Brown Dodgers, to play in a new Negro League. But Rickey, as Campanella reveals in his book, had something a little different in mind for Robinson.

Up in Campanella's room at the Woodside in a one-on-one game of gin rummy — half a cent a point — Robinson spilled the beans. The book: "'I signed,'" Jackie said quietly. "'But it's a secret. Mr. Rickey told me to keep it quiet, so you got to promise not to tell anybody.'

"Sure okay, I won't say anything," Campanella said. "It's okay for you, I guess. You've only been in the league one year ... I've got kids to think about. You can take a chance with a new league, and it don't make much difference. But it's like I told Mr. Rickey, I can't afford to.

"Jackie waited until I was finished," Campanella wrote. "Then he picked up the cards from the table and shuffled them idly. 'I didn't sign with the Brown Dodgers,' he said quickly. 'I'm going to play for Montreal,' (Brooklyn's top minor league team).

"Jackie wasn't calm now. His voice was loud with excitement. He knew he was revealing something important, something eventful. He watched me carefully, waiting for my reaction.

"'What do you mean, Montreal?' I asked.

"'I'm going to be the first Negro in organized baseball,' Jackie said. 'I'm flying up to Montreal tomorrow for the official signing ceremony. It's going to be a big thing — cameras and everything ... Do you realize what this means Campy? It's the end of Jim Crow in baseball.'"

Robinson signed the contract and the rest is in the record books. Campanella, gracious to the end, gave Robinson his word of silence until the announcement was made, adding, "I'm glad for you, Jackie, real glad."

"Don't be afraid of nothing," he told Robinson. "You're a good ballplayer, you'll make it."

A year or so later, Campanella made it too, signing with the Dodgers, and ending up, like Robinson, in the Hall of Fame. That's in the record books too.

END OF THE LINE FOR HAMMERIN' HANK
Bill's Cafe
3508 Broadway

Got to admit it — the stick-up man had a good line.

"Do you know who I am?" he asked one day in 1961, after walking into a Harlem bar named Bill's Cafe, revealing a .22-caliber pistol and demanding money from the register.

When the bartender said he didn't, the man replied, "Good, this is a stick-up. Put the money on the bar." Arrested within a few minutes, one block away with $37 in his pocket, he was charged with armed robbery, assault, and carrying a concealed weapon.

He was Hank Thompson, the talented but troubled former New York Giants' star of the 1950s. Stick to baseball and Thompson — he and Monte Irvin were the Giants' first black players — could carry a team with his potent bat. It was off the field that he had problems.

Thompson said later he had robbed the bar for transportation money to get back to see his mother in Fresno, California. Thanks to the intervention of Giants' owner Horace Stoneham and Commissioner Ford Frick, he got a slap on the wrist after the hold-up — probation. Two years later, Thompson got into a heap more trouble — this time, robbing a Houston liquor store of $270. He was caught within hours, but this time, the verdict was more extreme — Thompson was sentenced to 10 years in the Texas Penitentiary in Huntsville.

For Thompson, it was the climax to an aimless, troubled personal life. On the field, the agile third baseman's stats were impressive — known variably as Hammerin' Hank; and, with teammate, Bobby Thomson, as $1/2$ of the "Tom-Tom Twins," he hit 129 home runs in a nine-year career, including his best, 26, in 1954. In the '54 Series, in which the Giants swept Cleveland, Thompson hit safely in all four games, batting .364.

Off the field, the stats told a different story. The Houston heist led to his seventh arrest, which included his first at age 11 when he was caught stealing jewelry near his home in Dallas. Thompson would kill a man in a bar room brawl in 1948, assault a New York cab driver in 1953, and later admit that although he earned a quarter-million dollars from baseball, he threw it all away.

Thompson still had good years in New York. His lifetime average was .267 and, along with Irvin and Willie Mays, he became part of the first all-black major league outfield. And batting against Don Newcombe, he was the major leagues' first black batter to face a black pitcher. In 1957, after being sent to Minneapolis in the American Association, he quit baseball at 31.

It was in the Texas prison where Thompson faced reality. Attributing many of his problems to alcohol abuse, he joined Alcoholics Anonymous and became a mentor to first time offenders. And it was there that Thompson spoke up about his life, in a 1965 *Sport Magazine* article, "How I Wrecked My Life — How I Hope To Save It."

"The only person to blame is me," Thompson wrote. "So if I blame drink, I'm the guy ... who did the drinking ... Don't ask me to blame society, or the fact that I'm a Negro in a white world, or the fact that I have a grade school education, or the fact that I was washed up as a major leaguer when I was 31 years old. I'm the one who kicked society in the teeth."

Paroled in 1967, Thompson tried to get his life together. He finally got to Fresno, in 1968, and worked as a playground director. That year, he played in a San Francisco Giants' old-timers game, hoping that there just might be a job for him with the National League.

It was too late. In September 1969, Thompson suffered a seizure at his home and died a short time later at a hospital. He was only 43.

"SAY HEY" POUNDS THE SPALDEEN
Willie Mays hits New York
80 St. Nichols Place

Baseball legends come in all shapes and sizes, some believable and others far-fetched. Did Babe Ruth call his "shot" in the 1932 World Series? Possibly. No, probably. I mean, no way. Who knows for sure?

And what about Grover Cleveland Alexander striking out Tony Lazzeri to preserve a St. Louis win against the Yanks in game seven of the 1926 World Series? Was the old pitcher a tad tipsy that celebrated day? Hardly, because you can't pitch like that and be drunk. Then again, this was Alexander, so who's to know? Ah, the legends of baseball, where facts can get in the way of a good story.

There is one legend, however, that is secure — once upon a time, Willie Mays did play stickball on the streets of the Sugar Hill section of Uptown. Yes, he really did. Honest.

The mists of time conceal how exciting a ballplayer Mays was when he arrived in New York as a heralded Giants' rookie of 20. "Mays wasn't Joe Louis, slugging for democracy, or Jackie Robinson, stealing bases for collective self-respect," wrote William Rhoden in *The New York Times* ... "[While] black athletes were still a new commodity as mainstream athletes [they] no longer had to bear the entire weight of a nation's race consciousness."

That left Mays to simply be the best player of his generation, a graceful outfielder of enormous talent. He was the complete package — someone who could hit for power, field, and run just about better than anyone who ever laced up the spikes. His signatures were the basket catches he made and

It's another home run for Willie Mays of the Giants. (National Baseball Hall of Fame Library, Cooperstown, New York)

the way his cap fell off when he tore around the bases, topped off by a ready smile and a cheerful word for all. "Listen," somebody said, "if you could play ball like Willie Mays, you'd be laughing too."

How appropriate that Mays came to New York in 1951, the year of the Miracle of Coogan's Bluff, when the Giants came from 13$\frac{1}{2}$ games back in mid-August to take the National League pennant in the ninth inning of the third and final playoff game against the rival Dodgers.

At the time he hit New York, Mays was hitting .477 — not a misprint — at Triple A Minneapolis. When Giants' manager Leo Durocher telephoned him to announce the promotion, the understated Mays was apprehensive. "What are you hitting?" Durocher asked, not missing a beat. "Four-seventy-seven," says Mays. "Well," Durocher countered, "do you think you can hit two hundred points less up here?"

He did that rookie season, batting .274, including his first hit, a monster home run off Warren Spahn into the left-field stands at the Polo Grounds. Durocher again: "I never saw a f—ing ball go out of a f—ing park so f—ing fast in my f—ing life."

That Mays had time left for stickball fed the legend. "I had just turned 20," Mays explains in his 1988 autobiography, "[and] I didn't have a heck of a lot to do with my teammates, who were older and already settled in New York. So I played games with the neighborhood kids."

That first summer, Mays stayed with a couple named David and Anna Goosby in their house on St. Nicholas Avenue, near 151st Street, less than a half-mile from the Polo Grounds. The arrangements were made by the Giants' front office who wanted their young star to have a comfortable environment. Mays said Mrs. Goosby reminded him of his Aunt Sarah back home in Alabama; there was lots of home cooking, she washed his clothes, and simply opened the window and called him in from the street at dinner time.

Mays could usually be found playing stickball, the quintessential urban variation of the national pastime in which a pitcher typically throws a pink rubber ball called a "spaldeen" at the batter, who uses a manhole cover for home plate. With a broomstick for a bat, the hitter tries to hit the ball as far and as straight as possible, with each manhole cover generally counting as a base; in most cases a single is one manhole cover, a double is two and so forth.

"If you hit it two covers away, you were a 'two-sewer hitter' [which] meant you were pretty good," Mays writes in his autobiography. "I was a five-sewer hitter. So I was pretty damn good. And I never used to think much of playing with the kids in the street. That changed my image forever. I guess it made me seem like a grown-up kid. That wasn't too far from the truth back then."

Mays playing stickball draws a crowd. (National Baseball Hall of Fame Library, Cooperstown, New York)

SILENCED FOREVER — THE LIFE AND TIMES OF
"Silent" Mike Tiernan
2423 8th Avenue (& West 132nd Street)

No question that "Silent" Mike Tiernan was the very essence of a ballplayer on the field. The Trenton native hit better than .300 in eight of his 13 big league seasons, all with the late 19th-century Giants.

In his best year at bat, 1897, Tiernan hit a sparkling .361. In 1891, he led the National League in home runs with 17 — impressive for the dead ball era — and, in 1889, he was the National League leader in runs scored with 146.

"In the early days of the Giants, the name Mike Tiernan was on the lips of every baseball fan," wrote *The New York Times* long after he had retired. "To this day, old timers talk about the long drives which Silent Mike hit [at the Polo Grounds] in Harlem."

Tiernan earned his nickname through a decidedly un-New York attitude: He disliked publicity and was always reserved on the field, even when arguing with umpires. Tiernan started as a pitcher and switched to the outfield in his second year in the majors, so he could play every day and just hit.

In 1888 and 1889, with Tiernan manning rightfield, the Giants won National League pennants. Under Manager Jim Mutrie, he was part of a powerful team that included Roger Connor, John Montgomery Ward, Mickey Welch and Jim O'Rourke, all Hall of Famers.

Tiernan retired in 1889, owning a New York cafe after his baseball career. He died in 1918 at Bellevue Hospital at the age of 51, a victim of tuberculosis. The above address was his home.

ADDRESS HEARD 'ROUND THE WORLD
"Shufflin' Phil" Douglas puts pen to paper
145 Wadsworth Avenue

Poor Phil Douglas.

Lost in all the hoopla of the 1919 World Series fix is the distantly-related and truly unfortunate tale of a Giants' pitcher called "Shufflin' Phil," so named for his distinctive polio-induced gait.

Almost no one remembers Phil Douglas. But thanks in part to baseball's post-1919 paranoia about gambling and the cruel doings of John McGraw, Douglas was banned for life from baseball. Had it not been for a one-paragraph letter Douglas desperately wrote in 1922, he might even be in the Hall of Fame.

For a brief, shining moment, Douglas was a national hero. In the 1921 World Series, he won two of three three games he started against the Yankees, striking out Babe Ruth four times and helping the Giants to the Series triumph. In 1935, Bill Terry, then managing the Giants, named Douglas one of the best four pitchers in Giants' history; the others are Christy Mathewson, Rube Marquard, and Iron Man Joe McGinnity, all of whom have plaques at Cooperstown.

A lanky 6'5" and weighing 210 pounds, Douglas was a native Georgian with a popping fastball and a sneaky curve that bettors claimed was the outlawed spitter. He also had a big-league problem with alcohol.

After reaching the big leagues in 1912, Douglas typically unwound after games with what he called his "vacations" — benders in which he'd drink himself into a stupor and disappear for days at a time. No wonder he bounced around between five teams in his first nine major league seasons.

In 1919, Douglas was traded to the Giants, where he chalked up solid numbers, winning 14 games in 1920 and 15 in 1921. But it was the following season — 1922 — when Douglas, 11-3 through July, and apparently on his way to another good season, that things went terribly wrong.

The beginning of the end came July 30, when Douglas lost a game to the Pirates at the Polo Grounds and was bawled out afterward by McGraw. Shufflin' Phil's response: a particularly long one of his "vacations," when even his wife couldn't find him.

McGraw had had enough. He sent out five detectives, whose job it was to follow the pitcher and keep him sober. They found Douglas unconscious in the Manhattan apartment of a friend. Then, they dragged him, half-dressed, out of bed, threatening him with a beating if he didn't accompany them immediately to the 135th Police Station. Douglas went and passed out again.

The Giants had taken custody at the police station and then did the unforgivable — sending Douglas to the West Side Sanitarium, a Central Park West hospital, and forcing him to undergo a particularly brutal form of rehab called the Keely Cure. That included a series of stomach pumping, forced hot baths, and massive doses of sedatives.

Douglas' wife and two daughters weren't told of his whereabouts for two days, and Douglas was never told what drugs were used on him. He stayed five days at the sanitarium.

Douglas emerged dazed and weak from the drugs. Two days later, he reported on his scheduled pitching day to the Polo Grounds, but was obviously in no condition to do so. McGraw again lashed out, calling Douglas a drunk in front of his teammates.

That day's game, against the Reds, was rained out. Feeling despondent, Douglas lingered in the clubhouse long after his teammates had left. Then, he took pen to pad, using a piece of Giants' stationary to write a one paragraph note to Leslie Mann, a St. Louis outfielder he barely knew:

Dear Leslie:

I want to leave here but I want some inducement. I don't want this guy [McGraw] to win the pennant and I feel if I stay here I will win it for him. You know I can pitch and win. So if you see the fellows, and if you want to, send a man over here with the goods, and I will leave for home on the next train. Send him to my house so nobody will know, and send him at night. I am living at 145 Wadsworth Avenue, Apartment 1R. Nobody will ever know. I will go down to the fishing camp and stay there. I am asking you this so there won't be any trouble to anyone. Call me up if you are sending a man. Wadsworth 3210. Do this right away. Let me know. Regards to all.

— Phil Douglas

"I decided that I just couldn't pitch for McGraw," Douglas said later. "He was running me crazy ... He rode me every minute. He called me vile names. Everything I did seemed to be wrong."

The special-delivery letter reached Mann in a Boston hotel. He took it directly to Branch Rickey, his manager. Rickey, in a pennant race with the Giants, knew that the letter would get Douglas suspended at least, so he advised Mann to send it on to Baseball Commissioner Kenesaw Mountain Landis. Said Rickey of the letter: "I told [Mann] it was a hot potato, in fact dynamite."

Remember the times: It was a year or two after the Black Sox had been banned from baseball for life. Obsessed with ridding all gambling elements from the game, Landis hurried to Pittsburgh, where the Giants were playing the Pirates and contacted McGraw about the incident. On the morning of August 16, they asked Douglas about the letter.

By then, Douglas had all but forgotten about it. But, he admitted to writing the letter, explaining to Landis that, "a man has to live ... I guess I figured I was out of a job if [McGraw] let me go ... I reckoned with this letter, I might pick up some money and get along for a time."

"Douglas," said Landis, thrusting a finger in his face. "You are through with organized baseball."

And with that, his career was suddenly finished. It was Douglas' only hearing. There were no rebuttals, no witnesses, and no hearings. No money had been exchanged and nothing more came from Landis. The decision was final.

Douglas was left with little recourse, but to take a train home. A few days later, he spoke to reporters:

"I've never thrown a game in my life," he told them. "I'm as innocent as a child," he added, explaining that after he'd been suspended and placed in the sanitarium, he figured he'd been released and was only hoping to get some money to get by.

"McGraw had it in for me," Douglas said. "I was desperate when I wrote that letter ... I want the public to know that I am not guilty of any crooked baseball."

So Douglas just went back to Tennessee. In 1936, he applied for reinstatement, but was turned down. He worked as a laborer and a maintenance man with the state highway department, but ended up on relief. In his last years, Douglas had three strokes, the last one of which, in 1952, killed him in the rented backwoods log cabin, where he'd been living with his second wife.

In 1990, supporters petitioned Commission Fay Vincent to reinstate Shufflin' Phil, arguing that the cause of the letter had been the cruel sanitarium treatment. They were refused, with the comment that, "the events surrounding the matter cannot be recreated in sufficient detail to provide an adequate basis" for reversing Landis' decision.

THE POLO GROUNDS
"An absurd and lovely thing"
8th Avenue & West 157th Street

Its horseshoe shape was wrong for baseball. Its location at the foot of Coogan's Bluff on the northern fringe of Manhattan, meant a lot of potential customers could stand amidst the trees and boulders of the bluff and see the game for free.

Nor did it attract the kind of colorful characters that inhabited the smaller more intimate, more celebrated Ebbets Field in Brooklyn. And no, they never really played polo there.

So why do some segments of New York City baseball fans still pine for the oddly-named Polo Grounds? It could be, because as Roger Angell once wrote: "The Polo Grounds is an absurd and lovely thing."

"It is the only ballpark built against a cliff — Coogan's Bluff — so that a patron could walk downhill to his seat," Angell wrote. "You came slowly down the John T. Brush stairs to the cool of the evening, looking down at the flags and at the tiers of brilliant floodlights on the stands and, beyond them, at the softer shimmer of lights on the Harlem River."

As home to the Giants for most of the team's 75-year history in New York, the Polo Grounds hosted Bobby Thomson's 1951 "Shot Heard 'Round the World," countless World Series, big football games, heavyweight title fights, and even automobile racing, hurling, and Gaelic football. Given up for dead more times than an alley cat, the Polo Grounds — born of tragic and unusual circumstances in 1911 — made it all the way to 1963 and the birth of the Mets.

The Polo Grounds, in its modern form, took shape after fire of unknown but suspicious origins claimed the old park of that name, destroying even the players' bats. By then, the Giants of wealthy manufacturer John Day had been around in one form or another since 1888, playing first at a dinky little ballpark at East 110th Street and 5th Avenue, and later in other places, including Jersey City and St. George, Staten Island.

In 1889, Day built an all-wooden ballpark uptown by the Harlem River in a relatively unpopulated area called Coogan's Hollow, the last remaining portion of a farm granted to a John Lion Gardiner by the King of England in the 17th century. Got that, baseball fans? Day christened it, "The Polo Grounds."

It was quirky from the start. There was a double-decker wooden grandstand that wrapped from first base around to third; wooden bleachers that shot off into left-and right-center fields; and, a spacious carriage park, separated from the outfield by a long row of rope-linked hitching posts. Capacity was around 18,000, but another 4,000 or so could squeeze into the carriage park, onto the Bluff and yes, even the rickety grandstand roof.

But the Polo Grounds became famous mostly for the team that played there — the fiery, brawling Giants of John McGraw, for whom tempest and turmoil were typical. McGraw arrived in Manhattan from Baltimore in 1902, taking over a listless team. Yelled a spectator at the manager's first home game: "They're awake!"

By 1904, McGraw had turned things around, delivering the first of 10 pennants he would win with the Giants. That happened despite the April 14, 1911 fireball that destroyed both the Polo Grounds' wooden stands and its carriage drive circling the outfield.

The Polo Grounds in its modern state opened just 10 weeks later — on June 28, 1911 as Christy Mathewson shut out Boston before a crowd of 6,000. This time, spectators sat in the hurriedly-built concrete grandstand. The wooden bleachers built near the outfield remained from before the fire.

In 1913, the Giants took in as tenants, the Yankees, late of Hilltop Park and a rather bedraggled unit. That changed around 1920 with the arrival of a fellow named Ruth, who promptly exploded for 54 home runs, many of them sent high over the towering right-field roof of the Polo Grounds. Although McGraw's Giants continued to win — taking four straight pennants between 1921 and 1924 — Ruth stole their thunder. Mercifully, the Yankees moved across the Harlem River to a home of their own in 1923, leaving the Giants as sole occupants of their ballpark.

It's a full house at the Polo Grounds. (National Baseball Hall of Fame Library, Cooperstown, New York)

Some Polo Grounds facts worth knowing:

- It seems that one time, in the ballpark's early days, Iron Man Joe McGinnity developed a mighty thirst between pitching both games of a doubleheader for the Giants. Up he strode to the bar, asked for a drink and was politely refused. McGinnity then vaulted the bar, helped himself to three drinks and went out and won the second game.
- On May 30, 1921, a monument was dedicated to former Giant Eddie Grant, killed in battle in World War I. The monument stood in center field at the base of the clubhouse wall.
- The park's largest crowd was 60,747 for a Dodger doubleheader in 1937.
- On June 26, 1944, a three-sided game was played among New York's major league teams to raise money for World War II War Bonds. The crowd: more than 50,000. Final score: Dodgers 5, Yankees 1, Giants 0.
- With center field a mammoth poke at 410 feet, Luke Easter hit the first home run there, during a 1948 Negro League game. Only three others managed that — Joe Adcock, Lou Brock, and Hank Aaron. None hit the massive "Chesterfield" cigarette ad ("Always A Hit") that loomed over the area.
- Starting in 1946, groundskeeper Matty Schwab, his wife, and son occupied a tidy two-bedroom apartment under Section 3 of the left-field stands, just off the field exit near the foul line.
- During the Mets' tenure in 1962 and '63, Johnny McCarthy and his crew of groundskeepers painted Schawb's old apartment pink, installed a shower, and a plywood floor and called it the "Pink Room."
- Also in '62 and '63, the Howard Clothes sign on the outfield wall promised a boat to any player hitting the sign. Shades of Brooklyn's Abe Stark. No word on anyone actually getting a boat.

Just about any player of stature played in the Polo Grounds. Some, like Mathewson, Bill Terry, Mel Ott, Frankie Frisch, and Willie Mays called it home. And it was where Jack Dempsey was knocked through the ropes by Louis Firpo in 1923 and got up to win the fight; where Red Grange's spectacular play gave birth to professional football; and, where Notre Dame unleashed its famous Four Horseman against Army.

Sagging attendance was a real reason the Giants abandoned New York after the 1957 season. From a top figure of 1.5 million in 1947, the Giants slipped precipitously over the following decade, falling to less than 700,000 in their last season. Reasons varied, from the popularity of television, which kept people at home, to the crumbling neighborhood around the ballpark, which made people think twice before heading to a night game in reaches of upper Harlem.

No demonstrations or marches to borough hall met Horace Stoneham's decision to move the Giants to San Francisco. Nor do many writers look back nostalgically at the end of the era the way they do with the Dodgers.

Indeed, a sparse, decidedly unceremonious crowd of slightly more than 11,000 brought the team to a end on September 29, 1957 in a 9-1 loss to the Pirates. After the final out, souvenir-hungry fans ripped up the bases, the pitching rubber, clumps of outfield sod and even the Eddie Grant Memorial.

For the record, Bob Friend of the Pirates was the winning pitcher in the Giants' last game — nine years later, he was the winning pitcher at Shea Stadium's inaugural game — with Johnny Antonelli taking the loss. Dusty Rhodes drove in the Giants' last run. And the Giants' last official spectator: John McGraw's widow, Blanche, who lingered in her personal box seat long after the last out, and left clutching a bouquet of roses, her eyes moist with tears of emotion.

The Polo Grounds was vacant to baseball for four years, before the bumbling original Mets moved in as tenants in 1962. They left for the new Shea Stadium after the '63 season and the ancient ballpark was dismantled. Doing the dirty job was the aptly-named Wrecking Company of America, the same company that tore down Ebbets Field, but with little of the same pomp and circumstance that accompanied the grim task in Brooklyn.

Demolition started April 10, 1964 with the same wrecking ball used at Ebbets Field. Wrecking Corporation of America Vice President Harry Avirom, an avowed Dodger fan, summed up the divided feelings of New Yorkers toward their baseball teams at the time: "Getting at the Polo Grounds is something I've always wanted to do," he said. "This makes up for the sad day we went after Ebbets Field in 1960."

Today, the area is home to Polo Grounds Towers — four 30-story public housing units. There is an asphalt playground — Willie Mays Field — with six basketball backboards, right where Mays used to cover center field.

CHAPTER NINE

THE UPPER WEST SIDE

"My boy, one small breeze doesn't make a windstorm."

— *John McGraw, addressing a hot rookie, spring training, 1925*

SAY IT AIN'T SO JOE: BIRTH OF THE BLACK SOX
Ansonia Hotel
2109 Broadway (& West 73rd Street)

The story of the infamous 1919 Chicago White Sox is a familiar one. The basics: Eight members of the Chicago White Sox were banned from baseball for life after conspiring to throw that's season's World Series to the Cincinnati Reds.

Who would figure this landmark hotel with its Beaux-Arts style decorations, rounded-corner towers, and healthy supply of gargoyles, would play a prominent role in the fix? The Ansonia isn't associated much with baseball; sure Babe Ruth lived there, but so did Enrico Caruso, Igor Stravinsky, Arturo Toscanini, and a cast of characters noted for other things. Theodore Dreiser called the Ansonia home, as did showman Florenz Ziegfeld, his wife, and even his mistress.

Den of intrigue: the Ansonia.

Yet, here was baseball's most sensational affair kicking off at the Ansonia — a crucial September 21, 1919 meeting of plotting White Sox players. Those events took a further turn five days later with a meeting in the lobby between big-time gamblers, Arnold Rothstein and Sport Sullivan, which financed the clandestine plan.

The ringleader: White Sox veteran first baseman Chick Gandil, who began pulling in his fellow conspirators in and around the Ansonia, while the team was staying there during a late September series against the Yankees. Too preposterous to be imagined? Not for Gandil, with big underworld contacts and a team full of underpaid ballplayers.

The first player he approached was pitcher Lefty Williams, a staff mainstay. Williams was doubtful, believing at first that such a plan was too far-fetched to be tried. But, he was pulled in a few days later at a meeting of the eight players who assembled after dinner in Gandil's room. As Eliot Asinof recounts in *Eight Men Out*, his superb 1963 book on the Series: "In the history of American sport, it would be difficult to find another meeting that led to events so shattering."

If anyone could bankroll the Series, it was Rothstein, or "A. R.," as he was called. The 37-year-old king of New York mobsters amassed a fortune by controlling several gambling dens in the West 40s, conveniently protected by Tammany-controlled police. Convincing him to commit the $100,000 payment was the trick.

Leave that to Sullivan, a sophisticated, smooth-talking Bostonian. Their September 26 took place at Rothstein's home (355 West 84th Street, between Riverside Drive and West Side Avenue), where Sullivan told him that Gandil had committed his crooked teammates to the fix and they were eager to get involved. All they needed was one last thing: A. R.'s deep pockets.

Rothstein was convinced. He knew Sullivan and trusted him, and promptly set the signal to ensure that the plot was on — White Sox pitcher Eddie Cicotte, the starter in game one, was to to hit the game's first batter. Cicotte did the deed and drilled that first batter, Reds' second baseman Morrie Rath, with a fastball in the back — right between the shoulder blades.

A. R. got the signal while watching a report of the first game October 1 in a crowded room at — you guessed it — the Ansonia. It was all Rothstein needed; he didn't even like baseball and didn't plan to watch the rest of the Series.

And with that, Rothstein walked outside the Ansonia into the rain and caught a cab for one his gambling dens. He was never caught for his role in bankrolling the most infamous fix in American sports history.

JOE D. SETTLES DOWN — FOR AWHILE, ANYHOW
400 West End Avenue

If there ever was a nomad kind of ballplayer in New York, it was the Yankee Clipper — Joe DiMaggio. He lived, for the most part, in hotels, spent his time in saloons and kept to himself.

"He's one of the loneliest guys I ever knew," fellow Yankee Eddie Lopat once said. "And he leads the league in room service."

DiMaggio was part of another era — a manly, Runyonesque one, where socializing meant drinking with the boys, surrounding yourself with admirers and hangers-on and women. What a surprise then that DiMaggio actually settled down for a time, marrying the actress Dorothy Arnold in 1939 and living during the season at 400 West End Avenue (and 83rd Street).

Their November wedding in San Francisco, DiMaggio's hometown, made

Joe DiMaggio. (National Baseball Hall of Fame Library, Cooperstown, New York)

them the toasts of the town. Here were 25-year-old Joltin' Joe, already the young Yankee star and World Series hero, and his actress wife, tying the knot at the Cathedral of St. Peter and St. Paul. Outside was a throng of perhaps 30,000 — that's right, 30,000 — of their nearest and dearest friends.

The Clipper met Arnold in 1937 when the young ballplayer went to the Biograph Studios on 175th Street in the Bronx to play a bit role in a forgettable film, *Manhattan Merry-Go-Round.* His lines totaled three — "Well, I'm here," "What?" and "But I'm ...."

He got through it and in the process met the blond Arnold, a bit player herself and a Duluth, Minnesota native, whose real name was Arnoldine Olson. She had come to New York at 18, singing in clubs and on the radio and traveling the vaudeville circuit. Of that fateful first meeting with DiMaggio, as she later told a columnist, "I fell in love with him before I even knew who he was."

For DiMaggio, getting married meant giving up the hotel life. And it meant cutting back the saloon hopping and the hangers-on. To ease the transition, he and Dorothy became fast friends with Lefty Gomez and his starlet wife, June O'Dea, who lived nearby on 91st Street. He and Gomez shared a ride to Yankee Stadium on the days of home games, with their wives getting together themselves later for the ride to the ballpark.

The marriage didn't last, and in 1942, after three years, Arnold moved to Reno, claiming DiMaggio was cold, aloof, and almost never home. "We had a home," Dorothy said. "I wanted to make it a nice home. But he was never there." The really unfortunate part of the breakup: Arnold left with "Little Joe," DiMaggio's 13-month-old son. The couple divorced in 1944.

Others shared Arnold's assessment. "Joe was kind of a cold guy, everybody knows that," his teammate Tommy Henrich told writer Maury Allen years later. "He never asked me to go to dinner in all the years I was with the Yankees."

THEY MUST BE GIANTS
Original Polo Grounds
West 110th Street & 6th Avenue

Jim Mutrie didn't arrive in New York looking like the future father of the Giants. This late-19th century baseball tycoon first saw New York from the seat of a bicycle.

That was sometime during the summer of 1880 after Mutrie had pedaled into New York from his hometown of New Bedford, Massachusetts, where he had an demonstrated a keen interest in the emerging national pastime. But Mutrie also had driving ambition and an intriguing idea about how exactly to make baseball in New York a success. One problem though — that took money and he didn't have any.

So, Mutrie got cracking. No stranger to trying to huckster wealthy men into financing projects, he had recently tried without success to encourage industrialist August Belmont into bankrolling a baseball team. Once in New York, he went to work, using the same strategy on John Day.

Mutrie knew his business. His target was a prosperous young tobacco merchant, who owned a baseball team as a way of masking a real ambition to play. The problem was that Day was a better businessman than pitcher and became a consistent loser. How fortuitous then that after a bruising loss to Brooklyn, Day found himself seated in the grandstand next to the fast-talking Mutrie.

"Want to get a team that will beat those people who just knocked your brains out?" Mutrie asked. Day reared his head back and laughed. "Do I," he told the stranger. "I'd give a $1,000 if I could get one."

Mutrie was right where he wanted to be. His exact words of inticement are lost to history, but whatever he said, it worked, because the two men left the park together. Some weeks later, they formed an enterprise called the Metropolitan Exhibition Company. Its mandate: creation of a New York team to remember.

Bankrolled by Day and managed by Mutrie, they called their team, "The Metropolitans" or "Mets." When a supporter pointed out that the Mets were a collection of unusually large players, Mutrie agreed. "They're giants on the field as well," he said. So Giants they became.

Opening in 1880 as an independent club, the team played home games at a variety of fields, from New Jersey to Union Grounds and the Capitoline Grounds in Brooklyn, which had once been home to the Mutuals, a notable team from a previous generation. With such parks accessible only by streetcar or ferry — The Brooklyn Bridge wasn't yet built — the team barely drew from Manhattan, the fan base it most needed.

One day, Day was asked by a shoeshine boy why he headed all the way to Brooklyn and New Jersey to play his games. His only answer — no room in Manhattan. But when the shoeshine boy mentioned a polo field at 110th Street and 6th Avenue, where his team might play, Day was shrewd enough to investigate.

Day found the area was owned by James Gordon Bennett, Jr., the million-aire son of the founder and owner of *The New York Herald*, who used the field as a polo field for himself and his wealthy friends. Day liked the location and arranged to lease the field from Bennett.

Next, Mutrie built his team. He went to Washington, where he signed a score of good players and turned the Giants into winners. In fact, they became an immediate success in their new home, taking 16 games, losing seven and tying one of the season's last 24 games. The crowds came, and Day and Mutrie, the new tycoons of New York baseball, had themselves a hit.

Not that everything went smoothly; try weird. It turned out that the Polo Grounds — which stood on a rectangular sliver of land from 110th Street to 112th Street, bordered by the block between 5th and 6th Avenues — also served as home to another local team of note, the Nationals. For a time, the park's vast expanse was actually turned into two fields, divided by a canvas fence that essentially separated the two teams. The owner of both teams: Yup, John Day.

Mutrie's Giants prospered anyway. In 1882, they joined the American Association and the following year, at about the time they became the Giants, joined the National League.

See the Giants in those days and you'd catch Mutrie, with his trademark handlebar mustache, topped off by a stovetop hat, frock coat, gloves, and spats, as he roamed up and down the grandstand, cheering his team and adding a distinctive presence to Polo Grounds' festivities. No wonder the Giants were soon known by yet another moniker: "The People's Team."

The nucleus of Mutrie's first Giant teams came from raids on the Troy Haymakers, which he brought to New York almost in a body, including catcher Buck Ewing; pitcher "Smiling" Mickey Welch; and, first baseman Roger Connor, all future Hall of Famers. To that group, he added pitcher Tim Keefe, another eventual Cooperstown member.

In 1884, despite that powerful lineup, Mutrie's Mets, the AA winners, were defeated in three straight by the Providence Grays, NL champions, in the first World Series ever.

A more unfortunate fate awaited the Polo Grounds, which burned down in the spring of 1889. Mutrie left baseball a year later, but not before several more shrewd moves that assured the Giants another solid decade — acquiring two more Hall-of-Famers, John Montgomery Ward and Amos Rusie. The father of the Giants died in 1938 at the age of 86.

ODD COUPLE
Christy Mathewson and John McGraw move in
76 West 85th Street (off Columbus Avenue)

They are baseball's most notable odd couple — one standing well over 6',

Jack Armstrong handsome, the best pitcher of his time, and so celebrated for clean living that his wife once felt forced to admit that he was "no goody-goody," and — gasp — occasionally played checkers for money.

The other stood all of 5'7," had a bulbous nose, fought all comers, held grudges for years and may have been, next to Ty Cobb, the most loathed fig-

Seated are the Mathewsons. Standing are the McGraws. And so went one of the baseball's most unlikely friendships. (National Baseball Hall of Fame Library, Cooperstown, New York)

ure in baseball history. Yet, Christy Mathewson, the pitcher, and John McGraw, the Giants' testy manager, were of all things, inseparable best friends.

Starting in 1903, this unlikely pair of Giant heroes and their wives shared this spacious seven-room walk-up apartment, just one block to the elevated train that ran uptown to the Polo Grounds.

McGraw personified the rowdy team he managed for close to three decades. His genius as a leader was in taking and molding prospects from coal country or the big city into ballplayers of consummate skill, and, as one writer said, "the look of eagles." Most of the players that McGraw molded — like most players of the day — were the product of society's bottom rung. For them, the baseball life was preferable to the factory.

But not for Mathewson, his greatest star. As a product of a middle class Pennsylvania family, he was different from the start: He went to college — to Bucknell University, where he was a pitcher, an All-American football player, and the class president who married his campus sweetheart. Mathewson didn't need to play baseball for a living and could arguably have chosen a different career path with more lucrative results.

Just why McGraw and his new wife, Blanche, invited Mathewson and his wife, Jane, to share their new, furnished ground-floor apartment at Columbus Avenue and 85th Street, near Central Park, would intrigue a psychiatrist. The $50-a-month rent, was split between the couples; the Mathewsons paid for food and the McGraws, for utilities.

"We led normal lives, fed the men well, and left them alone to talk their baseball," Blanche McGraw wrote in her memoirs. "Their happiness was our cause."

Historians suggest that McGraw may have felt protective of his star pitcher, since baseball players of the era could be nasty, even to teammates and especially to rookies. Such a code applied to Mathewson, with his occasional air of superiority and given to moral pronouncements that some took for arrogance. "Hardly anyone on the team speaks to Mathewson," a teammate said. "He deserves it. He is a pinhead and a conceited fellow who has made himself unpopular."

But not to McGraw, the gambler and racetrack aficionado, who treated Mathewson as an equal — an almost unheard of arrangement between manager and player. Some said that McGraw, whose first wife, Minnie, had died tragically in 1899 of acute appendicitis, and never had children, looked on Mathewson as a surrogate son.

Both men became fa-
mous — Mathewson reach-
ing early-deity status by
shutting out the Philadelphia A's three times in the
1905 World Series and winning 373 games over his 16-
year major league career.
McGraw, meanwhile, led
the Giants to three World
Championships. Both were
early Hall of Famers.

And both men, while
fiercely competitive, re-
mained lifelong friends, although the McGraws left
the apartment at 76 West
85th Street in 1906, after
the birth of Mathewson's
son. The Giant skipper and
his wife then moved to the
Washington Inn, a residen-

*Out this door at 76 West 85th Street walked
Mathewson and McGraw.*

tial hotel near the Polo Grounds. As a tribute to their great friend, the
Mathewsons, who stayed on at West 85th Street, named the boy John Chris-
topher.

Sadly, John Mathewson, or Christy, Jr., had an abbreviated life, lending
tragic irony to the tradition of Mathewson men dying young. Like his father,
he attended Bucknell, but then went a different way, becoming an Air Force
pilot. The younger Mathewson died at 44 from burns sustained in a gas explosion at his home near San Antonio.

Matty, the pitcher, died at the age of 45 of complications from tuberculosis on the eve of the 1925 World Series. That same disease took his brother,
Henry, briefly a major leaguer, who died in 1917 at 31. The third brother,
Nicholas, nine years Christy's junior and reputedly the best athlete of the
bunch, committed suicide in 1908, a few months shy of his 20th birthday.

Henry's legacy was his part in the baseball trivia question, "What pitching
brothers in the major leagues have the most wins?" Why Christy, with 373
wins, and Henry, who went 0-1 with the 1907 Giants. The record has since
been broken by two sets of modern-day brothers — Gaylord and Jim Perry
and Phil and Joe Niekro.

BENNY KAUFF AND THE THEFT THAT NEVER WAS
788 West End Avenue

Okay, so Benny Kauff will never be confused with Shoeless Joe Jackson, Hal Chase, and other infamous characters of the early days of baseball. But Kauff's permanent dismissal from baseball even after the Giant outfielder was acquitted on charges of car theft outside 788 West End Avenue, remains an unjust stain on the national pastime.

Like Shoeless Joe and the 1919 Black Sox, Kauff was banned for life by Commissioner Kenesaw Mountain Landis, who declared the ballplayer ineligible for the vague reasons of actions "detrimental" to the game. But unlike the Sox players, some of whom were undoubtedly guilty of throwing World Series game, Kauff's career was abruptly terminated despite the court's declaration that he was innocent on all charges.

Few players of promise met such a sad end as Bernard M. "Benny" Kauff. He batted .311 in eight big league seasons, the last five of which he played for John McGraw's Giants. That was good, but not indicative of the promise he had showed a few years before when he was called, "The Ty Cobb of the Federal League."

A Middletown, Ohio native, Kauff turned pro in 1910, played briefly with the Yankees in 1911, and made a name for himself in 1914 when he jumped to the rival Federal League. There, he starred with the Indianapolis Hoosiers, where he batted .366 and stole 75 bases, a lethal combination of average and speed that attracted significant interest from McGraw, who purchased Kauff's contract from the Brooklyn Feds after the 1915 season. Kauff batted well for the Giants but not as his comparison to Cobb suggests.

His fast running and even faster talking made Kauff a natural for New York. "Flashy" fit well with the big city but not with Landis. That was mistake two. Mistake number one came had come when Kauff had jumped to the Federal League, whose demise Landis, as a federal judge, had helped to litigate and ultimately drive into the ground.

Kauff's ultimate mistake was the company he kept. The trouble started on the evening of December 8, 1919 with the theft of a Cadillac owned by James E. Brennan of Bronxville, Westchester County, who had parked in front of his father's home at 788 West End Avenue. Accusing Kauff of committing the crime were a couple of ex-cons, James Shields and James Whalen, associates of the ballplayer in the automobile business.

Shields and Whalen testified that they were having dinner with Kauff before the car was stolen. They said the ballplayer had told them he had a customer for the Cadillac, whereupon the group left the restaurant to steal one. The three men supposedly walked down Broadway and failed to see any similar cars but found one — Brennan's — parked a block west on West End Avenue. Shields testified they then stole the car, changed the tires and repainted the body, before selling it for $1,800 and splitting the profits three ways.

On the stand, Kauff vehemently denied the charges, saying he was the victim of dishonest employees who ran a car theft ring without his knowledge. Kauff said he had bought the car in question from a Cumberland Hotel resident and produced the bill of sale to prove it. He then sold the car to a Harlem resident and even refunded the purchase price when he learned from detectives that the car was hot. Even Kauff's wife testified she was having dinner with her husband on the night of the alleged theft.

The defense seemed airtight; the jury agreed, taking less than one hour to return a not-guilty verdict. But Kauff sensed he wasn't yet in the clear with Landis. "They made me the goat, but I know how to take my medicine," he told baseball writer Joe Vila after the trial. "I probably would have been allowed to play, if I had agreed to tell certain things to Judge Landis. But I'm no squealer and that's all there is to it."

Kauff guessed right: He was never reinstated and moved back to Ohio, where he worked as a salesman in Columbus. He died in 1961 at the age of 71.

FAREWELL TO A HERO — JACKIE ROBINSON
Riverside Church
Riverside Drive & West 122nd Street

Inside the statuesque, granite edifice of Riverside Church, the youngish Rev. Jesse Jackson, then with a shock of an Afro and dressed in a turtleneck, addressed the celebrity-laden congregation of 2,500.

"We must balance the roars of sorrow with the tears of joy," he said. "When Jackie took the field, something reminded us of our birthright to be free."

As Jackson spoke, Jackie Robinson's silver-blue coffin draped with red roses reflected the mood in the church that October 27, 1972 day — an outpouring of respect, pride, and admiration for major league baseball's first black player. Three days before, Robinson, 53, had died of a heart attack at his home in Stamford, Connecticut.

And outside sat the 57-year-old hearse driver, Charles Patterson. Not much of a baseball fan but a Harlem resident well aware of Robinson's tremendous legacy, Patterson said he was proud to be the driver delivering the pioneering ballplayer to the cemetery.

At breakfast that morning, Patterson said he had mentioned to his wife, Margaret, that he would be driving one of the cars at Jackie Robinson's funeral. "'I hope you're working with Robinson,' she had said. "'That would be an honor for a black man to drive Robinson's hearse.'"

And although Patterson had never seen Robinson play, he told *The Times*, "I understand what he meant. He and Martin Luther King did a lot for everybody."

Robinson did more than hit .311 during a 10-year Hall of Fame career with the Brooklyn Dodgers. As major league baseball's first African-American player, he fought a courageous, lonely struggle that changed not just his sport, but society as well.

"Jackie Robinson opened the door of baseball to all men," said Monte Irvin, himself a Hall of Famer and one of the first black men in the major leagues. "He was the first to get the opportunity, but if he had not done such a great job, the path would have been so much more difficult."

Irvin was among the athletes, politicians, civil rights leaders, and ordinary

There are no baseballs or stuffed bears at Jackie Robinson's grave in Queens. On the ground is a tiny American flag and a mini-Madonna. On top of the grave itself are stones, a sign of respect.

Riverside Church.

admirers who packed Riverside Church to remember Robinson. The occasion took on particular poignancy since Robinson's son, Jackie, Jr., had been killed the year before in an auto accident.

At the front of the church sat Robinson's widow, Rachel, an associate professor of psychiatric nursing at the Yale School of Medicine, and his other children, David and Mrs. Sharon Mitchell. Just behind the family, an all-star team of pallbearers: basketballer Bill Russell along with Don Newcombe, Pee Wee Reese, Larry Doby, Jim Gilliam, and Ralph Branca.

Up in the pulpit, Jackson held forth on how the years of Robinson's life — "1919 dash 1972" — would be engraved on the tombstone. "On that dash is where we live," he thundered. "And for everyone, there is a dash of possibility, to choose the high road or the low road, to make things better and to make things worse. On that dash, [Robinson] snapped the barbed wire of prejudice."

The service finished, the pallbearers hoisted Robinson's casket and slid it into the hearse. Quickly, the driver, Charles Patterson, slid it deeper and locked the door for the procession through the streets of Harlem and Bedford-Stuyvesant. His destination: Cypress Hills Cemetery, Queens, appropriately just a few miles from where Robinson played at Ebbets Field.

MYSTERY PUNCH
John McGraw fought here — or did he?
301 West 109th Street

John McGraw hit New York like a steam engine. A small-town boy who made it big as a scrawny, 120-pound third baseman with the brawling Baltimore Orioles of the 1890s, he arrived in New York in 1902 as the newly appointed manager of the last-place Giants.

Within a dozen years, he clawed his way to five pennants and narrowly missed two others — intimidating players from his own team and opponents alike, and making the Giants the most feared, most despised team in the land. His next dozen years were just as eventful, as McGraw's Giants willed and bullied their way to five more pennants.

But what hard-fought success this baseball genius of a little man — he stood only 5'7" and went by the moniker, "The Little Napoleon" — won on the ballfield, was matched by an equally pugnacious personality in his private life. McGraw gambled, drank to excess, and ran with the Broadway fast crowd of actors, hangers-on, and wise guys.

How fitting then that McGraw's most famous fight occurred not at the ballpark, but on the street outside the Upper West Side apartment he shared with his wife, Blanche. Here was a fight that ended with a typical Broadway flourish of mystery — an unconscious actor; a blooded, bruised baseball manager; and, one thoroughly confused police department.

Events kicked off the evening of Saturday, August 8, 1920 as McGraw celebrated the day's win over the Cubs at the Lambs, a club for actors. And it ended with actor and fellow Lambs Club member John Slavin found on the pavement with a severe head injury in the dawn of the next day. Police just called it, "a wild night."

This much is known — the actor and baseball manager had spent the evening at the Lambs and shared a cab back to McGraw's apartment. Neither claimed to be drinking and the cab driver swore the only argument between the two was a good-natured ribbing about who would pick up the fare. At that point, both men exited the cab — McGraw striding into his building, the driver never being paid and Slavin suddenly slumping to the pavement in agony.

Newspapers feasted on the incident: "Actor Near Death At McGraw's Door," screamed the next day's headlines. Not quite, but Slavin, a well-known vaudevillian of the day, was still rushed to nearby St. Luke's Hospital. The damage: a fractured skull, two missing teeth, a cut lip, and a punctured tongue.

McGraw fared a little better with two black eyes, facial bruises, and various cuts and scrapes himself. He spent the next few days in virtual seclusion, keeping away from the media and only journeying between his fifth-floor apartment and the Polo Grounds' clubhouse long enough to put Johnny Evers in charge of the team.

A week later, McGraw spoke. "I was clouted on the bean with a water bottle in the Lambs," he revealed. "I had bought four bottles of whiskey before that, and had emptied all four with outside help. I don't remember anything after that, until detectives woke me up in my apartment [the next day]."

Lambs Club members spun a different version. They said McGraw had entered the club, mistaken member William Boyd for a man with whom he held a grudge, and berated him with a stream of obscenties. They said that Slavin and another Lambs Club member, William Leggett, intervened and hustled McGraw into the taxi before there was real trouble.

Boyd, who was Hop-

The Lambs Club.

along Cassidy of later fame, said he was minding his own business when McGraw suddenly leaned over and clocked him on the nose. That was quite enough for the Lambs, which suspended McGraw for the second time in three months.

Police from the fourth Precinct never did figure out exactly how Slavin was hurt that night. Meanwhile, the case dragged into the following spring, after McGraw was charged, of all things, for having a bottle of whiskey while at the Lambs, a violation of the Volstead Act. A federal jury took five minutes to drop all charges.

BACK TO WORK FOR "TURKEY MIKE" – BRIEFLY
The death of Mabel Hite
526 West 111th Street

"Turkey Mike" Donlin lived up to his nickname. He didn't run, he strutted. And when he wasn't on the ballfield, starring for John McGraw's turn-of-the-century Giants, he drank heavily, went to jail often and generally personfied the stereotype of the era's hard-living ballplayer.

Once a wild-throwing minor league pitcher, the versatile Donlin became a star major league outfielder and sometime first baseman and shortstop. He spent a checkered 12-year career with six teams, but thrived as a consistent left-handed batter with the Giants. Donlin topped .300 in all but two of those seasons and compiled an impressive .333 lifetime average.

But Turkey Mike's most lasting prominence came off the field. He was a flamboyant, colorful personality who wore $350 suits, wed a vaudeville star, and got into more barroom brawls than a crew of sailors on shore leave. Such behavior often got him into hot water with both the law and the baseball hierarchy.

Donlin missed most of the 1902 season with the Reds because of a six-month jail sentence for assaulting a live-in girlfriend. McGraw was willing to overlook such behavior, and, in 1904, brought him to New York, where he fit in perfectly on the rowdy Giants.

New York took to Donlin, who along with Christy Mathewson, became the most popular Giants of all. Turkey Mike returned the favor, serving as team captain from 1906 to 1910, squiring actresses about town and plunging into the theater himself. It was shortly after another suspension from baseball

— this one in 1906 for drunkenly terrorizing a trainload of passengers headed to Troy, New York — that he met and fell in love with Mabel Hite, a leading vaudevillian of the day.

The daughter of an Ashland, Kentucky druggist, Hite hit the stage as a singer and comedienne, starting at the age of 11. By 1908, Hite and Turkey Mike were starring in their own show — one of the first "talking films" — at Brocker's old Bijou Dream on West 23rd Street.

It was a new start for Turkey Mike. He and Hite married and toured in a song and dance review during their honeymoon. And when his contract for the 1908 season arrived, he held out and didn't report all season, nor in the following season, choosing the theater instead. Lamented frustrated Giant fans: "If Donlin would only join the Giants, [we] would drink his health in pints."

By 1911, Donlin considered himself an actor and the impatient Giants sold the 33-year-old veteran to the Boston Braves. On the field, Donlin played sparingly, retiring again in 1913. Meanwhile, on the stage and in the movies, Donlin landed a few leading roles, one as an ambidextrous pitcher.

The new lifestyle suited him. "Marriage has made a man of Mike Donlin," a newspaper reported. "He is leading a temperate life and inspires confidence in his resolution to continue on the straight and narrow path for the rest of his life."

What could take him back to baseball? Hite's tragic death, that's what. The 27-year-old actress died October 22, 1912 of cancer, despite claims after converting to Christian Science, that she had been completely cured. It was on her deathbed that she read her husband the story of Napoleon's return from Elba and bade him to go back to baseball.

Donlin did, but the bat speed was gone. After a cup of coffee with the Pirates, Turkey Mike disappeared into the minors, before closing out his baseball career as a utility infielder in 1914 with the Giants. His batting average that final season: a measely .161.

Another sad part of the the Mabel Hite chapter reared in 1915, when Donlin went to court in the bizarre case of the desecration of his late wife's remains. It seems that one Ray Frye, an undertaker's assistant with Campbell's Funeral Home, had negligently left the urn that contained Hite's ashes in a Broadway restaurant.

The lure of Hollywood endured. Turkey Mike remarried in 1914, and devoted himself entirely to films, appearing in 20 more silent films and talkies. But the hard living caught up to Donlin; he died in 1933 at 55.

LOU GEHRIG: COLLEGE MAN
Columbia University
West 116th Street & Broadway

The ability to hit a baseball a country mile distinguished Lou Gehrig at each of his stops — from Yankee Stadium, where he starred for the Yankees, clear down to the vacant lots of Yorkville where he grew up and his school, the High School of Commerce (155 West 65th Street). And that goes for his college — Columbia University.

In 1922, Gehrig entered Columbia as the jewel of the city's baseball world, a player *The Times* called, "the Babe Ruth of the high schools." Enrolling in this Ivy League bastion of high learning mean he was able to join his mother, of all people. Christina Gehrig cooked and cleaned at the Phi Delta Theta fraternity house, where Lou joined her, waiting on tables to defray costs. A humbling experience, it left the taciturn Gehrig with a lifelong resentment of his wealthier classmates.

Gehrig's two years at Columbia confirmed his status as a jock deity in the making — not just as a baseball player known for prodigious home runs at South Field, but as a halfback, guard, and tackle for the Lions' football team. In fact, many of Gehrig's first press clippings came in football during the 1922 season under the tutelage of coach Buck O'Neil.

But it was Gehrig's baseball exploits during his one and only collegiate season of 1923 that achieved lasting recognition. His Columbia baseball career ran all of two months and six days, during which Gehrig batted .444, to go with a mind-boggling slugging percentage of .937, seven home runs, six doubles, two triples, and five stolen bases.

In those days, the Columbia baseball team played at South Field, nestled among the tall brick and concrete buildings of Columbia's busy, urban campus. Now the university's quad area, the field occupied two long blocks between Broadway & Amsterdam Avenue at West 116th Street. Gehrig's target: the steps of the Journalism Building, next to Thomas Jefferson's statue and a good 450-feet from home plate.

Gehrig's prodigious numbers quickly attracted the attention of Yankee scout Paul Krichell. On April 26, 1923, Krichell showed up for the game at Rutgers, intending to see a promising young left-handed Columbia pitcher named Gehrig. Instead, he saw a one-man hitting machine named Gehrig belt two home runs that disappeared into the trees outside the Rutgers field.

To be sure, Krichell showed up at Gehrig's next game two days later against NYU at South Field. The young slugger walloped another moon shot, sending the ball clear to Broadway and 116th Street. A month later, Gehrig signed with the Yankees.

CHAPTER TEN

QUEENS

"The Mets is a very good thing. They give everybody a job. Just like the WPA."

— Billy Loes, Mets pitcher, 1962

THE HOUSE WHERE HILDA LIVED
144-02 89TH AVENUE

Now it can be told — Hilda Chester, the leather-lunged fanatic of the fanatics who rooted for the Dodgers at Ebbets Field and became famous in the process, was actually from Queens. Yes, Queens.

Hilda rang a cowbell, knew not just the names of the players but their birthdays too, and rarely missed a Dodger home game. Along with the Dodger Sym-phony and the countless other bleacher-creature faithful of the 1940s and '50s to whom Erskine was "Oisk," Reiser was "Ree-sah" and all Giants were dirtbags, she helped to turn Ebbets Field into a colorful panalopy of characters.

Hilda stories are legion. During a game in the early 1940s, she shrieked to Reiser, got the attention of the Dodger centerfielder and dropped a piece of paper on the field, asking him to take it to manager Leo Durocher.

At the end of the inning, Reiser scooped up the paper and ran to the bench, stopping briefly to talk with Dodger general manager Larry MacPhail, who sat in the box seat by the home dugout. Once inside the dugout, he gave the note to Durocher.

In the next inning, Whitlow Wyatt, the starting pitcher for the Dodgers, got hit hard. So Durocher brought in Hugh Casey from the bullpen, and he got hit too, nearly blowing a big Dodger lead.

After the game, Durocher was hopping angry — taking out some of his anger on Reiser. "Don't you ever give me another note from MacPhail as long as you play for me," he ranted.

MacPhail? "That note was from Hilda," said Reiser.

"Hilda!" thundered Durocher. "You mean to say that wasn't from MacPhail?" The note, which Reiser neglected to even read, had said, "Get Casey hot, Wyatt's losing it."

That was Hilda, the best known civilian at Ebbets Field. But there was another, more tender side to her as well, as related by Leo Stanger of Summit, New Jersey, who grew up a Dodger fan in Brooklyn.

When Stanger was nine, he made his first trip to Ebbets Field for a 1941 Sunday doubleheader against the Cardinals, arriving hours early with his mother on a streetcar. Mom, who had no intention of seeing the game herself, looked for a gentle soul to accompany her son through the turnstile and into the park. Young Leo Stanger was turned over to Hilda.

"Hilda took me in and sent me on my way," Stanger says. "Most importantly, she assured my mother that she'd keep an eye out for me. Brooklyn was like that then. You could trust strangers and feel perfectly comfortable. In the case of my first game, Hilda was that stranger."

Ironically, not much is known about the private Hilda Chester, whose cowbell is displayed at the Baseball Hall of Fame. Marty Adler, president of the Brooklyn Dodgers Hall of Fame, doesn't know much; he heard that Hilda died some years ago in Ohio of complications brought on by Alzheimer's Disease.

The mention of her Queens address was a small item about her declining health that appeared in a 1969 edition of *The Daily News* when Hilda was 71. The three-line clipping is the only entry in her file in Coopertown's National Baseball Library.

HOLY COW! THE SCOOTER'S START
Dill Place & 78th Road

It's very chilly.

As a matter —
I'm telling you,
I've been freezing.
My hands are cold.
I have low blood pressure anyway.
And arthritis.
I really should be going home.

And so it goes for Yankee great Phil Rizzuto, New York's poet laurette of baseball and everyone's favorite announcer. Chances are he wished your aunt happy birthday on the air, as he discussed the perils of his sump pump or his latest golf game — all of it, in the middle of a big rally, when he didn't know the score anyway. Who cares? Everyone loves the Scooter, a true prince of a man and a deserving member of the Baseball Hall of Fame, whose rambling, stream-of-consciousness broadcasting style makes him a bona fide cultural icon.

The above poem, taken from a hilarious 1993 collection of Scooter-verse, *O Holy Cow*, is about going home. Although the Scooter resides these days in Hillside, New Jersey, his first home was a modest house at Dill Place and 78th Road in what is now Queens and once was Brooklyn. It was there that Philip Francis Rizzuto was born in 1917 to Italian immigrants.

Some 18 years later, the 5'5" Rizzuto was overlooked by most major league teams, told he was too small to ever play major league ball. "Look kid, this game's not for you," one big league manager told him. "You're too small. The only way you can make a living is by getting a shoeshine box." But Yankee general manager Ed Barrow thought differently after watching his tryout and offered the young ballplayer a Class D contract for $75 a month.

By 1941, Rizzuto was the Yankee shortstop — a fair hitter, a superb bunter, and a slick, flawless fielder. In 1950, he was the American League Most Valuable Player, batting .324 and leading the Yanks to a four-game World Series sweep of the Phillies. It was among the nine Series he played in 13 big league seasons.

Rizzuto's second career started quickly, in 1956, after the Yankees forced him to retire with his .273 lifetime batting average. WPIX requested he join Roy Campanella to work the remaining Giants games at the Polo Grounds. Told by Howard Cosell that, "… you look like George Burns and you sound like Groucho Marx," Rizzuto was hired the following year by the Yanks to call games on both radio and TV.

Had a great time up in Greenwich.
It's a nice little town.
And you know, what I like, Seaver,
About that town?
You can get two hours
On those meters in town.

You get the idea. As the poems from *O Holy Cow* demonstrate, Rizzuto's
broadcasting partners were strictly last name only, making Tom Seaver,
"Seaver," Bobby Murcer, "Murcer" and Bill White, well, just "White." And yet
it was all wonderfully intimate as the Scooter spun war stories and details of
his favorite Westchester golf courses, in between calling the balls the strikes
— sort of — in his distinctively wacky way, while boasting he knew nothing
of and cared even less for the National League.

The Hall of Fame called in 1994. The following year, Rizzuto, upset that
WPIX hadn't permitted him to skip a broadcast to attend Mickey Mantle's
funeral, called it quits after a wonderful, irreverent 54-year-run as a player
and broadcaster.

Wait!
I never finished.
This is a story about Dickie Thon!
I told you I played ball
With his grandfather.
And,
And he was so on the ball.
When he went to Puerto Rico
He realized they didn't
Have washing machines.

METS GO MODERN
Shea Stadium opens
Whitestone Expressway & Grand Central Parkway

How appropriate that on April 17, 1964, the day Shea Stadium, opened
for business, two things happened:

- The Mets lost; and,
- There was a big traffic jam.

The Mets lost a lot in those days, so their 4-3 loss to the Pittsburgh Pirates in that first game, attended by 50,312, was no surprise. That the park was built in Queens, a long way physically and emotionally from Manhattan's Polo Grounds, the Mets' home for their first two years of existence, was important: It was a gateway to the suburbs and a critical step in capturing a more suburban fan base.

More than three decades have passed since that first season at Shea, where thousands of baseball games have since been played. From those bad early days, the Mets got good, won an improbable World Series in 1969, took another in 1986 and managed some decent baseball in-between. Along the way, Shea Stadium has become one of the older National League stadiums and lamented of late as one of those spiritless, cookie-cutter, multi-purpose parks.

The house that Ed Kranepool built? No, it's just Shea stadium.

But when it was built, Shea was heralded as a gleaming futuristic looking place. "We got 54 restrooms — 27 for the men and 27 for the ladies and I know you all want to use them now," said Mets' manager Casey Stengel when asked for his first perception of the ballpark. "And the escalators. No stairs. I tell you, you'll all keep your youth if you follow the Mets."

Talk of a new stadium had started the decade before. Seeking to leave tiny Ebbets Field, Brooklyn Dodgers' president Walter O'Malley looked into building a new ballpark — first at Borough Hall, Brooklyn; and, then over the Long Island Railroad terminal along Atlantic Avenue, also in Brooklyn.

The city tried instead to interest O'Malley in Shea Stadium's current site, but no agreement was ever made. In 1957, in a business decision that continues to haunt and hurt Brooklyn, O'Malley moved his Dodgers to Los Angeles. At the same time, Horace Stoneham uprooted his Giants from the Polo Grounds for San Francisco.

With the Yankees suddenly the only game in town, serious effort was launched almost immediately by Manhattan lawyer William A. Shea to bring in a new New York franchise with the start of a third major league, to be called the Continental League. When that failed, Shea convinced the National League owners to expand their membership by two teams. So, along with Houston, a franchise was awarded to New York.

These days, Shea Stadium doesn't inspire a great sense of nostalgia. There is airplane noise from nearby La Guardia Airport. The facade is blue, a very odd color for a ballpark, and the nearest tree appears to be somewhere in the Bronx. A few fun facts anyway:

- On April 16, 1964, the day before it opened, William Shea christened the ballpark by pouring the contents of two small champagne bottles onto the infield. One contained water from the Gowanus Canal in Brooklyn — "you couldn't see the Gowanus Canal from Ebbets Field, but you could smell it," he said — and the other contained water from the Harlem River near the old Polo Grounds, once home of the Giants.

- That same day, with workmen still feverishly putting last-minute touches on the new ballpark, Mets starting pitcher Jack Fisher wondered if the showers would be done in time for opening day. After all, he said, "I may be the first one to try them out."

- He was. In that first game, Fisher did hit the showers early, pitching moderately well — lasting $6^2/_3$ innings in giving up three runs and 11 hits to the Pirates. For the record, his first pitch, delivered to Dick Schofield, the Pirate shortstop, was a strike. Calling the balls and strikes was umpire Tom Gorman.

- The stadium's first hit was a home run to start off Pittsburgh's second inning. It was delivered by Willie Stargell, who had four of his team's 16 hits that day. Roberto Clemente and Donn Clendenon had three each for the Pirates.

- Tim Harkness, the Mets first baseman, got his team's first hit off Bob Friend, the stadium's first winning pitcher. Friend went the distance for the Pirates that day, scattering seven hits and three runs.

DROPPING IN ON THE METS
A parachute and an arrest
Queens courthouse
125-01 Queens Boulevard

Twas Game Six of the Series when out of the sky,
Flew Sergio's parachute, a Met banner held high.
His goal was to spur our home team to success,
Burst Beantown's balloon claiming Sox were the best.

And so began Judge Phyllis Orlikoff Flug's poetic response to one of New York's truly surreal baseball moments. Flug's December 19, 1986 comments were directed to one Michael Sergio, a 37-year-old actor, who had parachuted into Shea Stadium in the first inning of that fall's World Series Game Six.

Judge Flug, of Queens Criminal Court, called it, "An Ode to a Criminal Trespasser," imposing a $500 fine and 100 hours of community service to Sergio.

The fans and the players cheered all they did see,
But not everyone reacted with glee.
'Reckless endangerment!' the D. A. spoke stern."
"'I recommend jail — there's a lesson he'd learn!'
Though the act proved harmless, on the field he didn't belong,
His trespass was sheer folly and undeniably wrong.

Sergio jumped because Met players had been quoted as saying they weren't getting the kind of fan reaction they wanted in the '86 Series. "So I gave it to them," he said, as he was being led away, handcuffed and taken in a police van to the 110th Precinct in Queens. Attached to his golden parachute get-up: a small banner reading, "Let's Go Mets."

Sergio didn't say as much immediately following after his high-profile arrest, refusing to tell the police about any accomplices or how he had arrived in the crowded skies above Shea Stadium, which is near La Guardia Airport. His first inning jump in which he landed on the infield, slapped high-fives with Mets' starter Ron Darling and was promptly hustled away, became a curious footnote to a memorable game.

Who can forget? It was the game when the Mets staged an improbable rally, scoring two runs with two outs in the bottom of the 10th to win, evening the Series. The winning run scored when Red Sox first baseman Bill Buckner, normally a sure-handed fielder but playing on sore legs, failed to handle Mookie Wilson's dribbler for what would have been the third out and Boston's first Series win since Babe Ruth was a Fenway mainstay. The Mets took Game Seven two nights later for their second world championship.

But jail's not the answer in a case of this sort,
To balance the equities is the job of this court.
So a week before Christmas, here in the court,
I sentence the defendant for interrupting a sport.

How exactly did Sergio do it? That was the question on the minds of Federal Aviation Authorities, who launched what they called a "special investigation" into the jump. Queens District Attorney John Santucci wasn't impressed, saying in a statement that "this act of theatrical self-promotion may have brought a momentary smile to some, but it could have meant injury, pain and tears if he had crashed into the stands or players."

The day after his jump, Sergio assured a battery of reporters who kept calling his home at 414 West 44th Street that there had been little chance of crashing, saying he had jumped more than 1,900 times. He was still elusive about his motivation for jumping in the first place, saying only that "it was a pivotal game."

That December, Sergio pleaded guilty to charges of criminal trespass in a plea deal in which prosecutors agreed to drop the more serious charge of reckless endangerment. Even so, Sergio noted, it was a Mets security guard who had signed a complaint against him, although the club added his stunt to their new video highlighting the team's 1986 season.

None of it made much difference in the end, reasoned Judge Flug, who imposed a $500 fine and 100 hours of community service the week before Christmas.

Community service, and a fine you will pay.
Happy holiday to all, and to all a good day.

As for her ode, it was a team effort, the judge's law secretary, Peter Kelly, said. "She came up with the idea and I gave her a rough draft," he explained. So Judge Flug did what judges do — cite precedent: "A Visit from St. Nicholas."

DON'T CHANGE THE CHANNEL
A death at the Mets
784 Senaca Avenue

Say, what you wish about the excitement that surrounded the 1969 Miracle Mets. It wasn't THAT exciting.

The scene: July 9, 1969; Mets vs. Cubs at Shea before more than 55,000 imploring the home-town Peskies to beat the first-place Cubs. Could they pull off the improbable and pull into first place?

At the home of Frank Gradock, 66, and his wife Margaret, 56, the excitement was evident. Frank wanted to watch the Mets, but Margaret did not. And when Margaret tried to get her husband to watch the soap opera, "Dark Shadows" instead, the response was quick, nasty, and tragic.

Frank Graddock beat up his wife. Police, called in to investigate a heated argument at the Graddock home, about 4:30 PM said both husband and wife had been drinking. Graddock was reported to have beaten his wife in the head and body with clenched firsts, before she went off to bed.

Then, about 1 AM the next morning, Graddock went to Margaret's bed and found her dead. An ambulance from St. John's Hospital was called, but it was too late, police said. Frank was charged with homicide, to end the awful episode.

And the Mets? They won, rallying with three runs in the ninth to edge the Cubs 4-3 and pull within four games of first place. And yes, they would take over first place that season on an improbable march to a World Series win.

CHAPTER ELEVEN

OUTER BOROUGHS AND ENVIRONS—
STATEN ISLAND, WESTCHESTER COUNTY, NEW JERSEY

"Why me? I don't smoke. I don't drink. I don't run around. Baseball is my whole life. Why me?"
— Ralph Branca, Dodgers pitcher, to a priest after
Bobby Thomson hit "The Shot Heard
'Round the World" off him, 1951

STATEN ISLAND

"THE GIANTS WIN THE PENNANT!" (REPEAT FOUR TIMES)
Bobby Thomson celebrates
Tavern on the Green
2566 Hylan Boulevard

Bobby Thomson grips his hands around an imaginary bat, sweeping them across his chest as if a fast ball was just that moment headed his way.

Never mind he's being called on yet again to remember the swing that produced baseball's most celebrated home run and New York's most dramatic sports moment of them all. And never mind that it's been that way for nearly 50 years.

Has it really been that long since the overcast October 3, 1951 afternoon, when Thomson, then a 28-year-old outfielder with the Giants, launched his dramatic three-run homer to beat the Dodgers in a playoff for the National League pennant, the famous "Shot Heard 'Round the World?"

"I haven't told too many people this, but I'm proud of that swing," recalls Thomson from the spacious back porch of his rambling home in the suburban New York town of Watchung, New Jersey. "My bat and hips were both back — just the way they should be — and boom, I swung. The ball was gone."

The medium-high pitch disappeared over the Polo Grounds' left field wall to win the pennant. The pitch, delivered at the expense of Dodger righthander Ralph Branca and the memorable scene of Thomson's joyous romp around the bases, have earned an enduring spot in the hearts of baseball fans everywhere. As Giants' radio announcer Russ Hodges called it: "There's a long drive ... It's gonna be ... I believe ... The Giants win the pennant! The Giants win the pennant!" (He said it three more times; you can hear it on the tape.)

So Thomson went out that night, celebrating his triumph at New York's finest night spots, right? He was the toast of New York. Who wouldn't? Thomson, that's who; instead, the Staten Island native who at the time lived with his mother, four sisters and a brother, went home to New Dorp, Staten Island, crossing by ferry. And that night, with a World Series game to play the next afternoon against the Yankees at Yankee Stadium, the new hero celebrated with his family.

After all, Thomson wasn't a superstar in the mold of a Mickey Mantle or Sandy Koufax. The Curtis High School product retired from baseball in 1960, after a solid 15-year major league career that included stints with the Braves, Cubs, Red Sox, and Orioles, a .270 lifetime batting average and 264 home runs.

On the other hand, what he did that afternoon in October 1951 did more than win the pennant — never mind that the Giants went on to lose that year's World Series in six games to the Yankees. It capped a stunning late-season comeback in which the team took 37 of its final 44 games to tie the Dodgers on the last day of the season and force the three-game playoff. And it may just have been the high water mark of the city's "golden decade" of baseball in which all three New York ballclubs were the best in the business.

Baseball back then was a simpler game without multi-million-dollar player contacts and assorted labor problems of today, Thomson admits. A case in point was in 1946, his rookie season with the Giants, when he commuted from home in New Dorp to the Polo Grounds, on the Staten Island Ferry and the subway. "It must have taken $2^1/_2$ hours to get there, but I made it," Thomson recalls.

After his "shot," Thomson slipped away, did a quick appearance on that night's Perry Como's television show and went home — taking the subway and the ferry. He did the trip alone. "It was a strange feeling after being inundated with people all day long," Thomson recounts in his 1991 book, the suitably-titled, *The Giants Win the Pennant.* "But now I was anxious to see my family."

The first family member he saw was brother Jim, a fireman, who was working and missed the game. Thomson's book again: "'Bobby,' he said, shaking his head. 'Do you realize what you did today? ... Do you realize something like this may never happen again?'"

That night, the Thomsons celebrated at the restaurant, where they often ate. The whole family was there and a lot of friends joined the party. Press pictures in the New York and Staten Island papers the next day show a beaming Thomson being toasted with champagne by his sisters and mother. Just about the only one without a drink is the slugger himself. After all, there was a game to play the next day.

MUTRIE'S DUMPING GROUNDS
A ballpark once stood here
B & O Rail Yards by the Ferry

Imagine a time when a ticket to a ball game also brought a free ferry ride to and from the game. It makes sense when trying to attract spectators from Manhattan to a major league game on Staten Island, which happened with the Giants for a spell in the late 1880s.

That was the dilemma facing Giants' founder Jim Mutrie, when, in 1889, he temporarily relocated his team to the St. George Cricket Grounds, just up from the boat dock, where the Baltimore & Ohio rail yards are today, next to the Staten Island Ferry.

The Giants were the kings of New York. Home through most of the 1880s was the original version of the Polo Grounds, named for a polo field owned and used by James Bennett and built between West 110 and 112th streets on the northern tip of Central Park. But, in April, 1889, the wooden park burned to the ground.

Mutrie's temporary solution was to look south to Staten Island's St. George Cricket Grounds. And so, for 25 games from April 29 to June 14, 1889, home for the Giants was this quirky little ballpark, where the field was stony and bare from second base to center field, thanks in part to a 1888 stage production of *Nero* that had ravaged the grounds.

Why Staten Island? Well, it was available. The Giants had played a few games there back in 1886 and 1887 when city officials had shut down the Polo Grounds for a nearby road project. And the primary reason — in 1886, the Giants' new owner, Erastus Wiman, just happened to own both the ferry service and a Staten Island amusement park.

By 1889, conditions at the St. George Cricket Grounds were so abysmal, they were funny. As the Giants took over, the scaffolding from *Nero* remained in place, lining the outfield. Because of swampy conditions in some parts of the outfield itself, boards were put down to absorb the water and provide outfielders with traction. And from the back of third base in both fair and foul territory, clear to the left field wall, the field actually sloped sharply downwards.

No wonder it was called "Mutrie's Dumping Ground." And no wonder Mutrie, ever the realist, looked hard and right away for a place to relocate his Giants.

Following a long June road trip, the Giants returned to New York — and mercifully, to a new field, way uptown at Coogan's Bluff. And despite the temporary troubles of adjusting to life on Staten Island early that season, they bounced back just fine, thank you — taking the 1889 World Series.

WESTCHESTER COUNTY

LOU GEHRIG TIES THE KNOT
5 Circuit Road
New Rochelle

Goodness knows few women were ever received into a family while facing more overt hostility from a mother-in-law than Eleanor Grace Twitchell of Chicago.

When Twitchell met the mother of her future husband, Lou Gehrig, for the first time, she thought Christina Gehrig was "built like a lady wrestler, with yellowish gray hair snatched back in a bun." Lou, an only child, was still living with his parents, in New Rochelle, at the time of his September 29, 1933 wedding. He was the apple of his mother's eye for whom no other woman was worthy.

Freud could have written volumes in trying to describe Gehrig's relationship with his mother. Only at his mother's insistence did he leave her bedside after she had surgery just before the 1927 World Series. "My place is at mom's side," he said. "She is worth more to me than any ball game, or any World Series that was ever invented."

Sportswriter Fred Lieb once described Gehrig returning home from a road trip and being met at the train station by his mother. "Mom and Louie kissed and hugged for fully 10 minutes as though they had been parted for years," he wrote. A 1928 profile in *New Yorker*, about the time he met Twitchell, said, "Gehrig does not drink, smoke, or gamble ... he has never had a girl."

Not until Twitchell and Gehrig were engaged was there any effort on the part of Ma Gehrig to welcome her to the family. Twitchell met Gehrig in Chicago during a Yankees' trip there in 1928. In contrast to stage-struck showgirls who gravitated to ballplayers, Twitchell was no bimbo, but a graduate of the University of Wisconsin, and more interested in horses, golf, and literature than baseball. She met Gehrig through a family connection during an infrequent trip to Comiskey Park.

Their romance was out of a storybook. By 1931, Eleanor, then working as a $40-a-week assistant at the Chicago World's Fair, and the quiet, introverted ballplayer, were an item. By 1933, they were engaged and intent on having a low-key wedding.

On Thursday, September 28, Gehrig went 1-for-3 in an 11-9 Yankee victory over Washington at Yankee Stadium. He left quietly after the fourth inning, presumably to prepare for his wedding day.

At issue was more than the ceremony itself. In protest, Gehrig's mother refused to attend, leaving both Lou and Eleanor bitterly disappointed, but determined to carry through. So that Thursday night, Lou placed a call to New Rochelle Mayor Walter Otto, to see if he would marry them the following day at their new fourth-floor apartment, near the Hudson Park Boatyard.

Otto agreed. Also invited was Fred Linder of Mt. Vernon and Blanche Austin, Eleanor's aunt, to stand in as witnesses.

Eleanor called it, "the classiest wedding ever held in Westchester County." She was half-kidding: Otto showed up with a marriage license and a screeching caravan of New Rochelle motorcycle cops. Lou wore short-sleeves and Eleanor dressed in an apron. As the ceremony kicked off, a bevy of workmen still fixing up the new apartment, paused for a few minutes in respectful silence. Hats were removed, the rite completed and Eleanor passed around dusty, unwashed glasses of warm champagne.

And with that, the happy couple made a quick exit escorted by the motorcycle cops — to Yankee Stadium for the afternoon's game. Gehrig promptly told his teammates about the wedding and went hitless in four plate appearances in a loss to the Senators. Even so, said a local paper, that was, "pretty good for a man who has just gotten married."

DARRYL STRAWBERRY STRIKES OUT
Federal courthouse
White Plains

How appropriate that the April 1995 day Darryl Strawberry was sentenced for income tax evasion, he showed up wearing pinstripes in Room 41 of United States District Court Building.

The stripes were of the muted variety in his shiny bluish-gray suit that blended with burgundy stripes on a white shirt. But Strawberry was fortunate, for after pleading guilty to failure to pay about $100,000 in income taxes on money earned at various card shows, he got a slap on the wrist — probation for three years, including six months' home confinement, substance-abuse counseling, and 100 hours of community service.

For Strawberry, it was just another example of a life careened out-of-control. As Dave Anderson reported in *The Times*, the ex-Met, ex-Dodger, and ex-Giant slugger, "…had swung a bat versus many good pitchers, but he had never faced a federal judge before."

The judge, Barrington D. Parker, Jr., dressed in a black robe and sitting high in a leather chair under the bronze United States' seal, lectured Strawberry that, "it's important that governmental and societal interests are protected," about his "egregious judgment," and his "puzzling immaturity." But when it came time to issue Strawberry's sentence, "he threw a batting practice pitch," as Anderson wrote.

Translation: no jail for Strawberry, despite a guilty plea to one felony count. Further translation: a fine of $350,000 in taxes, penalties, and interest on unreported earnings of $411,250 between 1986 and 1990. It was chicken-feed for a multi-millionaire.

The judge was right in one respect: Strawberry's "egregious judgment" personified the career of the all-time Met home run leader, who arrived in New York as the next Ted Williams and Mickey Mantle combined and struck out. Long before Strawberry's 1994 substance-abuse rehabilitation, he was in alcohol-abuse rehab. He allegedly waved a gun at his first wife, Lisa, during a domestic dispute, fought with his Met teammate Keith Hernandez during a team-photo session, was fined at least eight times for various team infractions, and usually sat out with the even the most minimal of injuries.

"At some particular moments," Strawberry told the judge in trying to explain his "slip" into drug dependency, "life was not worth it to be here living."

"Strawberry had arrived at the courthouse with his lawyers in a black sedan and before leaving, he was on the sidewalk talking into nearly a dozen microphones as television cameras rolled. "I'd like to apologize," he said, "to all my fans, to Major League Baseball and to all my friends and family. I look forward to turning my life around."

Moments earlier, Judge Parker had told him, "your future is entirely in your hands." But for Strawberry, once the toast of New York, that has always been the most dangerous place of all. He had the last laugh, however, returning to New York late in his career as a mainstay with the Yankees.

NEW JERSEY

BASEBALL'S BIRTHPLACE
Elysian Fields
Hoboken

Sure, baseball's first team, the Knickerbockers, played a brand of baseball that turned an old fashioned game of rounders to the faster, more democratic game of today. And sure, these Knickerbockers were the original Jack Armstrongs — dashing trend-setters in their uniforms of blue woolen pantaloons, white flannel shirts, and straw hats.

But history doesn't lie, and for all their look, pomp, and ceremony, the grim reality is that the Knickerbockers weren't a very good team. A case in point was the storied first game of modern baseball — a four-inning affair played June 23, 1846 at Elysian Fields, Hoboken. Final score: New York Base Ball Club, 23 — Knickerbockers, 1. Marvelous Marv Throneberry would be proud.

How the Knickerbockers actually found Hoboken is another story. For most of their previous four years, they had played at various sites around Manhattan — first in the fields surrounding Sunfish Pond, between what is now East 31st and 32nd streets and Park Avenue. But the team moved when faced with the effluent pollution oozing into surrounding streams from Peter Cooper's 33rd Street glue factory.

The next site, near 3rd Avenue, was soon closed to accommodate a new railroad right-of-way. Soon, the Knickerbockers found themselves forced from Manhattan by the rapid spread of urbanization, fueled by the real estate barons of the day. So it was to a short ferry ride across the Hudson to Hoboken.

It was ideal for this new game. Filled with flowers, trees, and enough room for picnicking, Elysian Fields was a beautiful place that an English visitor said, "... blasted the senses ... by reeking forth fumes of whiskey and tobacco."

Hoboken's hefty number of bars and restaurants along with entertaining diversions, like P. T. Barnum's various circus events, made it the ideal weekend retreat for New Yorkers. It was amidst such tranquillity that the Knickerbockers played their first recorded game — an October 1845 inter-squad game in which Alexander Cartwright contributed a run in an 11-8 loss. Still, the rigors of this new sport weren't enough to keep the team from retiring to McCarty's Hotel for a post-game meal of beer and cigars.

Out on the grassy meadow of Elysian Fields, the Knickerbockers were cheered on by the polite applause of their friends. Women were protected from the sun by a colored canvas pavilion. There was no grandstand, forcing those spectators without carriages to watch the action while standing.

That the Knickerbockers eventually managed to win a few games is incidental to their place in history. They were New York's team in the New York game and dominated baseball for more than a decade, putting their personal stamp on the game's history. Many of the clubs emerging in the 1850s copied the Knickerbockers in style and uniform fashion.

But if the Knickerbockers had their way, they wouldn't have been so popular. More interested in keeping baseball restricted to their own social classes, they soon found that baseball was getting too popular for that. The city was changing quickly, filling up with young men, mostly immigrants, who wanted to sample this new game called baseball. In 1856, *The New York*

Mercury proclaimed the game for the first time as "our national pastime." The game was here to stay.

JINTS IN THE MAKING — ROOSEVELT STADIUM
Droyers Point
Jersey City

Okay, it wasn't paradise exactly, but to a young kid from Jersey City, it was as about as close as you can get.

Here was John Betlow in his 70s, a lifelong Hudson County resident and a big booster of the area's positive steps toward urban renewal. Meet him (a few years ago) in the parking lot of Roosevelt Stadium, where the Jersey City Giants once played, and he'll bend your ear about skyscrapers going up and the expertise of local hospitals. But talk with him long enough and the conversation inevitably turns to a more distant time when towns like Jersey City and Newark were more neighborly, safer places boasting substantial numbers of stores, saloons, movie houses, and, yes, baseball teams.

"Ever heard of Jackie Robinson and Charlie Keller?" asks Betlow, gesturing toward a pile of crumpled concrete that was once a ballpark. "They played here, right here. So did Duke Snider, Monte Irvin, and Bobby Thomson. I can still see them whacking that ball and charging around the bases. It's sad what happened to baseball here, but the memories live on."

He refers in part to the late great Jersey City Giants, who called the big, barnyard of a ballpark home. Built as a WPA project in 1937 on the site of a landfill of dirt excavated from the Holland Tunnel and named for President Franklin D. Roosevelt, the Stadium served as home to three minor league teams, as well as 15 Brooklyn Dodger "home games" spread over two seasons, 1956 and 1957.

For Bobby Thomson, a Jersey City Giant in 1946, "Roosevelt was a huge park, a place you practically needed a shotgun or a cannon to get the ball over the fence. "My most vivid memory was of opening day — dressing in those snow-white uniforms and then stepping out of the dugout into a park, packed to overflowing," he says. "For a young guy like me, just out the service and without much professional experience, that was exciting."

Accounts differ on just how many people crammed Roosevelt for opening days — always quite the event in Jersey City. Estimates vary from

Thomson's 25,000-to-30,000 to 70,000. Typically, the events were packed at the command of Mayor Frank Hague who gave his policemen orders to sell tickets. They always sold more than their share for opening day, filling the park to capacity, with the profits from the extra tickets going straight to "The Boss."

In 1947, the Giants drew close to 340,000. Three years later, in their last season, the New York team's top minor league team finished fourth and drew only 64,000. Says Jack Swarz, the retired Giants' scouting director in a kind of epitaph for New Jersey baseball: "They drew enough most of the time, but it was just too close to New York, too close to three major league teams."

But for a time at least — back when the powerful Newark Bears were the Yankees' top farm team and the Giants' main rival, it was fun. Quirky too: Thomson lived on Staten Island when he played in Jersey City, and commuted by taking two or three buses, the Elizabeth Ferry, and then the Hudson Boulevard bus to the ballpark.

"There were times after a night game when I didn't get home until 3 AM," he says. "It was a heck of a hike, but it's what you did in those days."

Hall-of-Famer Duke Snider, who played in Roosevelt as a member of the Montreal Royals, remembers Roosevelt mostly for having the lights turned off quickly, so quickly that after a game outfielders were sometimes left stranded in the dark.

"I remember playing one night in 1946 and going after a ball in left-center field, and before catching it, having the lights go out just like that," he says. "I had a good line on the ball though and made the catch, but it was pretty tough. Anything to save a buck, I guess."

As a member of the Brooklyn Dodgers, Snider returned to Roosevelt Stadium in 1956, playing those 15 "home games" and becoming the lone Dodger to hit two home runs there. By playing away from their regular home, Ebbets Field in Brooklyn, the Dodgers were mounting a threat to move from the borough unless New York's civic leaders provided a new ballpark. "By then," says Snider, "we had a pretty good idea we were leaving."

The Dodgers did leave, as did the Jersey City Giants, moving to Ottawa in 1950, just a year after the Bears departed Newark for Springfield, Massachusetts. Roosevelt Stadium however, trudged on, as home to one of the more unlikely of teams, the Jersey City Jerseys of 1960 and '61. An International League farm team of the Cincinnati Reds, the Jerseys were the result of another in a litany of odd Jersey baseball footnotes.

You could say that the Jerseys owe their existence to the Cuban President

Fidel Castro. Some background: At midnight, July 25, 1960, during an extra-inning International League game at Gran Stadium, Havana, between that city's Sugar Kings and the Rochester Red Wings, Frank Verdi, a Red Wings' third baseman was accidentally shot from the stands during celebrations marking the first anniversary of the Cuban Revolution.

Although the bullet grazed Verdi's cap, leaving him unhurt, it was strongly recommended that the Sugar Kings, only two of whom were Cuban, move to the US. A ballpark was needed — and fast. So, on their next trip to the US, they moved to, you guessed it, Roosevelt Stadium. The newly-named Jerseys finished out the season there, drawing only 62,000 spectators — an average of less than 800 a game.

The tale of the 1977-78 Single-A Eastern League Jersey City Indians isn't much better. "I really thought the town would get behind us, but it didn't," says Mal Fichman, a Bergen County native and part-owner who urged the parent club, the Cleveland Indians, to settle in Hudson County. "What we didn't realize was that every night, the Mets or the Yankees were on TV. People weren't going to leave their living rooms for us."

The Indians finished last both seasons and drew miserably. The sole bright spot: 19-year-old Rickey Henderson, who hit .310 and led the '78 Eastern League with 81 stolen bases.

Roosevelt's deteriorating condition didn't help. When the Indians played there, half the ballpark's 25,000 seats were condemned, lights were left unfixed and the field was in constant disrepair, says Fichman. It was a sad end to the ballpark's odd but interesting history. Roosevelt Stadium was finally torn down in 1985.

GLORY DAYS, GLORY TEAM — THE NEWARK BEARS
Ruppert Stadium
Newark

"It was like a Yankees-Red Sox series," former Yankee pitcher Spec Shea recalled a short time before his death in 1994. "You wanted to beat them and hoped it would really show."

He wasn't referring to the Yankees-Red Sox. Try Newark Bears-Jersey City Giants of the International League of the late 1940s, an across-the-river microcosm to the intense New York major league rivalries of the same era.

Thank the team owners for that — the Yankees of the Bears and the Giants of Jersey City franchise. And give a nod to the players, who often resumed their rivalries once they got to New York.

For Shea, who played for the '48 Bears and later won 56 games in eight big-league seasons, "… we used to have a saying on the Yankees that if a player fell below a .280 batting average, he's going down to Newark."

"They just always seemed to have some kid down there hitting .340," said Shea. "Newark was that good. Year-in and year-out, they were a fabulous club."

The minor league crown jewel of the great Yankee dynasties of the 1930s and '40s, the Bears played their superior brand of baseball at Ruppert Stadium on Wilson Avenue in the Ironbound section of Newark. The ballpark, named for beer baron and Yankee owner Jacob Ruppert, was a pint-sized park with a capacity of 20,000 next door to a glue factory.

And yes, the team that played there was as good as they said. The Bears were the cream of the minor leagues, placing in the first division of the International League for 16 of 18 years. They won the bush league playoffs, "the Governors' Cup," four times, in 1937, '38, '40, and '45.

Indeed, the powerful '37 Bears are generally thought to be the greatest minor league team of all — it went 109-54 and won the pennant by $25\frac{1}{2}$ games. Every regular from the team made it to the majors, including Charlie Keller (.353 batting average, 13 home runs and league MVP that season), Joe Gordon, Atley Donald, and Spud Chandler.

But the history of Ruppert Stadium is more than just the Bears. Even with details sketchy, this much is known: Originally named Widenmayer's Park, it hosted precisely one major league game — a Highlanders-Tigers game on July 17, 1904 — and later burned down. Rebuilt in 1926 as David's Stadium, it was renamed Bears Stadium in 1932 and for Ruppert in 1934.

The Bears left in 1950. Ruppert Stadium made it all the way to the early 1970s when it was torn down, replaced by a mattress factory. Only a plaque commemorating the ballpark remains.

CHAPTER TWELVE

THE BABE SLEEPS HERE

"They have smelled the roses when they were in full bloom."
— Warren Brown, sportswriter, on ballplayers

A RUTHIAN FAREWELL – THE BABE IS BURIED
Gate of Heaven Cemetery
Hawthorne (Westchester County)

It was, well, a Ruthian farewell. A taxi driver echoed the feelings of the 100,000 or so who lined the rainy streets to watch Babe Ruth's August 19, 1948 funeral procession: "Even the skies wept for the Babe." Added Arthur Daley in *The New York Times*: "The Babe would have gloried in it; the final tribute would have left him shining-eyed and choked up because he always had the soft-hearted sentimentality of a small boy."

When Ruth finally succumbed at 53 to a two-year battle with throat cancer, the outpouring of grief at the passing of America's greatest sportsman matched that of a king. There were front-page stories in every newspaper and 77,000 people who filed past his coffin in an unprecedented lying-in-state at Yankee Stadium. And there was the big service at St. Patrick's Cathedral conducted by Cardinal Spellman, along with the uncounted thousands lining the 30-mile funeral procession from Midtown to Gate of Heaven Cemetery, Hawthorne.

The service lasted an hour. As mass ended, Ruth's mahogany casket was carried out of the Cathedral, and the rain that had fallen steadily through the morning suddenly stopped. Standing notably erect among the honorary pallbearers was Connie Mack, the 86-year-old manager of the Philadelphia A's and Ruth's longtime friend and rival.

It took several minutes for the mourners to get into the automobiles for the trip to the cemetery. The rain held off, only to begin again, once they were on their way. Some 250 policemen directed them up 5th Avenue from 51st Street to 120th Street, on to Madison Avenue and 138th Street, and across

Offerings at Babe Ruth's grave include a stuffed bear, an American flag, several baseballs, a mitt, two cigars, and a Darryl Strawberry-model Louisville Slugger bat.

the Madison Avenue Bridge into the Bronx. From there, the cavalcade of 25 cars traveled north up the Grand Concourse, past Yankee Stadium, scene of so many of Ruth's great moments, and into Westchester County.

The rain continued. And people continued to line the roads, many of them standing bareheaded and motionless out of respect. Others watched from rooftops and windows. When the procession reached the cemetery at 1:43 PM, it was met by another crowd — this one a tightly packed bunch of 6,000, who had waited since early morning.

Homage-payers crowded around the canopied plot in front of the receiving tomb, where the coffin, with "George Herman Ruth" on its silver name-plate, was placed for the brief committal service. Ruth wasn't actually buried until October 26, 1948.

Among the pallbearers were two former Yankee teammates, Waite Hoyt and Joe Dugan. "I'd give $100 for an ice-cold beer," whispered Dugan.

"So would the Babe," answered Hoyt.

The grave, in the cemetery's hill section, is within 200 feet of the grave of Mayor Jimmy Walker, an old friend of the Babe, who once told him, "never let those poor kids down." Ruth rarely did.

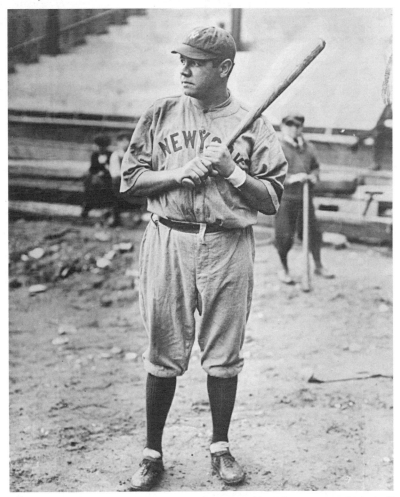

The one, the only, and the best there ever was: the Babe. (National Baseball Hall of Fame Library, Cooperstown, New York)

INDEX

S

About the Author

Jim Reisler's earliest baseball memory is of watching his father, a Giants fan and a New York native, demonstrate Mel Ott's famous "high-leg kick" batting stance and stubbing his big toe. Reisler, a former newspaper reporter, works in corporate communications in New York City and has written for a wide range of publications, including *Sports Illustrated* and *The New York Times*. He is the author of *Black Writers/Black Baseball* (McFarland & Company, 1994), an anthology of pieces by African-American journalists who covered baseball's Negro Leagues. A Pittsburgh native, Reisler is a graduate of Kenyon College and the Columbia University Graduate School of Journalism. He lives in Irvington, New York, with his wife, Tobie; daughter, Julia; and three cats.